Family Business Resilience in Times of Radical Change

Contemporary Issues in Family Business Entrepreneurship

Edited by
Stefan Märk and Mario Situm

Volume 2

Family Business Resilience in Times of Radical Change

Strategies to Manage Disruptions and Exploit Opportunities

Edited by
Stefan Märk and Mario Situm

DE GRUYTER

ISBN 978-3-11-077930-1
e-ISBN (PDF) 978-3-11-079034-4
e-ISBN (EPUB) 978-3-11-079040-5
ISSN 2751-7640

Library of Congress Control Number: 2025944719

Bibliographic information published by the Deutsche Nationalbibliothek
The Deutsche Nationalbibliothek lists this publication in the Deutsche Nationalbibliografie; detailed bibliographic data are available on the internet at http://dnb.dnb.de.

Cover image: BreakingTheWalls/iStock/Getty Images Plus
Typesetting: Integra Software Services Pvt. Ltd.
Printing and binding: CPI books GmbH, Leck

www.degruyterbrill.com
Questions about General Product Safety Regulation:
productsafety@degruyterbrill.com

MIX
Papier | Fördert gute Waldnutzung
FSC® C083411

Contents

Preface

It is with great pleasure that we present to you the second volume of our series "Contemporary Issues in Family Business Entrepreneurship." Following the inaugural volume, which focused on strategic transformation and business modeling, this edition delves into a theme of even greater urgency and relevance: Resilience in family businesses during times of radical change.

Titled "Family Business Resilience in Times of Radical Change: Strategies to Manage Disruptions and Exploit Opportunities," this volume is a timely response to the rapidly evolving landscape that family businesses must navigate today. The pressures of the VUCA and BANI environments – volatile, uncertain, complex, ambiguous, brittle, anxious, nonlinear, and incomprehensible – demand not only adaptability but also proactive resilience. These challenges stem not only from economic and technological transformations such as digitalization and Industry 4.0, but also from socio-demographic shifts, succession complexities, and increasingly unpredictable global crises.

Family businesses, as distinct economic actors embedded within a nexus of family, ownership, and enterprise, are especially vulnerable yet uniquely positioned to withstand and even thrive amidst disruption. This volume gathers research that goes beyond mere survival, focusing on how these enterprises can strategically harness resilience as a lever for sustainable innovation and transformation. The contributions span a wide range of topics from strategic renewal in radical change scenarios to leadership practices that foster employee resilience, to the intricacies of succession, social responsibility, and even moral dilemmas within family firms.

In doing so, this book showcases a rich mix of perspectives: theoretical reflections, empirical findings, case studies, and literature reviews that combine academic rigor with real-world applicability. The contributions address not only the classic three-circle model of family, ownership, and business, but also explore emerging intersections such as gender in succession, corporate social responsibility as a resilience strategy, and even the role of deviant behavior within family-led firms.

This volume is particularly valuable for researchers seeking to advance the field of family business studies, practitioners who support these firms in times of transformation, and family entrepreneurs themselves who are searching for strategic guidance in an increasingly complex world. We are convinced that the insights and models presented here will not only inform but inspire – helping family businesses to rethink their resilience not as a reactive necessity, but as a dynamic and strategic asset.

We thank the authors for their committed and insightful contributions, and all reviewers for their careful and constructive feedback. This volume would not exist without their intellectual generosity and dedication. Finally, we wish to emphasize

https://doi.org/10.1515/9783110790344-203

that this book is not a conclusion but a continuation of an ongoing dialogue. We invite scholars, consultants, and business families to join us in this conversation, contribute their experiences, and build new knowledge that will shape the future of family business entrepreneurship. We wish you an insightful and engaging read.

The Editors
FH-Prof. Dr. Stefan Märk
Prof. (FH) Dr. Dr. Mario Situm

Stefan Märk and Mario Situm

Strategy Development in the Light of Radical Change: A Perspective on the Evolution and Revolution of Family Businesses

Abstract: This study presents a systematic literature review on strategy development in family businesses, focusing on how these firms respond to evolutionary, revolutionary, and radical change. Based on 42 peer-reviewed articles, the findings show that family businesses primarily pursue incremental, evolution-based strategies rooted in long-term orientation, cultural continuity, and socioemotional wealth. These approaches foster resilience and adaptability in stable or moderately dynamic environments. However, the review reveals a significant gap in the literature concerning radical change and organizational revolution. Despite growing relevance due to digital disruption and global crises, few studies address how family firms manage abrupt, transformative shifts. Most existing research emphasizes gradual adaptation, leaving unanswered questions about strategic responses to disruptive, nonlinear developments. The study concludes that while evolutionary strategies support stability, they may limit responsiveness in times of radical change. Future research should focus on how family firms can balance tradition with transformation and develop capabilities for revolutionary renewal in increasingly volatile environments.

Keywords: Family business, Organizational evolution, Organizational revolution, Radical change, Strategy development

1 Introduction

All companies worldwide are facing unprecedented challenges. In addition to the well-established concept of VUCA (volatility, uncertainty, complexity, and ambiguity), the literature increasingly references the term BANI (brittle, anxious, nonlinear, and incomprehensible). Both indicate that businesses must navigate an increasingly complex environment. In this context, topics such as sustainability, resilience, crisis management, strategy, business models, and competitiveness are gaining importance (Situm, 2024). As a result, companies must strategically adapt to unavoidable technological (e.g., Industry 4.0, digitalization) and non-technological (e.g., demographic shifts, Silver Society) trends. Adaptability thus plays a crucial role in ensuring the future and sustainable survival of companies—including family businesses (Situm, 2021).

Especially in smaller (family) businesses, this adaptability is often lacking, as they do not necessarily have a strategic goal. Instead, decisions are made in the context of survival and operational necessity. Aspects such as growth and business development

https://doi.org/10.1515/9783110790344-001

play little or only a subordinate role (Down, 2013, pp. 91–92), because the presence of the family as the main stakeholder and thus the pursuit of non-financial goals prevail (Vazquez & Rocha, 2018). In family businesses, it is therefore not only the "fate" of the company itself that determines the overall strategy. It is the complex dynamics and the often divergent goals between the family, the family business, and the family wealth that shape the performance, growth, change, and transition of the business over time (Astrachan, 2010; Carlock & Ward, 2001; Davis, 2008; Venter et al., 2012). In particular, emotions significantly influence managerial decision-making (Morgan & Gomez-Mejia, 2014).

In the literature, this aspect is known as socioemotional wealth (Hernández-Perlines et al., 2023; Reina et al., 2023; Swab et al., 2020). For these reasons, the approach to (strategic) management in family businesses differs from that in non-family businesses (García et al., 2014), particularly in the sense that strategic planning is closely linked to continuity planning (Daspit et al., 2021; Brockhaus, 2004; Malone, 1989). Many of the trends mentioned include not only evolutionary developments but also revolutionary ones, which can trigger radical changes. This poses a significant risk, particularly for small and medium-sized (family) businesses, as their lack of adaptability, as outlined earlier, may lead them into a severe crisis. Without appropriate countermeasures, they risk disappearing from the market (Flagg et al., 2011; Smith & Graves, 2005; Yazdanfar & Öhman, 2020).

There is a unanimous consensus in the literature that a strong strategy is the foundation for protecting companies from severe crises. Therefore, every company, regardless of its size and type, should engage in strategic planning (Furrer et al., 2007; Hatten, 2025, p. 70; Spanos et al., 2004; Stafford et al., 2010). For strategy development to be successful, an open and inclusive approach should be adopted, actively involving managers and relevant stakeholders at all levels. This can help optimize communication between different hierarchical levels and actively manage cultural and political dynamics within the organization. As a result, the strategy process becomes more effective, adaptable, and future-oriented (Collier et al., 2004; De Feo & Janssen, 2001).

It is important to note that the strategic planning process is not a rigid tool within an organization. Strategic planning is only effective when combined with strategic thinking, and is based on clear objectives, resource focus, and continuous adaptation. Strategy development is a dynamic and continuously evolving process (Adamides, 2015; Bolland, 2020, p. 43). This is particularly relevant in times of radical change. Such transformations require a combination of strategic clarity, cultural adaptation, structural flexibility, technological support, and strong leadership. The success of change initiatives largely depends on how well these factors are interconnected and implemented (McAdam, 2003).

As previously mentioned, the literature recognizes that family businesses and non-family businesses differ in how they approach strategy development due to various factors. There is a need to further examine the role of individual actors in the strategic processes of family businesses. Particularly relevant is the connection between individual identity development and strategic decision-making, as well as the differences in this context between family and non-family businesses. Additionally, the underlying factors of individual identity work should be more clearly identified to better understand strategic mechanisms (Bettinelli et al., 2022).

Family businesses exhibit distinct characteristics in their strategic orientation and implementation, which bring both advantages and challenges. A deeper understanding of these dynamics requires targeted research to develop models that reflect the unique needs and mechanisms of family businesses (Harris et al., 1994). Chrisman et al. (2016) emphasize that family businesses are unique in strategy execution because family interests and business objectives are closely intertwined. Consequently, strategy and succession planning are strongly interconnected. Successful family businesses implement structured succession processes and engage in long-term strategic planning across generations to ensure sustainable growth (Ibrahim et al., 2004). There must be a balanced approach between strategy and succession planning. While a strong focus on internal succession ensures strategic continuity, it also carries the risk of reduced adaptability to changing market conditions. Therefore, both aspects should be managed in a balanced way to ensure strategic renewal and long-term competitiveness (Nordqvist et al., 2013; Smith & White, 1987).

The outlined research findings primarily focus on environmental and contextual conditions that are not subject to radical changes. This is likely due to the fact that, especially in recent years, numerous crises and shorter, more disruptive industrial waves have emerged, reducing the perceived necessity for in-depth research in this area. Research on family businesses still has gaps in the areas of strategic management and growth, particularly regarding success factors for sustainable development and innovation capability, as well as in professional business management and long-term strategic planning (Benavides-Velasco et al., 2013). This study aims to contribute by providing a systematic overview of strategy development in the light of radical change, considering both evolutionary and revolutionary dynamics in family businesses. Based on this objective, the following research questions will be addressed.

What is the current state of research on strategy development in family businesses in times of evolution, revolution, and radical change?

How should strategy development be implemented in family businesses during times of evolution, revolution, and radical change?

For this purpose, a systematic literature analysis was conducted using the Scopus database. The focus was placed on selected international journals specializing in family business research. This article is structured as follows: The next chapter provides a literature review focusing on the topics of strategy development and competitive advantage and evolution and revolution in times of radical change. This is followed by a description of the methodology, which precedes the presentation of the results of the systematic literature review. The article concludes with a summary of the key findings, an answer to the research question, the limitations of the study, and suggestions for future research projects.

2 Literature Review

2.1 Strategy Development and Competitive Advantage

Traditionally, strategy development follows a process that involves various analyses. It is essential for executive management to communicate a clear and inspiring vision across all levels of the organization (Coulson-Thomas, 1992; O'Shannassy, 2016), as it represents the organization's aspirations and future goals (Grant & Jordan, 2015, p. 14). In this context, it is important to recognize that visions and missions should be regularly reviewed, as significant changes in market conditions may necessitate their adaptation (Grimes et al., 2019; Märk & Situm, 2024). As part of the analytical process, it is crucial to realistically assess the market environment to effectively integrate both external and internal factors (Abell, 2006) and establish a solid foundation for strategic planning (Bittner et al., 2020; Veselinović et al., 2021).

Competitive analysis should be conducted from both the market-based view (outside-in perspective) and the resource-based view (inside-out perspective). Integrating these two perspectives enables companies to gain deeper insights into their competitive landscape and effectively manage both evolutionary adjustments and revolutionary transformations (Hooley et al., 1998; Peteraf & Bergen, 2003). A key concept within the resource-based view for the long-term and sustainable success of (family) businesses is the strategic utilization of resources, which can lead to a competitive advantage (Habbershon & Williams, 1999; Peteraf, 1993). A company can maintain a strong market position by either achieving lower costs than its competitors or by differentiating itself, allowing it to command a price premium in the market (Porter, 1991).

Competitive advantage is a fundamental requirement for a company's long-term competitiveness (Lockett & Thompson, 2010). In rapidly changing environmental and market conditions, this can only be achieved if the resource strategy is continuously adapted and the resource space is actively shaped (Van Witteloostuijn & Boone, 2006). Effective strategic management can only be successfully implemented if a company knows and understands its resources and capabilities (Duncan et al., 1998). Based on the findings of Feurer & Chaharbaghi (1996) and Sarason & Tegarden (2003), it has been demonstrated that strategic planning and strategy development can only provide a competitive advantage when they are flexible, resource-based, and adaptable to dynamic market conditions. Unstructured or inconsistent strategies result in poor business performance (Anwar et al., 2016).

Resources serve as key components of entrepreneurial resilience and enhance an entrepreneur's dynamic capabilities, which include the ability to access and reconfigure resources to address new challenges and opportunities (Deakins & Scott, 2024, p. 163). However, it is essential to recognize that competitive advantage does not arise from resources themselves but rather from their specific utilization in firm-specific performance processes. Resources are only valuable if they contribute to strategically relevant performance (Newbert, 2008; Ployhart, 2021) and meet the criteria of the VRIN framework – valuable, rare, inimitable, and non-substitutable (Kraaijenbrink et al., 2010; Lin & Wu, 2014). These insights highlight the importance of the resource-based view in the strategy development process, not only as a theoretical paradigm but also as a foundation for understanding how companies can achieve competitive advantage (Barney,-ney, 2001).

As environmental and market conditions are increasingly affected by radical and disruptive influences, they evolve at a much faster pace. Therefore, it is necessary to validate previously established strategies in shorter cycles, utilizing flexible, agile, and iterative approaches (Henkel, 2023; McGrath, 1998). Strategic planning is not a one-time activity but rather a continuous, dynamic process (London, 2002; Madai et al., 2020). Only by adopting this approach companies can identify strategic opportunities and take calculated risks, both of which are crucial for sustained success in dynamic markets (Cohan & Rangan, 2006).

A highly effective way to implement strategic planning in faster cycles is through an incremental approach to strategy development. This method provides organizations operating in dynamic and uncertain environments with a practical alternative to large-scale strategic transformations while ensuring flexibility, adaptability, and lower risks. However, this approach is only feasible when cyclical changes do not result in radical transformations (Rees & Porter, 2006). In cases of disruptive shifts, more fundamental strategic adjustments may be required (Greenwood & Hinings, 1996).

Small and medium-sized enterprises (SMEs) face particular constraints when developing strategies. SMEs possess unique characteristics that influence their performance management practices, such as limited resources, short-term priorities, and a strong internal focus. To achieve sustainable growth and performance, they require a balanced combination of strategic planning, clear communication, and continuous adaptation (Ates et al., 2013; Rangone, 1999). In family businesses, the strategy development process must be viewed through the broader lens of family and business overlap. The concept of "Familiness" represents a valuable strategic resource, playing a crucial role in overcoming challenges (Down, 2013, pp. 90–91; Reisinger & Lehner, 2015).

In family businesses, the concept of entrepreneurial orientation (EO) plays a relevant role in strategy development. EO encompasses a company's innovativeness, risk-taking, and proactiveness in strategic decision-making and serves as a key framework for explaining business strategies and performance in family firms (Hernández-Linares & López-Fernández, 2018; Schepers et al., 2014). Family-run businesses tend to be more resilient to economic crises, especially when family members are actively involved in management. However, a strong entrepreneurial orientation (EO) can weaken this advantage, as it creates internal tensions and leads to changes in strategic direction (Revilla et al., 2016). EO also changes significantly across generations. While the first generation is strongly shaped by the founder, the competitive environment and external resources play a larger role in later generations. To remain innovative and competitive in the long run, companies in later generations should strategically integrate non-family managers and investors (Cruz & Nordqvist, 2012).

Zellweger & Sieger (2012) state in this context that a flexible adaptation of entrepreneurial orientation across generations is crucial for sustainable competitiveness. A balance between EO (Entrepreneurial Orientation) and SEW (Socioemotional Wealth) is therefore necessary. While EO generally enhances firm performance, a strong focus on SEW (e.g., prioritizing family control over profitability) can weaken or even nullify this effect. Family businesses must therefore develop a well-balanced strategy that considers both entrepreneurial growth and the long-term preservation of family values (Cater & Schwab, 2008; Schepers et al., 2014). In summary, it can be stated that in family businesses, the owners' goals significantly influence strategic decisions and, consequently, the long-term success of the company (Lee & Marshall, 2013).

2.2 Evolution and Revolution in Times of Radical Change

Radical change can be understood as a shift from an existing fundamental structure to an entirely new one. It involves a transformation from a state that cannot be clearly assigned to any specific structure to one with a distinctly defined and recognizable structure. The considerations of pace, sequence, and linearity of the change process are based on this concept of radical change (Amis et al., 2004; Greenwood & Hinings, 1996). Radical organizational changes do not always occur as planned but can unintentionally emerge from small, local adjustments, especially in unstable environments (Plowman et al., 2007). Radical changes in uncertain times can be successfully implemented through a clear vision, consistent leadership, and iterative adjustments (Corbett, 2013; Gross & Geiger, 2017). Closely intertwined with radical change are the concepts of evolution and revolution. Revolutionary phases in organizations are characterized by profound disruptions that radically alter existing structures and management practices. Evolutionary phases promote stability and growth, revolutionary times force a break with outdated models, such as the transition from centralized to decentralized structures.

Companies should utilize evolutionary phases to better account for dynamic, path-dependent developments. Even during evolutionary phases, strategy must be pursued as a continuous process of experimentation, selection, and adaptation (Barnett & Burgelman, 1996). In family businesses, evolutionary development also inevitably involves the formation of the three subsystems – family, management, and ownership – as outlined in the Three-Circle Model by Taguiri & Davis (1996) (family business system evolution). These subsystems are often the source of many challenges that family businesses must navigate (Schuman et al., 2010, p. 77). However, these subsystems can coexist and do not necessarily conflict with one another. In fact, when balanced properly, they can be crucial for high performance in family businesses (Uhlaner et al., 2012; Zahra, 2005). Family businesses possess a unique strategic dynamic that fosters their longevity but can also hinder them during times of radical change. A differentiated approach to incremental and disruptive changes is necessary to ensure their long-term competitiveness (Belling et al., 2021).

The success of a revolution determines whether an organization can achieve sustainable growth. During this phase, management must develop new practices that serve as a foundation for future expansion. Revolutions can be delayed but not avoided – they are essential for overcoming structural barriers and enabling progress (Greenwood & Hinings, 1996; Greiner, 1998). To remain successful after a revolution, companies need organizational strength. Building such strength is a continuous process that requires vision, innovation, cultural transformation, and adaptability. Companies that strategically utilize their resources, nurture talent, and maintain a clear vision can ensure long-term resilience and competitiveness (Sharma & Sahoo, 2013).

Within the evolutionary and revolutionary perspective, there is a connection to the resource-based view (RBV). Resources generally develop incrementally through continuous adaptation to changing market conditions. Both evolutionary and revolutionary adaptation processes are crucial for ensuring long-term success and competitive advantage (Mathews, 2002). In this context, Porter (1991) introduces the concept of the "dynamic theory of strategy", emphasizing that environmental factors must be carefully considered in corporate decision-making. Strategies should not be viewed merely as reactions to external conditions, but rather as a long-term, evolutionary process that enables companies to build and adjust competitive advantages over time.

Radical change presents family businesses with significant challenges, as they generally respond more slowly and implement necessary changes inadequately due to the concept of "familiness" (Belling et al., 2021). This is because it reflects the result of the specific regulation of the interplay of different systems in an overall context (Frank et al., 2010). As a result, there is a risk that corrective measures will be initiated too late, which can negatively impact the performance and development of the business.

3 Methodology

To comprehensively answer the research question and achieve the objective of this study, a systematic literature analysis was conducted. This method is particularly suitable for gaining a clear overview of the current state of research on the key concepts of Organizational Evolution, Organizational Revolution, Radical Change, Strategic

Change, and Strategy Development. The systematic literature analysis enables the creation of a transparent and reproducible foundation for synthesizing existing scientific knowledge (Fisch & Block, 2018; Knopf, 2006; Thomé et al., 2016). The chosen approach (Figure 1) follows the established scientific standards of Tranfield et al. (2003) and Bramer et al. (2017) and adheres to a multi-stage process that ensures relevant publications are identified, assessed, and analyzed in terms of their content.

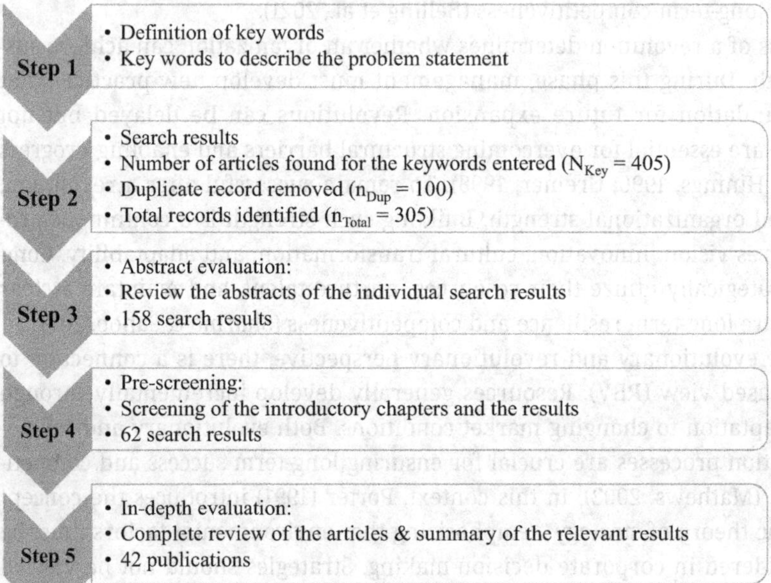

Figure 1: Literature filtering process.

Step 1 – Definition of key words:

The first step of the systematic literature analysis involved defining key terms that served as the foundation for the literature search (Mishra, 2020). These terms were carefully selected to represent the core concepts of the study—Organizational Evolution, Organizational Revolution, Radical Change, Strategic Change, and Strategy Development (Amis et al., 2004; Greenwood & Hinings, 1996; Greiner, 1998). The keywords were deliberately chosen to capture both theoretical and practical perspectives on the strategy development process.

– Organizational Evolution and Strategy Development and Family Business
– Organizational Revolution and Strategy Development and Family Business
– Radical Change and Strategy Development and Family Business

Step 2 – Search results:
The search for relevant publications was conducted in the recognized scientific database Scopus. Scopus covers the greatest number of journals compared to other international databases (Guz & Rushchitsky, 2009) and is a widely used and well-established source for academic literature in the fields of Business, Management, and Accounting (Kraus et al., 2020; Paul & Criado, 2020). Focusing on a single database is sufficient for the purpose of this study, as only journals specializing in the field of family business with a strong reputation within the research community were considered (Rovelli et al., 2022).

In accordance with the Chartered Association of Business Schools (CABS), the selected journals include: *Journal of Family and Economic Issues* (2 Stars), *Family Business Review* (3 Stars), *Journal of Family Business Strategy* (2 Stars), and *Journal of Family Business Management* (1 Star). The search was limited to English-language journal articles. To ensure that all relevant publications were comprehensively captured, the search process followed the recommendations of Bramer et al. (2017).

- No time restriction: The analysis included both recent and historical publications to trace developments and trends in the research field.
- Filter criteria: The search was limited to journal articles from the relevant research areas (as described above).
- Total extracted articles: A total of 405 articles (N_{Key}) were retrieved from the database based on the selected keywords.
- Removal of duplicates: 100 duplicate entries (n_{Dup}) were systematically eliminated.
- Final dataset: A total of 305 search results (n_{Total}) were identified from the database.

Step 3 – Abstracts evaluation:
In the third step, the identified publications were assessed based on their abstracts to ensure their relevance to the research question (Thomé et al., 2016). The evaluation specifically considered the following criteria:

- Clear relevance to key concepts: Only publications with a direct connection to the core concepts were included.
- Focus on strategy development, evolution, revolution, and radical change: The selection prioritized studies addressing these aspects.
- Exclusion of niche publications: Studies focusing exclusively on specialized niche areas without a clear link to the research question were excluded.

After this evaluation, 158 relevant publications remained.

Step 4 – Pre-screening:
In a fourth step, the previously selected publications underwent a preliminary content review (Tranfield et al., 2003). The objective was to ensure that only studies contributing meaningfully to answering the research question were included. The criteria for the preliminary screening included:

- Full alignment with the defined keywords: The publication had to match the key concepts precisely.
- Relevance to the underlying research question: Only studies that contributed directly to answering the research question were included.
- Methodological quality of the studies: The research needed to demonstrate a rigorous and transparent methodology.

After completing the screening process, 62 publications remained for the final analysis.

Step 5 – In-depth evaluation:
The remaining 62 articles were read in full and analyzed regarding their theoretical and empirical contributions. The focus was placed on:
- The underlying theoretical frameworks used in the studies.
- The operationalization of key concepts, examining how Organizational Evolution, Organizational Revolution, Radical Change, Strategic Change, and Strategy Development were defined and measured.
- Key findings and practical implications derived from the studies.

Following the in-depth evaluation, the 42 core publications were systematically categorized into thematic clusters to structure the key insights and contributions of the studies more effectively (Greenstein & Davis, 2013, p. 37). The clustering process was guided by both theoretical considerations and empirical findings, ensuring a comprehensive synthesis of research on strategy development in family businesses under conditions of evolution, revolution, and radical change. The final thematic clusters are as follows:
- Strategic adaptability & transformation in family businesses
- Management in and after situations of crises
- Succession & long-term orientation
- Management of innovation

The clustering process followed an iterative and deductive approach, grounded in existing theoretical frameworks while allowing for emergent themes from the empirical studies. The decision to form these clusters was based on (Snyder, 2019):
- Conceptual Coherence: Studies were grouped based on shared theoretical foundations and core concepts such as socioemotional wealth, ambidexterity, and strategic fit.
- Empirical Focus: Publications addressing similar empirical phenomena (e.g., crisis responses, internationalization strategies) were assigned to the same category.
- Practical Implications: Studies were clustered according to their real-world applicability, ensuring that key findings could be translated into actionable insights for family businesses.

By structuring the heterogeneous landscape of family business strategy research into these seven key clusters, the analysis provides a clearer theoretical and empirical synthesis, facilitating a more structured discussion of strategic development in family businesses. This categorization lays the groundwork for deriving meaningful insights into how family firms navigate, adapt, and thrive in times of evolution, revolution, and radical change.

4 Results

The results of the literature review are structured and presented in the following chapter according to the developed clusters.

4.1 Strategic Adaptability and Transformation in Family Businesses

The strategic management of family businesses is shaped by the close interweaving of family and business logics. The influence of the family affects not only goal setting but the entire strategy process (Sharma et al., 1997). Strategy is therefore understood less as a singular decision-making act and more as an ongoing process of adaptation, operating within the tension between stability and change.

In dynamic and uncertain environments, family businesses have demonstrated the ability to pursue both explorative and exploitative activities simultaneously. This ambidexterity is considered a strategic core competence that enables long-term transformation in the sense of “organizational evolution” (Canale et al., 2024). Evolutionary change does not occur abruptly but unfolds as an incremental process, driven by intergenerational values, a sense of responsibility, and a long-term orientation.

Digital transformation in family businesses typically does not follow a disruptive pattern. Instead, it manifests as a gradual development, in which technologies are strategically embedded and accompanied by cultural adaptations (Begnini et al., 2024). The implementation of artificial intelligence is also seen not as a rupture, but as a gradual shift, closely tied to values, heritage, and entrepreneurial objectives (Tuncalp, 2024). This change is part of an evolutionary transformation in which ethical considerations, intergenerational integration, and cultural cohesion play central roles.

Corporate culture is also central to strategic development. The so-called Family Business Culture (FBC) represents a strategic resource that provides stability across generations while supporting adaptive processes (Alipour et al., 2024). It contributes to the development of dynamic capabilities by fostering social bonds, knowledge transfer, and values-based leadership (Chirico et al., 2012). Adaptability, however, is not determined by internal factors alone. Family businesses operate in environments that require ongoing reflection and strategic realignment. Studies show that even in unstable, resource-scarce contexts, strategic responses are possible, although often slowed by ownership logics (Wang et al., 2020). This highlights the need to actively manage strategic paradoxes. As Gil et al. (2024) demonstrate, sustainable transformation arises not from resolving contradictions, but from their productive coexistence.

Long-term development is also shaped by interaction with the institutional environment. Historical analyses show how family businesses position themselves within their market category over decades and mobilize cultural resources for strategic reorientation (Haag et al., 2023). Radical change, such as entrepreneurial reinvention, is only possible when existing cultural patterns allow sufficient openness to learning processes (Hall et al., 2001). Structural inertia can be both an obstacle and a stabilizing force. Especially with increasing family influence, decision-making structures often remain unchanged, even when strategic realignments are initiated (Lindow et al., 2010). Successful organizational evolution thus requires not only strategic clarity but also structural flexibility.

Finally, long-term resilience arises not from singular resources, but from the combination and reconfiguration of human, social, and financial capital (Mallon & Fainshmidt, 2024). Strategic identity, particularly in the form of Entrepreneurial Orientation, develops over generations and reflects the cultural imprint of the organization (Short et al., 2009; Casillas et al., 2010). Taken together, these findings point to a dynamic, diverse, and context-bound developmental trajectory of family businesses, whose strategic adaptation is deeply embedded in cultural, structural, and relational contexts.

4.2 Management In and After Situations of Crises

Crises act as significant turning points for family businesses, triggering strategic, cultural, and structural changes. Unlike in stable periods – often characterized by a risk-averse mindset – crisis situations can lead to increased innovation and a greater willingness to take risks. Leppäaho & Ritala (2022) argue that this interplay between stability and change is not coincidental but can be interpreted as a manifestation of organizational evolution. In this view, crises serve not only as stressors but also as catalysts for incremental – and at times radical – transformations.

In particular, external shocks – such as economic recessions, geopolitical tensions, or global pandemics – force family businesses to reassess and realign established structures. Hadjielias et al. (2022) illustrate, using the Eurozone debt crisis and the COVID-19 pandemic as examples, how familial social capital transforms in times of crisis. By reorganizing roles, trust, and relationships, new network structures emerge that enhance both internal and external collaboration capabilities. This adaptation reflects an evolutionary learning logic, in which resilience stems not from mere resistance but from active transformation and relationship management.

Similarly, Czakon et al. (2023) emphasize the role of strategic resilience as a long-developed pattern in family businesses. Coping with so-called "wild cards" – extreme and unpredictable events – is not based on impulsive strategic shifts but on a repertoire of decision-making routines built over generations. Through experiential knowledge, shared values, and a long-term perspective, a stable foundation emerges – one that integrates change rather than resists it. This is a core feature of organizational evolution.

A central element of crisis resilience lies in leadership. Block & Ulrich (2023) show that family-led businesses tended to suffer smaller financial market losses during the COVID-19 crisis compared to other types of firms. They attribute this to a pronounced stewardship-oriented management style, characterized by personal identification, a strong sense of responsibility, and strategic flexibility. In this context, leadership becomes a key function in adaptive strategy development, one that is evolutionarily stabilized over time through accumulated experience.

Zainal (2022) expands on this perspective by highlighting the role of innovation capacity and future-oriented thinking. Family businesses that had already developed a strong innovation orientation prior to the crisis were able to respond more quickly and effectively during the pandemic. Creativity, willingness to take risks, and strategic openness are not traits that emerge in the midst of a crisis, but are instead the result of long-term learning and development processes. This evolutionary perspective underscores the importance of forward-looking strategic work during stable times as a foundation for resilience in exceptional situations.

Overall, the findings make clear that family businesses do not view crises solely as threats but also as opportunities for further development. Resilience is not limited to short-term reactions, but should be understood as a deeply embedded, evolutionary process. The ongoing reflection and adaptation of strategic, cultural, and structural elements lay the groundwork for sustainable crisis management – and thus for long-term business success.

4.3 Succession & Long-term Orientation

Succession processes are among the most complex challenges for family businesses and mark critical phases of organizational transformation. These transitions involve not only the transfer of responsibility but also the reorganization of power structures, strategic orientation, and cultural imprint. Serhan et al. (2023) interpret such transitions as expressions of a strategic paradox, in which continuity and change do not contradict but rather mutually reinforce each other. The process follows a logic of organizational evolution, where existing values, rituals, and structures are not only preserved but also developed further or reinterpreted.

In their study, Kessler & Zipper-Weber (2023) demonstrate how succession can also trigger profound strategic realignments – such as in the form of internationalization. Initiated by a so-called SEW "loss mode," a dynamic emerges that enables new strategic learning processes and the development of dynamic capabilities. These adaptive patterns show that succession does not necessarily equate to stability, but can also serve as a catalyst for innovation and change. It can be understood as an evolutionary process.

Sunon et al. (2022) emphasize the profound impact generational transitions can have on structure and strategy. Even without radical disruptions, these phases often mark turning points in a company's development, especially when emotional attachment, value orientation, and governance issues intertwine. This underscores that organizational evolution in family businesses is strongly shaped by soft factors – ones that may not be immediately measurable, but are observable over the long term.

A central driver of this development, according to Barros-Contreras et al. (2022), is the so-called "Familiness Learning Mechanism." This describes a process of organizational learning shaped by familial closeness, emotional attachment, and shared experiences. Through knowledge accumulation, social integration, and cultural embeddedness, a stable, incremental change occurs – enabling strategic adaptation. This mechanism is a core element of evolutionary development.

The complexity of succession is further explored in the study by Blanco-Mazagatos et al. (2016), which shows that increasing distance between active and passive family members can lead to new lines of conflict that impact governance structures. This change typically unfolds gradually, but has far-reaching consequences for decision-making logics, forms of cooperation, and ownership structures – an evolutionary process that can be accelerated by generational transitions.

Shahzad et al. (2024), using case studies from Pakistan, demonstrate that successful succession requires structured planning, early involvement, and clear responsibilities. Where these conditions are lacking, disruptions occur; where they are in place, they facilitate further development. Succession can thus be seen as a critical transitional process, in which governance, culture, and strategy are closely interwoven, collectively shaping an evolutionary development path.

Governance philosophy itself is also part of this transformation. Steier & Miller (2010) show how succession often leads to a shift from community-oriented to more formalized structures. This transformation does not happen abruptly but unfolds in phases, during which power dynamics, decision-making processes, and strategic objectives change step by step – a pattern that can be interpreted as evolutionary.

Ahrens et al. (2018) additionally highlight the role of the outgoing owner, whose influence often remains even after the formal handover. Whether this influence is stabilizing or inhibiting depends on factors such as the company's maturity, the relationship with the successor, and the organization's learning capacity. Here too, leadership transition does not automatically bring clarity, but initiates negotiation processes that are part of organizational evolution.

Finally, Cherchem (2017) emphasizes that the strategic orientation of a family business is significantly shaped by cultural evolution. Especially in the context of intergenerational leadership, normative assumptions – such as proximity versus professionalism – shift, thereby transforming the foundation of entrepreneurial decision-making. This cultural transformation is not coincidental, but part of a long-term adaptation process that strengthens organizational resilience and strategic capacity for action.

4.4 Management of Innovation

Innovation is considered a central element for the long-term competitiveness of family businesses, with the innovation process typically unfolding in an evolutionary rather than disruptive manner. Paunović et al. (2023), using the example of Serbian family businesses, show that these firms often rely on incremental process innovations to increase efficiency and enhance customer proximity. Strategic development is thus based on gradual adjustments and continuous learning, rather than abrupt changes.

A recurring pattern is the distinction between family businesses and founder-led firms. Block et al. (2013) emphasize that founder firms tend to be more risk-oriented and initiate more radical innovations, whereas family firms focus more on stability and proven innovation pathways. This distinction points to different organizational development trajectories: while founder firms aim for disruption, family firms pursue value-based, sustainable development.

Brinkerink (2018) adds to this differentiation with the concepts of "deep" and "broad search." Family businesses are characterized by deep learning, meaning they deepen existing competencies, but often struggle with broader, more exploratory search efforts. This limits the scope of innovation but ensures high implementation efficiency – a classic feature of evolutionary innovation strategies.

Cultural and social factors also play a decisive role. Diéguez-Soto et al. (2016) show that family management can both hinder and support innovation processes. While it may impede the commercialization of new ideas, it simultaneously strengthens execution in operational processes. This ambivalence highlights the importance of tacit knowledge and social bonds in shaping innovative structures.

Gusenbauer et al. (2023) show that family businesses make specific use of historically accumulated knowledge for innovation purposes. The ability to recombine past experiences fosters continuous renewal and enhances innovation capabilities without relying on disruptive impulses. Kammerlander et al. (2015) add that cultural narratives can foster innovation readiness across generations – particularly when they are interpreted through a family-centric lens. The study by Kosmidou and Ahuja (2019) highlights that innovation in family businesses arises from specific configurations. Factors such as succession planning, environmental changes, or professionalization act as moderators of different innovation paths. This dynamic diversity reflects an evolutionary innovation logic oriented toward contextual conditions.

At the same time, there are also barriers. Miroshnychenko et al. (2024) identify a tendency toward innovation conservatism, which can negatively affect market performance – particularly in institutionally weaker environments. However, they also show that a strong institutional setting can mitigate this effect. This results in a picture of context-dependent, evolutionary innovation processes. Another key element is the balance between exploration and exploitation. Moss et al. (2014) stress that strategic consistency in balancing these two dimensions is critical.

It is not the exact weighting, but the consistency of behavior that enhances performance – further evidence of the evolutionary nature of innovation in family businesses. Innovative collaborations, especially in vertical partnerships, are described by Pemartín et al. (2024) as particularly effective. Family businesses leverage their stable networks and tacit knowledge bases to realize long-term cooperation advantages. This development is rooted in structural stability and strategic learning capacity – typical elements of organizational evolution.

Innovation attitudes also vary fundamentally. Rondi et al. (2019) identify four strategic innovation types, shaped by factors such as family cohesion, goal divergence, or succession. These attitudes evolve over time and shape innovation behavior in stable patterns. Brinkerink et al. (2020) show that the perception of organizational identity significantly influences innovation capability. Firms with high "Organizational Identity Elasticity" – meaning a strategic adaptability of identity – are particularly capable of responding to disruptive changes.

Finally, Dieleman (2019) highlights the role of governance structures built over the long term. Trust, oversight, and networks create a framework in which innovation is systematically developed. Scholes et al. (2021) add that elements such as family management and family guardianship significantly influence the direction of strategic innovation – particularly with regard to integrating new technologies or entering new markets.

In summary, innovation in family businesses does not occur randomly or abruptly, but as the result of long-term, evolutionary development paths. Change emerges through cultural stability, strategic learning processes, and context-sensitive governance – allowing innovation capacity not only to be preserved, but to be deliberately enhanced.

5 Summary and Conclusion

This study systematically examined how family businesses approach strategy development in the context of evolution, revolution, and radical change. Through a comprehensive systematic literature review encompassing 42 peer-reviewed articles from leading family business journals, the study explored how family-owned firms navigate strategic transformation in increasingly complex and uncertain environments. Central to the analysis was the distinction between gradual, evolutionary change and sudden, disruptive revolutionary change, with particular attention paid to the mechanisms that enable or inhibit strategic adaptability in family enterprises.

The findings confirm that most family businesses tend to engage with change through evolutionary, incremental processes rather than through radical transformation. Strategic development in family firms is typically embedded in long-term thinking, emotional attachment, and the intergenerational transfer of values, which reinforces a preference for continuity over disruption. This confirms earlier observations by Sharma et al. (1997) and Chirico et al. (2011), who described strategic behavior in family firms as a gradual, path-dependent process deeply shaped by the family's cultural and emotional framework. The prevalent use of the resource-based view (Habbershon & Williams, 1999; Barney, 2001) in family business literature also reinforces the idea that sustainable competitive advantage is achieved through the accumulation and preservation of unique, firm-specific resources over time.

The literature shows that family firms often demonstrate high levels of resilience and internal cohesion in times of external crisis. Studies by Hadjielias et al. (2022) and Block & Ulrich (2023) emphasize the role of stewardship, long-term commitment, and family social capital in navigating turbulent times. However, these studies frame crisis response largely within an evolutionary logic – where firms adjust through internal learning, role redistribution, or incremental innovation. Even in the context of global crises, such as the COVID-19 pandemic, family businesses were more likely to restructure within existing frameworks than to fundamentally alter their strategic direction. This tendency aligns with findings by De Massis et al. (2015), who observed a general conservatism in family firms' innovation and change processes.

In contrast to the well-researched themes of continuity, succession, and incremental innovation, the study finds that the topics of radical change and organizational revolution remain significantly underexplored in the family business literature. While several theoretical frameworks – such as those proposed by Greenwood & Hinings (1996) and Amis et al. (2004) – offer valuable perspectives on organizational revolution, their application within family business research is limited. Most existing studies implicitly assume a relatively stable or gradually shifting environment, leaving a clear gap in understanding how family firms respond to highly disruptive, nonlinear shifts – such as those brought about by digitalization, climate change, or geopolitical upheaval.

Only a small subset of the analyzed literature directly addresses revolutionary change, and even then, the treatment is often conceptual or secondary. For example, Belling et al. (2021) discuss the constraints that familiness imposes on adaptability but stop short of analyzing how family firms might overcome these constraints during episodes of radical transformation. Similarly, while the resource-based view and concepts like socioemotional wealth (Berrone et al., 2012) have been extensively used to explain strategic inertia or incremental adaptation, they are rarely applied to study processes of deep structural disruption or business model reinvention.

This underrepresentation is particularly notable given the increasing pace and intensity of disruptive environmental shifts. As firms across sectors are compelled to respond to digital revolutions, ecological transformation, and social realignments, it is imperative to understand how family firms – often characterized by slower decision-making cycles and deeply embedded traditions – cope with such changes. The current literature lacks sufficient empirical evidence or conceptual models to assess how family firms initiate, manage, or resist revolutionary change, highlighting a critical area for future research.

In answering the research questions, the study concludes that the current body of research on strategy development in family businesses is heavily weighted toward evolutionary models of change, with limited engagement in the domains of revolutionary transformation and radical strategic realignment. The implementation of strategy in family firms continues to reflect long-term, stability-oriented frameworks, emphasizing continuity, internal learning, and cultural cohesion. These approaches offer advantages in terms of resilience and sustainability but can also hinder the rapid strategic shifts required in radically changing environments.

There remains a substantial research gap regarding how family firms manage or fail to manage radical transformations. Questions such as what triggers a revolutionary change in a family firm, how family structures facilitate or impede such shifts, and what leadership dynamics emerge in moments of rupture are yet to be sufficiently addressed. Moreover, the intersection of radical change with issues such as intergenerational leadership conflict, external professionalization, and the erosion of socioemotional wealth presents fertile ground for empirical exploration.

The study is not without limitations. By focusing on selected journals within the Scopus database and English-language publications, potentially relevant interdisciplinary and non-English sources may have been overlooked. The clustering of thematic insights, while grounded in theory, involves interpretative judgment and may reflect some degree of subjectivity. Additionally, the reliance on published academic literature excludes practitioner perspectives and gray literature that might provide further insight into radical change processes in real-world family firm contexts.

Future research should prioritize the systematic study of radical change and organizational revolution in family businesses. Longitudinal case studies, comparative cross-industry analyses, and multi-level frameworks that incorporate psychological, structural, and institutional variables are needed to better understand how and under what conditions family firms can successfully navigate disruptive change. Investigating the interplay between strategic identity, entrepreneurial orientation, and governance innovation in moments of transformation could contribute significantly to both theory and practice. By shifting focus from merely preserving the past to also enabling future reinvention, research can help equip family businesses to remain competitive and resilient in a world increasingly defined by discontinuity and upheaval.

References

Abell, D. F. (2006). The future of strategy is leadership. *Journal of Business Research, 59*(3), 310–314.

Adamides, E. D. (2015). Linking operations strategy to the corporate strategy process: A practice perspective. *Business Process Management Journal, 21*(2), 267–287.

Ahrens, J.-P., Uhlaner, L., Woywode, M., & Zybura, J. (2018). "Shadow emperor" or "loyal paladin"? – The Janus face of previous owner involvement in family firm successions. *Journal of Family Business Strategy, 9*(1), 73–90.

Alipour, K. K., Barber III, D., Batchelor, J. H., Peake, W., Jones, S., & McIlveene, T. (2024). Family business culture: a strategic resource and driver of firm performance. *Journal of Family Business Management*, Vol. ahead-of-print No. ahead-of-print. https://doi.org/10.1108/JFBM-03-2024-0064.

Amis, J., Slack. T., & Hinings, C. R. (2004). The pace, sequence, and linearity of radical change. *Academy of Management Journal, 47*(1), 15–39.

Anward, J., Shah, S., & Hasnu, S. (2016). Business strategy and organizational performance. *Pakistan Economic and Social Review, 54*(1), 97–122.

Astrachan, J. H. (2010). Strategy in family business: Toward a multidimensional research agenda. *Journal of Family Business Strategy, 1*(1), 6–14.

Ates, A., Garengo, P., Cocca, P., & Bititci, U. (2013). The development of SME managerial practice for effective performance management. *Journal of Small Business and Enterprise Development, 20*(1), 28–54.

Barnett, W. P., & Burgelman, R. A. (1996). Evolutionary perspective on strategy. *Strategic Management Journal, 17*(Special Issue: Evolutionary Perspective on Strategy), 5–19.

Barney, J. B. (2001). Resource-based theories of competitive advantage: A ten-year retrospective on the resource-based view. *Journal of Management, 27*(6), 643–650.

Barros-Contreras, I., Basco, R., Martín-Cruz, N., & Hernangómez, J. (2022). Strategic management in family business. The missing concept of the familiness learning mechanism. *Journal of Family Business Management, 12*(1), 67–89.

Begnini, S., Oro, I. M., Tonial, G., & Dalbosco, I. B. (2024). The relationship between the use of technologies and digitalization strategies for digital transformation in family businesses. *Journal of Family Business Management, 14*(4), 710–726.

Belling, M., Pidun, U., & zu Knyphausen-Aufseß, D. (2021). Unbindling strategic change in family firms: The influence of familiness on the strategic change process. *Schmalenbach Journal of Business Research, 73*(10), 381–411.

Benavides-Velasco, C. A., Quintana-Garciía, C., & Guzmán-Parra, V. F. (2013). Trends in family business research. *Small Business Economics, 40*(1), 41–57.

Berrone P., Cruz C., & Gomez-Mejia, L. R. (2012). Socioemotional wealth in family firms: Theoretical dimensions, assessment approaches, and agenda for future research. *Family Business Review, 25*(3), 258–279.

Bettinelli, C., Lissana, E., Bergamaschi, M., & De Massis, A. (2022). Identity in family firms: Toward an integrative understanding. *Family Business Review, 35*(4), 383–414.

Bittner, B., Nagy, A., Kovacs, T., & Hajnalka, M. (2020). Methodology for the external environmental analysis as a part of strategy planning. *The Annals of the University of Oradea. Economic Sciences, 29*(1), 461–466.

Blanco-Mazagatos, V., de Quevedo-Puente, E., & Bautista Delgado-García, J. (2016). How agency conflict between family managers and family owners affects performance in wholly family-owned firms: A generational perspective. *Journal of Family Business Strategy, 7*(3), 167–177.

Block, J., & Ulrich, L. (2023). Are family owners and managers good stewards in global crises? Evidence from stock market reactions to Covid-19. *Journal of Family Business Strategy, 14*(1) 100534.

Block, J., Miller, D., Jaskiewicz, P., & Spiegel, F. (2013). Economic and technological importance of innovations in large family and founder firms: An analysis of patent data. *Family Business Review, 26*(2), 180–199.

Bolland, E. J. (2020). *Strategizing: New thinking about strategy, planning and management*. Bingley, UK: Emerald Publishing.

Bramer, M. W., Rethlefsen, M. L., Kleijnen, J., & Franco, O. H. (2017). Optimal database combinations for literature research searches in systematic reviews: A prospective exploratory study, *Systematic Reviews, 6*(1), 245.

Brinkerink, J. (2018). Broad search, deep search, and the absorptive capacity performance of family and nonfamily firm R&D. *Family Business Review, 31*(3), 295–317.

Brinkerink, J., Rondi, E., Benedetti, C., & Arzubiaga, U. (2020). Family business or business family? Organizational identity elasticity and strategic responses to disruptive innovation. *Journal of Family Business Strategy, 11*, 100360.

Brockhaus, R. H. (2004). Family business succession: Suggestions for future research. *Family Business Review, 42*(2), 165–177.

Canale, F., Müller, C., Laveren, E., & Cambré, B. (2024). The role of the family and the institutional context for ambidexterity in Latin American family firms. *Journal of Family Business Strategy, 15*(1), 100567.

Carlock, R. S., & Ward, J. L. (2001). *Strategic planning for the family business: Parallel planning to unify the family and business*. New York, NY: Palgave MacMillan.

Casillas, J. C., Moreno, A. M., & Barbero, J. L. (2010). A configurational approach of the relationship between entrperneurial orientation and growth of family firms. *Family Business Review, 23*(1), 27–44.

Cater, J., & Schwab, A. (2008). Turnaround strategies in established small family firms. *Family Business Review, 21*(1), 31–50.

Cherchem, N. (2017). The relationship between organizational culture and entrepreneurial orientation in family firms: Does generational involvement matter? *Journal of Family Business Strategy, 8*(2), 87–98.

Chirico, F., Nordqvist, M., Colombo, G., & Mollona, E. (2012). Simulating dynamic capabilities and value creation in family firms: Is paternalism an "asset" or a "liability"? *Family Business Review, 25*(3), 318–338.

Chrisman, J. J., Chua, J. H., De Massis, A., Minola, T., & Vismara, S. (2016). Management process and strategy execution in family firms: From "what" to "how". *Small Business Economics, 47*(3), 719–734.

Cohen, P., & Rangan, S. U. (2006). Follow the legend: Seven strategy lessons from top entrepreneurs. *Business Strategy Review, 17*(4), 56–61

Collier, N., Fishwick, F., & Floyd, S. W. (2004). Managerial involvement and perceptions of strategy process. *Long Range Planning, 37*(1), 67–83.

Corbett, J. (2013). Leading radical change in uncertain times. *Public Administration Review, 73*(3), 388–389.

Coulson-Thomas, C. (1992). Strategic vision or strategic con?: Rhetoric or reality? *Long Range Planning, 25*(1), 81–89.

Cruz, C., & Nordqvist, M. (2012). Entrepreneurial orientation in family firms: A generational perspective. *Small Business Economics, 38*(1), 33–49.

Czakon, W., Hajdas, M., & Radomska, J. (2023). Playing the wild cards: Antecedents of family firm resilience. *Journal of Family Business Strategy, 14*(1), 100484.

Daspit, J. J., Chrisman, J. J., Ashton, T., & Evangelopoulos, N. (2021). Family firm heterogeneity: A definition, common themes, scholarly progress, and directions forward. *Family Business Review, 34*(3), 296–322.

Davis, J. A. (2008). Toward a typology of family business systems. In: J. Tàpies & J. L. Ward (Eds.), *Family values and value creation: The fostering of enduring values within family-owned businesses* (pp. 127–154). New York, NY: Palgrave MacMillan.

De Feo, J. A., & Janssen, A. (2001). Implementing a strategy successfully. *Measuring Business Excellence, 5*(4), 4–6.

De Massis, A., Frattini, F., Pizzurno, E., & Cassia, L. (2015). Product innovation in family versus nonfamily firms: An exploratory analysis. *Journal of Small Business Management*, *53*(1), 1–36.
Deakins, D., & Scott, J. M. (2024). Resources for entrepreneurship. In: D. Deakins & J. M. Scott (Eds.), *Entrepreneurship: A contemporary & global approach* (pp. 163–194). Thousand Oaks, CA: Sage Publications.
Diéguez-Soto, J., Manzaneque, M., & Rojo-Ramiírez, A. A. (2016). Technological innovation inputs, outputs and performance: The moderating role of family involvement in management. *Family Business Review*, *29*(3), 327–346.
Dieleman, M. (2019). Reaping what you sow: The family firm innovation trajectory. *Journal of Family Business Strategy*, *10*(4), 100248.
Down, S. (2013). *Enterprise, entrepreneurship and small business*. London, UK: Sage Publications.
Duncan, J., Ginter, P. M., & Swayne, L. E. (1998). Competitive advantage and internal organizational assessment. *Academy of Management Executive*, *12*(3), 6–16.
Feurer, R., & Chaharbaghi, K. (1996). Competitive environments, dynamic strategy development capabilities and business performance. *Benchmarking for Quality Management & Technology*, *3*(3), 32–49.
Fisch, C., & Block, J. (2018). Six tips for your (systematic) literature review in business and management research. *Management Review Quarterly*, *68*(2), 103–106.
Flagg, D., Kudrimoti, S., & Margetis, S. (2011). Do management decisions matter when firms are in distress? *Review of Management Innovation & Creativity*, *4*(9), 1–19.
Frank, H., Lueger, M., Nosé, L., & Suchy, D. (2010). The concept of "Familiness": Literature review and systems theory-based reflections. *Journal of Family Business Strategy*, *1*(3), 119–130.
Furrer, O., Pandian, R. J., & Thomas, H. (2007). Corporate strategy and shareholder value during decline and turnaround. *Management Decision*, *45*(3), 372–392.
Garcìa, J. O., Castejón, P. J. M., & Pérez, C. P. (2014). The culture of conflict in family business. *Revista de Empresa Familiar*, *4*(2), 25–35.
Gil, M., Thor, K., & Gemheden, A. (2024). Managing the tensions between tradition and innovation in family firms. *Journal of Family Business Management*, Vol. ahead-of-print No. ahead-of-print. https://doi.org/10.1108/JFBM-09-2024-0213.
Grant, R. M., & Jordan, J. (2015). *Foundations of strategy*. West Sussex, UK: John Wiley & Sons. Inc.
Greenstein, T. N., & Davis, S. N. (2013). *Methods of family research*. Thousand Oaks, CA: Sage Publications.
Greenwood, R., & Hinings, C. R. (1996). Understanding radical organizational change: Bringing together the old and the new institutionalism. *The Academy of Management Review*, *21*(4), 1022–1054.
Greiner, L. E. (1998). Evolution and revolution as organizations grow. *Harvard Business Review*, *76*(3), 3–11.
Grimes, M. G., Williams, T. A., & Zhao, E. Y. (2019). Anchors aweigh: The sources, variety, and challenges of mission drift. *Academy of Management Review*, *44*(4), 819–845.
Gross, N., & Geiger, S. (2017). Liminality and the entrepreneurial firm: Practice renewal during periods of radical change. *International Journal of Entrepreneurial Behavior & Research*, *23*(2), 185–209.
Gusenbauer, M., Schweiger, N., Matzler, K., & Hautz, J. (2023). Innovation through tradition: The role of past knowledge for successful innovations in family and non-family firms. *Family Business Review*, *36*(1), 17–36.
Guz, A. N., & Rushchitsky, J. J. (2009). Scopus: A system for the evaluation of scientific journals. *International Applied Mechanics*, *45*(4), 351–362.
Haag, K., Achtenhagen, L., & Grimm, J. (2023). Engaging with the category: Exploring family business longevity from a historical perspective. *Family Business Review*, *36*(1), 84–118.
Habbershon, T. G., & Williams, M. L. (1999). A resource-based framework for assessing the strategic advantages of family firms. *Family Business Review*, *12*(1), 1–26.

Hadjielias, E., Hughes, M., & Scholes, L. (2022). External crises and family social capital reconfiguration: Insights from the European debt crisis and the Covid-19 pandemic. *Family Business Review*, *35*(3), 275–305.
Hall, A., Melin, L., & Nordqvist, M. (2001). Entrepreneurship as radical change in the family business: Exploring the role of cultural patterns. *Family Business Review*, *14*(3), 193–208.
Harris, D., Martinez, J. I., & Ward, J. L. (1994). Is strategy different for the family-owned business? *Family Business Review*, *7*(2), 159–174.
Hatten, T. S. (2025). *Small business management: Creating a sustainable competitive advantage*. Thousand Oaks, CA: Sage Publications.
Henkel, C. B. (2023). Strategy development in family businesses. In: T. Zellweger & P. Ohle (Eds.), *Financial management of family businesses: Transparency – compliance – performance – strategy – governance* (pp. 151–154). Wiesbaden: Springer.
Hernández-Linares, R., & López-Fernández, M. C. (2018). Entrepreneurial orientation and the family firm: Mapping the field and tracing a path for future research. *Family Business Review*, *31*(3), 318–351.
Hernández-Perlines, F., Araya-Castillo, L., Millán-Toledo, C., & Ibarra Cisneros, M. A. (2023). Socioemotional wealth: A systematic literature review from a family business perspective. *European Research on Management and Business Economics*, *29*(2), 100218.
Kammerlander, N., Dessì, C., Bird, M., Floris, M., & Murru, A. (2015). The impact of shared stories on family firm innovation: A multicase study. *Family Business Review*, *28*(4), 332–354.
Kessler, A., & Zipper-Weber, V. (2023). Born-again global internationalization in family businesses as a process: A dynamic capabilities perspective in the context of socioemotional wealth. *Journal of Family Business Management*, *13*(3), 1366–1391.
Knopf, J. W. (2006). Doing a literature review. *Political Science & Politics*, *39*(1), 127–132.
Hooley, G., Broderick, A., & Möller, K. (1998). Competitive positioning and the resource-based view of the firm. *Journal of Strategic Marketing*, *6*(2), 97–115.
Ibrahim, A. B., McGuire, J., Soufani, K., & Poutziouris, P. (2004). Patterns in strategy formation in a family firm. *International Journal of Entrepreneurial Behaviour & Research*, *10*(1/2), 127–140.
Kosmidou, V., & Ahuja, M. K. (2019). A configurational approach to family firm innovation. *Family Business Review*, *32*(2), 154–173.
Kraaijenbrink, J., Spender, J.-C., & Groen, A. J. (2010) The resource-based view: A review and assessment of its critiques. *Journal of Management*, *36*(1), 349–372.
Kraus, S., Breier, M., & Dasí-Rodríguez, S. (2020). The art of crafting a systematic literature review in entrepreneurship research. *International Entrepreneurship and Management Journal*, *16*(3), 1023–1042.
Lee, Y. G., & Marshall, M. I. (2013). Goal orientation and performance of family businesses. *Journal of Family and Economic Issues*, *34*(3), 265–274.
Leppäaho, T., & Ritala, P. (2022). Surviving the coronavirus pandemic and beyond: Unlocking family firms' innovation potential across crises. *Journal of Family Business Strategy*, *13*(1), 100440.
Lin, Y., & Wu, L.-Y. (2014). Exploring the role of dynamic capabilities in firm performance under the resource-based view framework. *Journal of Business Research*, *67*(3), 407–413.
Lindow, C. M., Stubner, S., & Wulf, T. (2010). Strategic fit within family firms: The role of family influence and the effect on performance. *Journal of Family Business Strategy*, *1*(3), 167–178.
Lockett, A., & Thompson, S. (2010). Through the looking glass: Contestability theory and the resource-based view. *Journal of Management Inquiry*, *19*(2), 98–108.
London, C. (2002). Strategic planning for business excellence: Take the right road to reach your destination. *Quality Progress*, *35*(8), 26–33.
Madai, H., Bittner, B., Kovacs, T., & Nagy, A. (2020). Methodology for the internal environmental analysis as a part of strategy planning. *The Annals of the University of Oradea. Economic Sciences*, *29*(1), 551–556.
Mallon, M. R., & Fainshmidt, S. (2024). Breaking new ground in family business research with neoconfigurational theorizing and analysis. *Journal of Family Business Management*, *14*(2), 266–285.

Malone, S. C. (1989). Selected correlates of business continuity planning in the family business. *Family Business Review, 2*(4), 341–353.

Märk, S., & Situm, M. (2024). Long-term guidance in flux: The evolving significance of mission and vision in strategic management. In: S. Märk & M. Situm (Eds.), *Family business transformation: Strategic orientation and business modelling* (pp. 1–16). Berlin/Boston: Walter de Gruyter GmbH.

Mathews, J. A. (2002). A resource-based view of Schumpeterian economic dynamics. *Journal of Evolutionary Economics, 12*(1), 29–54.

McAdam, R. (2003). Radical change: A conceptual model for research agendas. *Leadership & Organization Development Journal, 24*(4), 226–235.

McGrath, M. (1998). Strategic planning within a postmodern context. *Journal of Humanistic Education & Development, 37*(2), 78–84.

Miroshnychenko, I., de Oliveira, R. T., De Massis, A., & Überbacher, R. (2024). Family involvement and firm performance: A worldwide study unveiling key mechanisms. *Family Business Review, 37*(4), 449–475.

Mishra, S. (2020). Reviewing the literature. In: R. N. Subudhi & S. Mishra (Eds.), *Methodological issues in management research: Advances, challenges, and the way ahead* (pp. 11–25). Bingley, UK: Emerald.

Morgan, T. J., & Gomez-Mejia, L. R. (2014). Hooked on a feeling: The affective component of socioemotional wealth in family firms. *Journal of Family Business Strategy, 5*(3), 280–288.

Moss, T. W., Payne, T. G., & Moore, C. B. (2014). Strategic consistency of exploration and exploitation in family businesses. *Family Business Review, 27*(1), 51–71.

Newbert, S. L. (2008). Value, rareness, competitive advantage, and performance: A conceptual-level empirical investigation of the resource-based view of the firm. *Strategic Management Journal, 29*(7), 745–768.

Nordqvist, M., Wennberg, K., Bau, M., & Hellerstedt, K. (2013). An entrepreneurial process perspective on succession in family firms. *Small Business Economics, 40*(4), 1087–1122.

O'Shannassy, T. (2016). Strategic intent: The literature, the construct and its role in predicting organization performance. *Journal of Management & Organization, 22*(5), 583–598.

Paul, J., & Criado, A. R. (2020). The art of writing literature review: What do we know and what do we need to know? *International Business Review, 29*(4), 701717.

Paunović, M., Mosurović Ružičić, M., & Lazarević Moravčević, M. (2023). Business process innovations in family firms: evidence from Serbia. *Journal of Family Business Management, 13*(1), 166–184.

Pemartín, M., Monreal-Pérez, J., & Sánchez Marín, G. (2024). Family firms and the collaborative advantage: Unveiling innovation efficiency across partnership types. *Journal of Family Business Management, 14*(6), 1173–1202.

Peteraf, M. A., & Bergen, M. E. (2003). Scanning dynamic competitive landscapes: A market-based and resource-based framework. *Strategic Management Journal, 24*(10), 1027–1041.

Peteraf, M. A. (1993). The cornerstones of competitive advantage: A resource-based view. *Strategic Management Journal, 14*(3), 179–191.

Plowman, D. A., Baker, L. T., Beck, T. E., Kulkarni, M., Solansky, S. T., & Travis, D. V. (2007). Radical change accidentially: The emergence and amplification of small change. *The Academy of Management Journal, 50*(3), 515–543.

Ployhart, R. E. (2021). Resources for what? Understanding performance in the resource-based view and strategic human capital resources literatures. *Journal of Management, 47*(7), 1771–1786.

Porter, M. E. (1991). Toward a dynamic theory of strategy. *Strategic Management Journal, 12*(Special Issue: Fundamental Research Issues in Strategy Economics), 95–117.

Rangone, A. (1999). A resource-based approach to strategy analysis in small-medium sized enterprises. *Small Business Economics, 12*(3), 233–248.

Rees, D. W., & Porter, C. (2006). Corporate strategy development and related management development: The case for the incremental approach, part 1 – the development of strategy. *Industrial and Commercial Training, 38*(5), 226–231.

Reina, W., Pla-Barber, J., & Villar. C. (2023). Socioemotional wealth in family business research: A systematic literature review on its definition, roles and dimensions. *European Management Journal*, *41*(6), 1000–1020.
Reisinger, S., & Lehner, J. M. (2015). Navigating a family business through a changing environment: Findings from a longitudinal study. *Review of Managerial Science*, *9*(2), 411–429.
Revilla, A. J., Pérez-Luño, A., & Nieto, M. J. (2016). Does family involvement in management recued the risk of business failure? The moderating role of entrepreneurial orientation. *Family Business Review*, *29*(4), 365–379.
Rondi, E., De Massis, A., & Kotlar, J. (2019). Unlocking innovation potential: A typology of family business innovation postures and the critical role of the family system. *Journal of Family Business Strategy*, *10*(4), 100236
Rovelli, P., Ferasso, M., De Massis, A., & Kraus, S. (2022). Thirty years of research in family business journals: Status quo and future directions. *Journal of Family Business Strategy*, *13*(3), 100422.
Sarason, Y., & Tegarden, L. F. (2003). The erosion of the competitive advantage of strategic planning: A configuration theory and resource based view. *Journal of Business and Management*, *9*(1), 1–20.
Schepers, J., Voordeckers, W., Steijvers, T., & Laveren, E. (2014). The entrepreneurial orientation–performance relationship in private family firms: the moderating role of socioemotional wealth. *Small Business Economics*, *43*(1), 39–55.
Scholes, L., Hughes, M., Wright, M., De Massis, A., & Kotlar, J. (2021). Family management and family guardianship: Governance effects on family firm innovation strategy. *Journal of Family Business Strategy*, *12*(4), 100389.
Schuman, (2010). *Family business as paradox*. London, UK: Palgrave MacMillan.
Serhan, C., Nader, R., & Gereige, W. (2023). Modeling the effect of continuity and change as paradoxical forces in the inter-generational transition process of family businesses. *Journal of Family Business Strategy*, *14*(4), 100582.
Shahzad, F., Akhlaq, A., & Ghaffar, C. (2024). Exploring business succession dynamics in family-owned businesses: Lessons from Pakistani case studies. *Journal of Family Business Management*, Vol. ahead-of -print No. ahead-of-print. https://doi.org/10.1108/JFBM-09-2024-0214
Sharma, P., Chrisman, J. J., & Chua, J. H. (1997). Strategic management of the family business: Past research and future challenges. *Family Business Review*, *10*(1), 1–35.
Sharma, R., & Sahoo, C. K. (2013). Regenerating organizational strength the employee centric way. *Strategic HR Review*, *12*(2), 61–69.
Short, J. C., Payne, T. G., Brigham, K. H., Lumpkin, G. T., & Broberg, C. J. (2009). Family firms and entrepreneurial orientation in publicly traded firms: A comparative analysis of the S&P 500. *Family Business Review*, *22*(1), 9–24.
Situm, M. (2024). Editorial: Strategic pathways for the future – Sustainability, resilience, and innovation in corporate governance and business strategy. *Corporate & Business Strategy Review*, *5*(4), 4–5.
Situm, M. (2021). Editorial: New challenges and opportunities in strategic decision making. *Corporate & Business Strategy Review*, *2*(1), 4–6.
Smith, M., & Graves, C. (2005). Corporate turnaround and financial distress. *Managerial Auditing Journal*, *20*(3), 304–320.
Smith, M., & White, M. C. (1987). Strategy, CEO specialization, and succession. *Administrative Science Quarterly*, *32*(2), 263–280.
Snyder, H. (2019). Literature review as a research methodology: An overview and guidelines. Journal of Business Research, 104, 333–339.
Spanos, Y. E., Zaralis, G., & Lioukas, S. (2004). Strategy and industry effects on profitability: Evidence from Greece. *Strategic Management Journal*, *25*(2), 139–165.

Stafford, K., Bhargava, V., Danes, S. M., Haynes, G., & Brewton, K. E. (2010). Factors associated with long-term survival of family businesses: Duration analysis. *Journal of Family and Economic Issues*, *31*(4), 442–457.

Steier, L. P., & Miller, D. (2010). Pre- and post-succession governance philosophies in entrepreneurial family firms. *Journal of Family Business Strategy*, *1*(3), 145–154.

Sunon, K. H., Islam, M. T., & Kabir, A. M. (2022). Impact of family succession on financial performance: Empirical evidence from Bangladesh. *Journal of Family Business Management*, *12*(2), 337–354.

Swab, G. R., Sherlock, C., Markin, E., & Dibrell, C. (2020). "SEW" what do we know and where do we go? A review of socioemotional wealth and a way forward. *Family Business Review*, *33*(4), 424–445.

Taguiri, R., & Davis, J. (1996). Bivalent attributes of the family firm. *Family Business Review*, *9*(2), 199–208.

Thomé, A. M. T., Scavarda, L. F., & Scavarda, A. J. (2016). Conducting systematic literature review in operations management. *Production Planning & Control*, *27*(5), 408–412.

Tranfield, D., Denyer, D., & Smart, P. (2003). Towards a methodology for developing evidence-informed management knowledge by means of systematic review. *British Journal of Management*, *14*(3), 207–222.

Tuncalp, D. (2024). Directing the future: Artificial intelligence integration in family businesses. *Journal of Family Business Management*, Vol. ahead-of-print No. ahead-of-print. https://doi.org/10.1108/JFBM-03-2024-0051.

Uhlaner, L. M., Kellermanns, F. W., Eddleston, K. A., & Hoy, F. (2012). The entrepreneuring family: A new paradigm for family business research. *Small Business Economics*, *38*(1), 1–11.

Vazquez, P., & Rocha, H. (2018). On the goals of family firms: A review and integration. *Journal of Family Business Strategy*, *9*(2), 94–106.

Veselinović, J., Mitić, M., Bačvarević, B. B., & Zlatanović Marković, V. (2021). Strategic planning as the inevitability of modern management. *Megatrend Review*, *18*(4), 57–70.

Van Witteloostuijn, A., & Boone, C. (2006). A resource-based theory of market structure and organizational form. *The Academy of Management Review*, *31*(2), 409–426.

Venter, E., van der Merwe, S., & Farrington, S. (2012). The impact of selected stakeholders on family business continuity and family harmony. *Southern African Business Review*, *16*(2), 69–96.

Wang, K., Pellegrini, M. M., Xue, J., & Wang, C. (2020). Environment uncertainty and a firm's strategic change the moderating role of political connection and family ownership. *Journal of Family Business Management*, *10*(4), 313–327.

Yazdanfar, D., & Öhman, P. (2020). Financial distress determinants among SMEs: Empirical evidence from Sweden. *Journal of Economic Studies*, *47*(3), 547–560.

Zahra, S. A. (2005). Entrepreneurial risk tanking in family firms. *Family Business Review*, *18*(1), 23–40.

Zainal, M. (2022). Innovation orientation and performance of Kuwaiti family businesses: Evidence form the COVID-19 pandemic. *Journal of Family Business Management*, *12*(2), 251–265.

Zellweger, T., & Sieger, P. (2012). Entrepreneurial orientation in long-lived family firms. *Small Business Economics*, *38*(1), 67–84.

Bernhard Baumgartner

The Importance of VUCA and BANI in Developing Sustainable and Long-term Oriented Strategies in Family Businesses

Abstract: The purpose of this chapter is to explore Family Business strategy advisors' actions and interactions with family actors and non family managers for strategy work in Family Businesses (FB). Combining the strategy as practice perspective with the concept of emotional engagement practices and changes in the structure of the FBs, this chapter interprets two cases with a family firm collaborating with an external interim CEO (=CRO) over a period of two years. The CRO's work is to build trust and emotional connections that shape relational dynamics within the restructuring of the Family Businesses. The implications for strategy work during the restructuring period will be outlined, taking into account the evolving nature of relational dynamics over time.

Keywords: Interim CEO (CRO, advisor), Family Firms, Strategy-as-Practice, Trust and Emotions, Strategizing

1 Introduction

Over the past several decades the world has undergone numerous changes and transformations in the way it operates. A concept introduced in the 1980s, known as VUCA (Volatility, Uncertainty, Complexity, Ambiguity), served as a guiding framework for navigating these shifts on the path to prosperity. VUCA proved to be a valuable tool for understanding modern life, particularly in the context of globalization. Unlike other models, VUCA emphasized the need for continuous adaptation to remain competitive and, most importantly, to stay in business. This approach significantly shaped many Family Businesses (FBs), influencing their evolution into what they are today.

Strategy in FBs may now be viewed through the lens of the "strategy-as-practice" (SAP) perspective (e.g., Jarzabkowski et al., 2007; Vaara & Whittington, 2012). SAP highlights the complexity of strategic work in FBs, defined as "actions, interactions of multiple actors, and the situated practices that they draw upon" (Jarzabkowski et al., 2007, p. 8). Strategic work in FBs is carried out by both family actors and non-family managers. The latter are increasingly involved, as their contributions tend to be more specific and objective. Non-family managers often initiate strategic innovations. However, their external perspectives are frequently overlooked in strategic discussions due to emotional resistance from family actors, who may perceive change as a threat. This tension is a common occurrence in restructuring cases, regardless of the size of the FB.

https://doi.org/10.1515/9783110790344-002

Several studies have shown that “family leaders are generally entrenched in inherent values, traditions, and ways of thinking” (Hall et al., 2006, p. 254), leading to isolated decision-making and a reluctance to change strategic directions (Fang et al., 2021). This reluctance to consider the views of non-family managers can result in what Ingram et al. (2016, p. 3) describe as falling into the strategic “simplicity trap.” In this context, strategy advisors such as Chief Restructuring Officers (CROs), hired by the family to provide specialized knowledge and services related to restructuring (planning, implementation, and control), can play a vital role. They can facilitate the involvement of both family actors and non-family managers in developing strategies for the FB’s successful future. However, the specific ways in which CROs facilitate these interactions and influence strategy work over time remain underexplored and warrant further research.

Recent insights suggest that CROs can ease tensions between family actors and non-family managers while fostering trustful relationships. As such, they serve as key connectors within this triad of actors. This role is particularly important today, as intra-family relationships are increasingly “embedded in a social context of exchange with other actors” (Nason et al., 2019, p. 846), including non-family managers and CROs. The goal, therefore, is to examine how FBs can master their future in an ever-changing business environment – a process often driven by non-family managers introducing new approaches. It is essential to evaluate whether VUCA remains a relevant guiding concept or if newer paradigms, such as the BANI or TUNA models, are emerging as more suitable frameworks for addressing the challenges ahead. These new models propose a shift in understanding our world:
- BANI stands for Brittle, Anxious, Non-Linear, and Incomprehensible
- TUNA stands for Turbulent, Uncertain, Novel, and Ambiguous

The BANI concept was introduced by Jamais Cascio, an American anthropologist, futurist, and author. He was inspired by numerous contemporary crises – climate change, pandemics, global instability, wars, and rising inequality. Cascio argued that the VUCA model is no longer sufficient to address the pressing issues of a rapidly evolving world. Instead, he proposed BANI as a more accurate conceptual tool to understand and respond to current and future complexities.

2 Conceptual Foundations: Understanding VUCA and BANI Frameworks

The VUCA acronym was first mentioned in 1987 by the U.S. Army War College to describe the forthcoming challenges in a post–Cold War world. The leadership of the U.S. was looking for a way of dealing with the Communist world in the near future. The concept was based on theories concerning leadership by Warren Bennis and Burt

Nanus. The VUCA term at that time referred to the change in military organizations. Since then, VUCA has become a concept used in business, leadership, and other fields to describe situations characterized by volatility, uncertainty, complexity, and ambiguity. The global economy, market dynamics, the political landscape, and even the stock market are examples of VUCA environments.

In a VUCA world, change is the prevalent dynamic and is unpredictable. Everything seems to be – and is – in flux, and nothing is certain. That is why it leads to disorientation and becomes difficult to navigate. Adaptation becomes vital for leaders, and change is a constant challenge to be implemented without complete information. The VUCA world is very difficult to navigate. However, some strategic approaches can help leaders effectively steer through the stormy conditions of global issues. Information plays a key role in such situations – what is happening around you and in your immediate environment. You must develop strong relationships with your team members and communicate effectively.

This turbulence, along with its disruptive wake, will most probably not last just for a decade but is likely to become our normative state, causing us to redefine what the new normal will be. Now we are looking into the specifics of VUCA, to gain an in-depth understanding of the VUCA model, its origins, and its relevance in contemporary society. Let us examine the intricacies of volatility, uncertainty, complexity, and ambiguity, and how they impact decision-making, strategic planning, risk management, and problem-solving within FBs.

- VOLATILITY: Refers to the rapid changes and unpredictable nature of the challenges organizations encounter. Fast change is real and often unexpected, making it difficult for organizations to anticipate and adequately prepare for adaptation.
- UNCERTAINTY: Associated with unpredictable events and issues. Forecasting the future has never been an easy task, but it becomes increasingly difficult even to guess what the future might bring. It results from a lack of clear data or a surplus of conflicting data.
- COMPLEXITY: Interrelated and interwoven forces and issues make cause-and-effect relationships very unclear and hard to evaluate. Organizations must navigate through an intricate web of stakeholders, regulations, market trends, and other important factors.
- AMBIGUITY: Points to unclear realities and potential misunderstandings rooted in mixed messages and a lack of clarity. This may lead to confusion and misinterpretation, which in turn makes decision-making even more difficult.

Despite these four roadblocks, VUCA offers a guideline for fostering awareness and preparedness in various sectors of our economy and beyond. The VUCA framework remains instrumental in many areas, including decision-making, planning, risk management, driving change, and problem-solving. It helps articulate how organizations perceive their current and potential challenges and provides a basic structure for planning and policy-making. When these elements interact in various ways, they can either complicate decision-making or enhance an organization's ability to strategize, plan, and make progress. It also lays the groundwork for effective management and leadership by enabling organizations to anticipate key issues, understand the consequences of specific actions, appreciate the interrelation of various factors, prepare for diverse scenarios and challenges, and interpret and tackle relevant opportunities.

The VUCA framework shapes the ability of organizations to respond to the four elements it defines. However, it is not just about understanding the challenges – it is about developing the capabilities to thrive amidst these challenges. It emphasizes the need for resilience, adaptability, and learning from failure, which are not always obvious qualities in leaders or organizations (see Figure 1).

BUT is the concept still at the forefront of our daily challenges?

The four elements of VUCA have defined the characteristics of our global environment. Rapid technological advancements, geopolitical challenges, environmental concerns, societal shifts, and economic fluctuations all contribute to the VUCA nature of our current world (Reeves et al., 2016; Situm, 2021; Schmutte, 2020, pp. 35–36).

- Volatility can be observed across the global landscape – from technological changes to unpredictable political developments happening right at our front doors.
- Uncertainty permeates our private and professional lives. Issues such as climate change and other crises make the future increasingly difficult to predict.
- Complexity defines our interconnected world. Global supply chains and the complex interplay between various sectors of the economy are on the rise. Cause-and-effect relationships become very difficult to trace (Exler et al., 2023).
- Ambiguity prevails in the modern world. The sheer volume of information at our fingertips also reveals that much of it is incomplete or unclear, leading to potential misunderstandings and misinterpretations.

Living in a VUCA world should not be considered entirely negative. It provides us with opportunities for innovation, further growth, and development. Although it presents challenges, it also encourages adaptation, resilience, and the ability to thrive during times of change.

- Can VUCA help us better understand, navigate, and leverage the challenges and complexities of our contemporary world?
- VUCA uses a collection of terms that can be misleading, as not all elements are present in every situation.
- Volatility does not always imply a high degree of uncertainty or ambiguity in an industry.
- Uncertainty does not always increase the need for problem-solving activities.

– Complexity does not necessarily coincide with volatility or ambiguity.
– Ambiguity, for instance, in the field of quantum computing, does not inherently make the situation volatile.

Examples show that while all four elements can coexist, they may also occur independently of one another, each requiring distinct strategies for effective management. It is not the mere presence of VUCA conditions, but the degree to which they disrupt the status quo, that necessitates a change in our decision-making techniques. VUCA can also limit our way of thinking. At times, we become too defensive – falling victim to our environment rather than responding creatively. The electric vehicle industry may serve as a case in point. Initially, it was uncertain whether electric cars would succeed. An uncertain regulatory environment, volatile oil markets, and the complexity of developing a new engine concept were seen as opportunities, not threats. Sometimes, VUCA overstates the unpredictability of change. The four elements are not always so pervasive that they cannot be mastered. Solutions for organizations lie in robust systems, continuous process evaluation, and a strong, consistent commitment to understanding and meeting customer needs.

BANI, a new paradigm, is asserting itself as the primary model to describe the issues of our modern world. This leads us to examine the complexities of our current existence. Our fragile systems are at stake. The model highlights the brittle components of our daily lives, particularly within organizations. It also addresses the prevalent anxiety permeating society, the non-linear nature of the challenges we face, and the difficulty of comprehending our constantly changing world. Attempting to proactively understand and accept the principles of BANI can help individuals and organizations flourish in an environment that demands adaptability, resilience, and a full comprehension of the factors shaping our lives. To explore BANI more deeply, we are compelled to rethink our strategies, seek new implementation methods, and develop mechanisms to cope with emerging challenges. Traditional tools may no longer be sufficient in this evolving landscape. BANI encompasses the defining characteristics of our contemporary world:

Brittle, Anxious, Nonlinear, Incomprehensible

The concept offers a deeper understanding of the unique traits of our rapidly changing world. These elements impact both individuals and organizations, offering a framework to respond effectively.

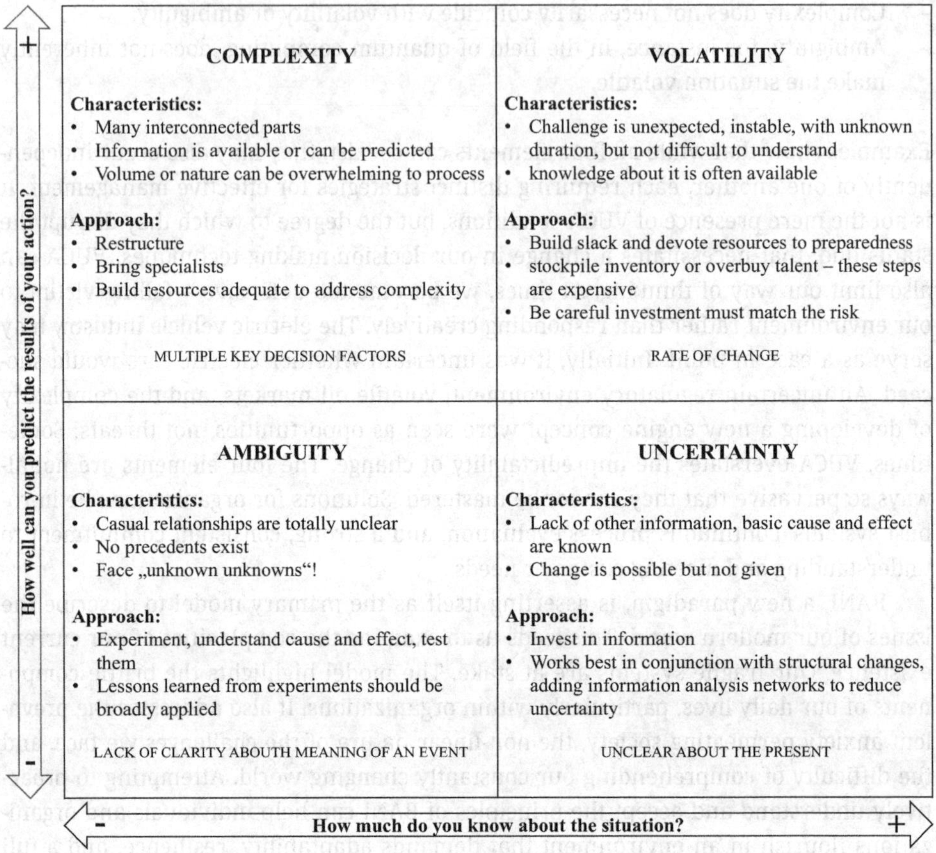

Figure 1: VUCA Framework: Navigating Volatility, Uncertainty, Complexity, and Ambiguity.

Brittle

A brittle system may appear stable over a long period but gradually becomes porous and develops small fractures, ultimately breaking unexpectedly. Such a collapse can have far-reaching and devastating consequences, leaving individuals and organizations utterly unprepared. Three main factors contribute to brittleness:

– Overemphasis on Profit and Efficiency: The relentless pursuit of profit and efficiency is often a central objective for many organizations. However, when prioritized at the expense of other critical factors, this mindset creates significant vulnerabilities. It can lead to shortages of skilled and motivated workers. This internal brittleness weakens organizations from within, rendering them unable to adapt and thrive in dynamic environments. To mitigate this risk, emotional in-

telligence, thought leadership, and empathy are essential for fostering a workplace that values both profitability and sustainability.
- Global Interconnectedness and Cascading Effects: In our interconnected world, any disruption or failure in one part of the system can trigger a chain reaction across sectors and regions. The 2008 financial crisis exemplifies how an ostensibly isolated issue can quickly escalate into a global economic downturn. This highlights the need for resilient, robust structures capable of withstanding disruptive shockwaves (Situm & Möllers, 2024)
- Emotional Intelligence and Adaptability: Brittleness can also be alleviated by prioritizing emotional intelligence and empathy within organizational values and mission statements. Doing so can improve employee relations, strengthen supportive work environments, and enhance adaptability – an essential trait for future success.

Anxious

Anxiety is linked to uncertainty, which arises from the fear that something significant might suddenly emerge or unravel. Anxiety acts as a mechanism for safeguarding security in an unpredictable environment. When systems are perceived as fragile, this fear may result in passivity, causing individuals and organizations to become risk-averse instead of addressing problems head-on. Fear and anxiety can then lead to inaction, excessive analysis, and hinder forward momentum.
- Negative Impact on Decision-Making: Despair is often prevalent during periods of heightened fear and anxiety, which negatively influences the decision-making process. This may result in overly cautious decisions that lack the creativity and innovation needed to succeed in the future.
- Media's Role in Fostering Anxiety: The media plays a significant role in amplifying societal anxiety. It frequently employs fear-inducing narratives and language that promote uncertainty. Constant exposure to negative or sensational news often overshadows positive developments, deepening feelings of anxiety.
- Overcoming Anxious Tendencies to Foster Innovation: While pessimism is a natural human response and serves a protective function, it can also become a barrier to innovation – in areas such as artificial intelligence, data science, big data, and business model innovation. Overcoming these mental roadblocks is critical for creating a successful organizational future.

Nonlinear

Non-linearity contributes to the growing fear and confusion in the modern world. This complexity stems from the reality that the systems in which we operate are inherently intricate. In such complex systems, the relationship between cause and effect is often blurred or hidden.

- Challenging Cause-and-Effect Assumptions: Linear models are frequently applied in an attempt to solve complex problems, yet they often fail to capture the true nature of these systems. The relationship between cause and effect is multifaceted, involving numerous variables, interactions, and synergies. A single cause may lead to multiple outcomes, making it difficult to predict or recognize the precise impact of specific actions.
- Unpredictability in Outcomes: Non-linearity implies that implemented measures may not produce results in a straightforward or expected way. Significant efforts may yield minimal results, while seemingly minor decisions may lead to disproportionately large impacts.

Incomprehensible

What does "incomprehensible" mean in a non-linear world? Let us try to unravel this concept. Incomprehensibility represents the culmination of complexity in our non-linear reality and goes a step beyond ambiguity. There are numerous examples of incomprehensibility in our daily work lives. Actions considered non-essential to a planned outcome may unexpectedly lead to results that contradict the original objective. The most baffling aspect is the absence of a definitive explanation for this phenomenon.

- Importance of Understandability: Clarity and orientation are crucial in times of rapid change. Understandability reduces surprise, which can amplify the negative effects of unforeseen events. It helps pave the way for sustainable solutions.
- The Overwhelming Nature of Incomprehensibility: When we are unable to understand or interpret a situation, it often feels overwhelming. This is especially true in today's data-rich environment, where the sheer volume of information – combined with unpredictable structures – can make comprehension feel impossible.

The BANI framework helps us understand the challenges and uncertainties emerging from the Fourth Industrial Revolution, which is being driven by digital technologies, artificial intelligence, the Internet of Things (IoT), and tools such as ChatGPT. This new wave introduces elements of non-linearity, anxiety due to rapid change, and incomprehensibility tied to the growing complexity of systems. The BANI world offers a lens to navigate these broader implications of change, characterized by brittleness, anxiety, non-linearity, and incomprehensibility. Together, these components provide a usable toolkit for individuals and organizations striving to thrive in an era marked by complexity and uncertainty. BANI should be considered as part of strategic planning and leadership models, especially given the continuously evolving nature of the world. To foster a deeper understanding of both VUCA and BANI, a direct comparison of the two frameworks is essential (see Table 1).

Table 1: Comparison between VUCA and BANI World based on selected aspects.

ASPECT	VUCA World	BANI World
Foundation and Origin	Originated in the late 1980s, focused on geo politics	Emerged more recently in response to challenges incl. digitalization
Framework	Volatility, Uncertainty, Complexity, Ambiguity	Brittle, Anxious, Nonlinear, Incomprehensible
Components	Focusing on external factors	Addressing internal and external dynamics
Change Perspective	Primarily external disruptions and adaptability	Extends to internal fragility, psychological anxiety, and non-linear change
Response	Adaptability, agility, reacting to external changes	Resilience, anxiety management, embracing complexity addressing internal issues
Focus	External environment, market, competition, geopolitics	Broader focus on external and internal dimensions, including organizational dynamics

The goal of this chapter is to gain a better understanding of strategic actions and interactions applying the VUCA and BANI model with family and non-family actors for strategic work in FBs. The Research Questions are the following:

Research Question 1: How can CROs' activities shape the relevant dynamics between family actors and non-family managers in a changing business environment?

Research Question 2: How can these relational dynamics help FBs to adapt new survival strategies in a VUCA and BANI world?

To answer these questions, we draw upon SAP research (e.g., Jarzabkowski et al., 2013; Vaara & Whittington, 2012) to conceptualize strategy, CROs' actions, and interactions with family actors and non-family managers in strategizing. To combine this perspective with the concept of emotional engagement practices (Sloan & Oliver, 2013) helps to explain how CROs can create trustful connections and emotional bonding with actors in strategy work, respectfully, in restructuring of FBs. In using this theoretical approach, this chapter describes and interprets two cases of an Austrian and German FB operating in the machinery industry for the food and pharmaceutical industry, and also in the second case in the power plant industry over a period of four, respectively of two years.

For these two cases, the names of the companies cannot be disclosed, since an NDA was signed, which is still valid at this point in time. As CRO, it is very important to establish a trustful collaboration and connection with the family actors, as well as with family members and non-family managers. These relational dynamics changed the strategy work by bringing the actors closer to each other. The two cases were especially, in one part of the business system, very similar. That is why this chapter focuses on the change process in adapting a new way of building value-added for the

FBs. Further, it provides insight into extending strategy research in FBs by digging deep into the family–non-family relational dynamics and their emotional dimensions.

It tells the CRO's activities that shape these dynamics and affect strategy work by a) activating empowerment with non-family managers, b) activating openness to change activities with family actors, and c) providing shared spaces of strategic discussions. It further provides insight into trust-building in restructuring cases by showing that trustful and emotional connections with the CRO originate from relational security. These forms are somehow nurtured by trustful and empathic behaviour towards family actors and non-family managers, allowing them to get more control over strategy work and, on the other hand, providing a safe way towards new strategic discoveries. It also shows the way of strategizing in an environment dominated by family actors and the role played by CROs as strategy experts and their activities that enable trusting as a "leap of faith" (Nikolova et al., 2015).

3 Theoretical Background

3.1 Family Actors and Nonfamily Managers in Strategy Work during Restructuring the FB

The concept of strategy work has its roots in the SAP perspective (e.g., Jarzabkowski & Spee, 2009; Vaara & Whittington, 2012), which focuses on what actors do when they enact strategy, seen as "a situated, socially accomplished activity" (Jarzabkowski et al., 2007, p. 7). However, it is also the structure of the FB that dominates strategy work. Structures were established to function both internally and externally. These structures were seldom questioned, even when dealing with VUCA elements. They were considered foundational building blocks and rarely challenged or altered. Structure also holds social and emotional significance, particularly in maintaining the FB over time, as it was initially shaped by family actors.

The social factor plays a vital role in FBs, especially when considering the long-term individual actions taken by family actors. The relationship between these two elements – individual action by family actors and social structures within an FB – can be understood through Anthony Giddens' structuration theory. Giddens proposes to reconcile the opposition between structure and agency, viewing them as mutually constitutive: structure influences human behavior, and humans are capable of changing the social structures they inhabit. Structure both enables and constrains action, while simultaneously being (re)constituted through action. Structuration explains the motivations for actions, the choices – both real and perceived – shaped by structural opportunities and constraints, and the interactions involved.

3.2 Key Concepts in Structuration Theory

A central problem in social theories is how to evaluate the opposition or dualism between agency and structure. Many individuals, including leaders – not only in FBs – experience that their activities are both constrained and enabled by social structures. When considering such managerial actions by FB actors or non-family managers, agency must be understood as both enabled and constrained by, and constitutive of, structures such as organizational designs and institutional embeddedness – phenomena particularly observable in FBs. Actors possess the capacity for sociologically meaningful autonomous action because they have "free will," a common dilemma in FBs. If that is the case, how can their agency be constrained by structure, if not through voluntary choice?

Do such actions in FBs originate from initiatives taken by FB actors? If one postulates that structure determines human behavior, then how can there be space for agency? The paradox of embedded agency has been widely discussed as a theoretical issue in the literature on institutional entrepreneurship (Battilana, 2006; Greenwood & Suddaby, 2006). Structuration theory is one of several theoretical approaches proposed to address this problem. In examining Giddens' theory, we aim to outline his conceptualization of duality, agency, structure, and time-space, which are the constitutive elements of structuration theory.

3.3 Duality

To explain social outcomes, one needs to study individuals and their interactions. What is the place for agency, if structure is dominant? What is structure, if it cannot always be reduced to the outcome of aggregate human interaction? These issues are frequently observed in FBs, particularly during critical situations. Rather than applying an artificial approach to reconcile the opposition between the two perspectives, structuration theory seeks to transcend it. Giddens proposed the concept of the duality of structure, "in which structure is both the medium and the outcome of the reproduction of practices" (Giddens, 1979, p. 5), and structuration as the process through which social structures and human agency interact in mutually constitutive ways. No priority is given to one over the other.

Furthermore, structuration signifies that human agents operate within a preexisting interpreted world – a phenomenon observable not only in non-family businesses but especially in FBs. They constitute that world through the meanings they assign to it (Giddens, 1976). Social structures are established at the very moment they are reproduced by agents, while social agents simultaneously constitute themselves through structural action. Duality implies that both structure and agency are considered simultaneously. Structuration refers to giving attention to both past and present – as avenues for innovation and change, or structural reproduction (Whittington, 2015). It represents the moment in which agency and structure are reproduced (Haugaard, 2002).

3.4 Agency

Agency is one of the fundamental concepts of structuration theory. It refers to the extent to which social agents are able to make a difference in the everyday course of events – that is, their ability to change or to do otherwise. Giddens ties this ability directly to the exercise of power. An agent ceases to be an agent when lacking the ability to act otherwise. This notion of agency is based on a set of assumptions about how and why agents can act.

Giddens considers agents to be reflexive and capable beings, rather than the "cultural dopes" that "ensue from strong forms of structuralism" (Mutch, 2014), or the "structural dopes of even more stunning mediocrity" (Giddens, 1979, p. 52). Agents are seen as intentional, reflexive, and rational beings who behave according to their knowledge of their situation and the expected outcomes of their actions.

In structuration theory, agency assumes that agents have knowledge about what they do, why they do it, and the structural context in which – and upon which – they act. They are capable of applying this knowledge and exercising reflexivity in the production and reproduction of social practices. Agents use such knowledge to understand the foundation of their everyday lives and to guide the continuation of day-to-day action (Giddens, 1984).

Giddens suggests that "knowledgeability" is related to two modes of consciousness: practical and discursive. Discursive consciousness refers to the most explicit form of knowledge and is immediately available to the agent – it is the ability to articulate knowledge. The reflexivity of action, through which individuals reflect upon, monitor, and modify their behavior on an ongoing basis, falls within the domain of discursive consciousness (Giddens, 1984).

On the other hand, practical consciousness involves tacit, unarticulated, and taken-for-granted knowledge. It facilitates everyday exchanges among social agents and serves as mutual knowledge. Social agents possess a significant amount of knowledge about social life. The process through which they use this mutual knowledge to understand the fundamentals of their everyday life and to maintain continuity in their actions is referred to as the rationalization of action.

3.5 Structure

Structure is anything that possesses fundamental endurance and has the effect of imposing order on an organization or any other similar form of social setup. The structuralist understands structure as a set of underlying codes or ordered relations beneath the surface level of society, which must be interpreted through their surface-level manifestations. One way of understanding structure, according to Giddens, is through the analogy of language and its relationship to speech. Just as language both enables and constrains speech – and speech in turn reconstitutes language – so too does structure provide the conditions and possibilities for social action.

Giddens differentiates three forms of interaction in which agency is performed: communication, power, and sanctions. He proposes that the properties of interaction are directly related to the properties of structure and the modalities of structuration. Structures and interactions are mediated by the modalities of interpretive schemes, facilities, and norms. Modalities are the means through which structural dimensions are expressed in interaction (Whittington, 2015). For example, the use of power (interaction) involves drawing upon facilities derived from allocative and authoritative resources (modality), which are linked to domination (structure). Similarly, the application of sanctions (interaction) draws on norms (modality) that are linked to legitimation (structure). Giddens argues that, in actual social practices, there are varying degrees of combination among all three kinds of structure. He emphasizes the reciprocal relationship between all these structural properties (Whittington, 2015).

3.6 Time Space

Significant to the theory of structuration is the concept of time-space. Giddens stated that social interaction occurs across time and space; it is both contextual and situated. It is important to understand not only the objects and persons present during interactions but also those who are absent. During social encounters, there is an intersection of interacting agents according to their time-spaces at different levels. Structure refers to the structuring properties that provide the binding and continuity of time and space in patterned social relations, such as social systems (Giddens, 1979). Regular activities bring people together within these systems, which are reproduced over time through continued interaction. Social systems can exist at various levels and may even be overlapping or contradictory (Whittington, 2015).

To summarize, structuration theory is a sociological theory concerned with how people behave in groups. Giddens argues that human behaviour cannot be separated from structures or institutions. While human behaviour is the result of individual action and based on personal choice, the influence of social structure cannot be ignored. The theory seeks to examine how social structures are represented and replicated in human interaction and is based on social practices that integrate individual behaviour (agency) with social structures.

4 Research Design

4.1 Case Study Context and the Mediating Role of Trust

In this chapter, the case studies build on in-depth interpretive research, which holds the potential to explore organizational phenomena in practice. Studies have shown that family actors are more accepting of the advisor's influence when affective forms of trust are present (e.g., de Groote & Bertschi-Michel, 2021; Salvato & Corbetta, 2013; Strike, 2013). Such trust grows through feelings of liking the advisor, the CRO, as "a good person" (de Groote & Bertschi-Michel, 2021, p. 143). The advisor then acts as a mediator of family emotions. Trust in the advisor is also required from non-family actors to allow advisors, particularly CROs, to move seamlessly between multiple strategic arenas. This suggests that advisors may also possess the power to break down a family's resistance to change, affect relationships, and thus support the strategizing process (McCracken, 2015).

The case studies selected for this chapter are very similar in their business models but differ significantly in their operating mechanisms. The first company, a U.S.-based daughter company of a leading German machinery supplier for the food and pharmaceutical industry, is independent from the family business in Germany, though owned by the same family. It is currently run by the second generation but remains heavily influenced by the founder. The second company, also a family business, is based in Austria and is run by the third generation, while the second generation remains consistently present in the company.

The cases were selected because they provide a thorough understanding of the "deeper social dynamics" characterizing strategy advisors' (CROs') actions and interactions in FBs, for two main reasons. First, the German company is firmly established in the global industry. This is also true for the Austrian company, although its main focus lies in the DACH region (Deutschland, Österreich und Schweiz – translated into Englisch: Germany, Austria and Switzerland). Over time, it became clear that strategy-making in both companies relied on continuously evolving interactions between family actors and non-family managers. Second, while existing data sets were available, a deeper understanding of the two companies was necessary.

4.2 Data Collection

At the time of entering the companies, a very detailed data collection program was established with the support of external consultants to understand the current situation. In the case of the U.S. company, this was triggered by information provided by the CFO of the parent company. The U.S. company was clearly outperforming the parent company by a factor of five. In the Austrian case, the financial figures indicated the need for an immediate restructuring program.

The interviews aimed to evoke contextual narratives, particularly in the first case, where the founder played a crucial role in strategizing. He determined the strategic direction of the company. During the interviews, notes were taken on the informants' nonverbal responses (e.g., body language, facial expressions, tone of voice, etc.), as it was important to understand their emotional reactions (King et al., 2019, pp. 76–77). Documentary research was also conducted, including both publicly available documents (if any) and internal documents produced by the companies and the consultants (Flick, 2018, pp. 312–313).

4.3 Data Analysis

The data analysis was employed by abductive reasoning (Locke et al., 2008), which allowed for sensitivity to the data while also using theory as a source for interpreting patterns within an interactive process (Kennedy & Thornberg, 2018). All material was reviewed multiple times to develop a preliminary general understanding, which served as the basis for the initial narrative of the cases, covering aspects of the companies' performances. This process allowed for the assessment and de termination of strategic directions (e.g., forecasting, scenario planning) and the building and monitoring of goals (e.g., performance targeting, business planning).

The findings were discussed in detail with the CEO and CFO, and in the first case, also with the founder of the company. It became evident that trust was emerging as a key driver in the interactions between the advisor (CRO) and the CEO/CFO. The data were re-examined and coded in the database by noting instances where trust was expressed (e.g., "Now I feel more comfortable that an outsider is taking charge of the company"). Notable findings emerged regarding the association of trust with the various actors' positive expectations for the future – such as "taking more control over strategic actions" in pursuit of long-term success.

As it turned out in the case of the U.S. company, the financial figures reported to the parent company by the founder were incorrect. There had been a misinterpretation of profit. Documents had not been sent over an extended period to the parent company, as consolidation had not previously been necessary – the U.S. company was still owned independently by the founder. After the generational succession, the founder's son – now running the parent company – was given the U.S. entity by his father. At that point, consolidation of the U.S. company into the parent company in Germany became mandatory. The U.S. company now constituted a restructuring case, and immediate action was required to implement a successful action program.

This chapter does not describe the cost-cutting measures, which were necessary in both cases following the analyses, but instead focuses on the future strategic direction in the VUCA world, while remaining alert to the emerging BANI world. What strategic direction should the companies take following a comprehensive analysis of both competitors and internal capabilities? Key actors involved in shaping the strategic implications were nominated unanimously by the family actors and the CRO. A three-phase approach was agreed upon. These phases are interconnected in that the actions of one phase (i.e., the CRO's practices) lead to changes (i.e., the emergence of trustful connections in strategic arenas), which then influence the actions of the subsequent phase (Langley, 1999). The three phases are as follows:

- Phase 1: Involving the empowerment of non-family managers through the enactment of caretaking practices
- Phase 2: Involving the broadening of family actors' perspectives through the enactment of pathfinding practices
- Phase 3: Involving the creation of shared spaces for strategic discussion

5 Findings

The findings are organized around the three phases from data analysis.

5.1 Phase 1. Empowering Nonfamily Managers

For the majority of non-family managers, the VUCA model was unfamiliar. This was also true for the family actors. However, they were aware of market dynamics – its players, customers, suppliers, and roadblocks – and acted accordingly, though typically with a short-term focus. In both cases, the family actors were emotionally attached to their companies' traditional products and product lines. Their primary goal had always been to strengthen these products – "to build a better mousetrap" – by investing heavily in technological development and new production equipment.

Strategic decisions were typically made by the CEO and family actors, and in the U.S. case, also by the founder. Although formal meetings were held – comprising CFOs, heads of production, family members, operations management, etc. – they rarely included actual debate on strategic issues. In this context, nearly all non-family members felt excluded from strategic discussions. Financial managers, in particular, struggled to have their voices heard, especially when planning, controlling, and monitoring financial resources for so-called strategic initiatives. The CRO initiated the introduction of strategic planning practices to foster greater strategic thinking regarding the financial viability of the two companies' strategies. Although initially not fully convinced, the CEO of the Austrian unit formally agreed to collaborate with the CRO, as specified in the signed contract.

In the U.S. case, the situation was different. The founder had left the company, and once the unit was integrated into the structure of the parent company, the founder's son – now CEO of the parent company – joined in to navigate the three phases. He decided to appoint the CFO of the U.S. unit as a member of the strategy team. The

CRO and the CFO acted as strategic actors who gradually implemented new planning practices (e.g., creating business and financial plans, formulating target objectives, constructing future scenarios). These practices included setting performance targets, gathering material on future scenarios, and analyzing competitor information.

Crucially, the CFOs were fully involved in the strategic process, and their confidence grew as they came to rely on the CRO's support. This enabled them to fulfill their expectations of exerting some form of control over strategic actions and gaining a voice in future strategic discussions. The CRO proposed, in both cases, engaging in planning activities that would allow for easier access to financial resources, thus helping both companies manage and control the financial feasibility of new strategic initiatives.

Through in-depth conversations with team members to develop future scenarios, the team and the CRO frequently identified a range of detailed strategic variables (e.g., industry growth rate, market share, repeat buying behavior). Data were provided by the CFO, while the CRO made adjustments to the Excel models. Cause-and-effect relationships led to extensive discussions across multiple variable sets. Simulations were run regularly to assess the current VUCA environment. This structured approach was new to both companies – formally addressing aspects of VUCA and analyzing its implications for the FB.

Building these simulations collaboratively and discussing possible outcomes served as an empowerment mechanism, encouraging all team members – not just a select few – to develop strategic thinking around cause-and-effect relationships. Feelings of assurance contributed to growing trust in the CRO, who became the go-to figure for developing and guiding deep discussions about dynamics that could influence the companies' futures. This was observed in both cases.

It is often the case that a restructuring concept is presented and then left for implementation by the former CEO or a management team – an approach not typically accepted by financial institutions. In contrast, in both cases here, the CRO guaranteed his physical presence, not only during formalized ad hoc meetings but also during informal encounters. The CRO remained consistently present, as he was responsible for implementing the action program and guiding the companies' future direction. He served as a partner for interpreting emerging issues from daily operations and providing actionable suggestions. This continuous presence acted as an empowerment mechanism, reinforcing trust within the team. Whenever a problem arose that needed to be addressed, the team could rely on the CRO for support – either endorsing their proposals or guiding them back to the strategic, action-oriented drawing board without assigning blame for individual shortcomings.

These rational and relational dynamics had strong implications for strategy work throughout the first phase. Importantly, the practices of caretaking that occurred within these strategic arenas helped build the confidence of team members, enabling them to contribute meaningfully to the company's overall strategy.

5.2 Phase 2. Broadening the Family Actors` Perspective

In both companies, the business was solely focused on selling machines within their respective industries. Sales departments were occupied with calculating project costs and sending offers to prospective customers. The CRO observed, in both cases, a large volume of quotations being sent out to the market. When asked about follow-up responses from customers, the sales departments' replies were concerning: "The customers are not providing us feedback, so we wait until we get an answer from them." This approach was supported by the family actors, as they were accustomed to receiving some form of customer response in the past. It had become a routine practice – one that drew the attention of the CRO.

Instead of waiting passively for a response, the sales team – now part of the strategic team – was instructed to follow up promptly to determine the status of the offer. Regular sales trips to customers were not part of their agenda and only occurred on an ad-hoc basis. This new action-oriented plan was a surprise to both companies – especially to the Austrian family business, and somewhat less so to the U.S. company. The CRO initiated a project titled "New Friends," which initially involved the family actors, and was later expanded to include the CFOs and the strategic team. The project increased the frequency of interactions between the CRO and the strategic team, thereby creating a new strategic arena that was further expanded to incorporate additional strategic planning practices (e.g., competitor analysis, market analysis, financial simulations).

These practices included day-to-day micro-level activities such as identifying competitor offerings, forecasting sales volume, and discovering potential new customers – activities in which all actors were jointly engaged. While working with the team and the family actors, the CRO began to demonstrate how planned strategic decisions could be reviewed and questioned to allow for alternative routes. He would occasionally present examples of comparable machine and line suppliers, offering proactive comparisons that encouraged the family actors and strategic team to reflect critically. One such example involved a strategic action from an elevator company that, at the time, transformed its industry – then composed of around 400 competitors.

With profit margins extremely low due to fierce competition, one company shifted its strategy by promising that their elevator would never break down, i.e., never stop unintentionally. This company began offering a service – now known as Total Preventive Management – for not only their own brand but also for competitors' products. Today, there are perhaps ten major players left in that market. The CRO conveyed this example in a forceful, direct manner – especially when offering critiques of specific strategic actions. He recalled telling the family actors and team members: "You have the choice to focus on your quotes or talk to your customer early on to find out what they want, what they would like to have, or what both the supplier and customer can be happy with." This example, along with the elevator company story, served as a mechanism for openness to change, instilling in the team and family actors a sense of bewilderment due to the disruption of their existing beliefs – yet simultaneously stimulating curiosity toward previously unnoticed issues. In this way, the CRO built trust by reassuring the family actors and the team of the generative potential that lies in uncertainty when rethinking strategic decisions.

During the meetings focused on analyzing strategic options for a successful future, the CRO engaged the family actors and the team in meaningful conversations by introducing powerful and evocative imagery. He repeatedly referenced the "Red and Blue Ocean" concept as a metaphor for forward integration of the business – offering extended services to customers. This new approach, inspired by the elevator company's transformation, presented a potential strategic advantage for both companies. They could be first in the market and first in the minds of their customers, delivering positive cash flow from the moment a new production line was launched.

This could be achieved not merely by installing the line and training the customer's personnel for three weeks, as was customary, but by running the line with the supplier's experts for a specific period. During this active handover, the customer's employees would receive intensive training, including failure analysis concepts. The advantage for the customer is immediate cash flow after installation – guaranteed by the supplier, i.e., the two companies in their respective industries. The additional cost of the supplier's personnel operating the line is compensated by the early revenue generation it enables.

The image of the Blue Ocean symbolized an unexplored market space outside the companies' traditional boundaries – a space rich with opportunity. Importantly, it did not imply the loss of the "sailor's" identity, but rather an enrichment of it. The metaphor had a strong impact on the family actors and the strategic team, who became eager to experiment with this idea in the near future. Moreover, strategic activities such as crafting communication strategies to reach customers with this new value proposition began to involve other organizational members – especially those working in sales, maintenance, and service – within the strategic arena of the "New Friends" project.

This collective effort reinforced the feeling that the challenges ahead were to be tackled together, as a community. Consequently, it became clear that a new organizational structure was emerging, aligned with structuration theory, where agency resides within the individuals driving and enacting change. These activities acted as mechanisms of openness to change, stimulating in the family actors and strategic team a sense of courage and ambition to pursue a destination beyond familiar boundaries – without compromising the identity of the FBs. For both the family actors and the strategic team, the CRO became a reliable guide, not only pointing to the path forward but also challenging the companies' current structures, encouraging them to step beyond their comfort zones. This strengthened their confidence in navigating new, previously unimaginable "waters."

Through this approach, the CRO provided a practical introduction to the VUCA world. Although the family actors were initially cautious believers, they came to understand over time that change was essential for securing a successful future. These relational dynamics had significant implications for strategic work during the second phase. The CRO established new arenas for strategic discussion, directly involving family actors. This fostered their confidence and helped dismantle resistance to change. Although structural change remained a source of concern for some, the broad acceptance of the new strategic direction by the team eased these fears.

The new approach – extending service to customers – represented a concrete opportunity that preserved the identity of the family business while simultaneously building trust with employees, even though a new structure would inevitably be required. As postulated in structuration theory, every strategic action necessitates a corresponding structural form – a principle already introduced earlier in this chapter.

5.3 Phase 3: Establishing Shared Space for Strategic Discussions

The trustful discussions during the previous phases between the CRO and the family actors, as well as the strategic team, raised awareness of the importance of considering the VUCA world. In order to continue on this path, other voices needed to be heard. These voices came from different departments and proved beneficial in discovering new strategic routes. This encouraged the family actors to strengthen planning processes and practices, and it contributed to a more constructive approach to questioning strategic decisions. The family actors in both cases supported this ongoing process of strategizing. In the U.S. case, as mentioned before, the family actors intervened positively, which had significant implications for strategy work. Team meetings, especially in the U.S. company, were progressively transformed into a dominant strategic arena, reflecting the dynamics of the market.

The meetings became a space where an increasing debate on strategic issues between family actors – particularly in the Austrian company – and non-family managers unfolded.

In the U.S. company, the CRO also served as the CEO, and the team meetings generated new ideas on how to gain market share by offering valuable services to the customer base. Unsurprisingly, the U.S. unit and its department heads became the change leaders and implemented a new company structure through their trusted activities. The family actors in the parent company agreed to move forward – according to the CEO and CFO of the parent company, they had no other choice anyway.

6 Discussion and Conclusion

The US unit began with a single project for a major beverage company and, after three months, delivered highly successful results. The increased cash flow during this period was equally shared between the US unit and the customer. In recognition of their professionalism, the customer awarded the operating team both a formal commendation and a financial bonus. Encouraged by this success, employees at the US company proposed new organizational structures to better serve their customer base. This new strategy led to a significant increase in service-related business. Every new offer included a detailed procedure to avoid initial negative cash flows, assuming the team could manage the operation during the start-up phase.

Among the US company's customers, a competitive dynamic emerged – each wanted to be the first to receive support from the US unit to boost productivity on their existing lines. The company continuously adapted its structure to meet these new demands. The CRO introduced a bonus program tied to cash flow: if a previously agreed percentage of sales was reached, that portion was distributed among all employees. This had a multiplier effect on the sales team, ensuring that no customer inquiries went unanswered. The dynamic aligned everyone, fostering collaboration and driving the creation of structures designed to outperform competitors.

VUCA (Volatility, Uncertainty, Complexity, Ambiguity) was embedded in the company's culture. Teams reacted swiftly and positively, with no fear of failure – only fear of missing opportunities to innovate for customer benefit. The parent company's family stakeholders viewed the US unit as a "racehorse," but did not adopt its strategy. The US unit served the US, Canada, all of South America, and the Caribbean. Later, the CRO appointed a new CEO and faced further challenges in the US.

The CRO later described the VUCA environment as a gift, prompting the company to reflect on and embrace change. Cross-functional teams – R&D, Sales, and Operations–collaborated with the Service Team on-site to understand the practical issues of transitioning production lines. Even in difficult times, the US company remained successful. BANI (Brittle, Anxious, Nonlinear, Incomprehensible) did not pose a major challenge, as the teams were already accustomed to adaptation and transformation. This set them apart from the parent company, which struggled with bureaucracy, excessive management layers, and weak strategic collaboration.

The parent company retained a rigid, hierarchical structure, incapable or unwilling to transition to a more flexible "water lilies" management model – where decentralized, team-based leadership thrives. VUCA severely impacted the parent company, forcing family stakeholders and non-family managers to face reality. Only then did they begin implementing adaptable strategic action programs. While the parent company continues to adapt to VUCA, it now faces the emerging BANI challenge.

The Austrian company's structure remained unchanged due to the family actors' reluctance to implement a new strategy, despite the CRO presenting successful service-based business cases. Strategic meetings revealed that non-family managers, who had long-standing trust in the family actors, hesitated to think outside the box. Although they listened to the benefits of generating additional revenue through service offerings, fear of failure held them back.

This fragmented industry, filled with similar undifferentiated companies, somehow persisted year after year. Low profit margins seemed not to matter much to family businesses (FBs). The CRO repeatedly proposed future-oriented strategies and even suggested pilot projects with prominent clients, but these efforts were in vain. The VUCA environment was already influencing the business: volatility in customer behavior, uncertainty about order timings, increasing legal complexity, and pervasive ambiguity. Despite this, suppliers maintained weak relationships with customers, lacking direct, strategic engagement. This left room for larger players to take over through customer-centric strategies.

The family actors, unwilling to act or change, remained passive. Strategic meetings continued, often ending with the family actors citing past successes as reasons not to change. The CRO persistently explained VUCA and its implications for FBs in one-on-one discussions with family actors. Eventually, they agreed to include department heads in strategic meetings. Gradually, team members began sharing their ideas. The CRO supported this process, encouraging the family actors to respond positively. However, in the end, non-family managers deferred to the family actors' views. VUCA was dismissed as a myth, created by outsiders. The fragmented nature of the industry persisted, and the company did not adapt its structure to meet future challenges such as BANI.

Over time, the situation worsened, and the company needed external financing. The CRO returned to help find an investor. After losing majority ownership, the family actors handed leadership to non-family managers. Over the next two years, the company implemented critical structural changes. When BANI disrupted the business world, especially in fragmented industries, many companies failed or were absorbed by larger entities. Despite financial support, the Austrian company eventually had to shut down.

These two cases highlight the emotional dimensions shaping relationships between family actors, non-family managers, and advisors like the CRO in implementing strategic change. The CRO often remained on the periphery of strategy debates but played a vital role in restructuring efforts (Exler et al., 2017). All stakeholders agreed that ad hoc collaborations were necessary to promote mutual understanding. CROs can empower non-family managers by offering support, persuasion tools, and encouragement to think strategically. This, in turn, renders old structures obsolete and facilitates the creation of new ones. Repeated action programs led to successive structural changes, with early adopters driving success.

When non-family managers feel valued and reassured in their strategic roles, their engagement within the FB increases. The CRO fosters open, honest dialogue, highlights overlooked issues, and encourages innovative thinking. This builds trust and supports strategic redirection. Emotional support from the CRO enables family actors to consider new approaches and appreciate non-family managers' contributions.

This chapter provides insight into how CROs shape relational dynamics that influence strategic work and structural transformation in FBs. It outlines how CRO practices enable collaboration between family and non-family actors, leading to a shared action plan and successful organizational change. Trust-building is central to this process. A CRO's ability to care for and guide both parties supports emotional connection and fosters collaborative strategy work.

Both cases reveal the benefits of strong three-way relationships between family actors, non-family managers, and the CRO. While some FBs are open to external advice, others resist change. The CRO plays a crucial role in redefining FB structures and ensuring future viability. In the US case, this led to clear success. In the second case, the family's attachment to the status quo limited the potential of both the non-family managers and the CRO. It is recommended that family actors and non-family managers view the CRO not as a threat but as an empowering ally. By facilitating strategic engagement, CROs help build confidence and autonomy within the FB. This enables action and organizational change, strengthening emotional and relational bonds across the company.

In closing, the author acknowledges the limitations of this chapter and suggests directions for future research. While two case studies provide deep insights into differently managed FBs, personal and professional traits of actors involved may influence outcomes. Trust-building remains challenging, especially when family actors are reluctant to relinquish routine processes. Still, this framework may aid future case studies in understanding how trust and strategic collaboration reshape FBs in VUCA and BANI contexts. Future research should explore how emotional connections influence strategic relationships and how external institutional forces affect successful FB restructuring. Ultimately, this chapter underscores the importance of the CRO's role as a multifaceted advisor who integrates various resources to drive change. These themes merit deeper exploration in future research on FB strategy and transformation.

References

Batilana, J. (2006). Agency and institutions: The enabling role of individual`s social position. *Organization, 13*(5), 653–676.

De Groote, J. K., & Bertschi-Michel, A. (2021). From intention to trust to behavioural trust: Trust building in family business advising. *Family Business Review, 34*(2), 132–153.

Exler, M. W., Situm, M., & Bagari, J. (2023). Auswirkungen extern induzierter Krisen auf die Beschaffungsstrategien: Ergebnisse einer empirischen Studie mit Unternehmen in Deutschland und Österreich. *Krisen-, Sanierungs- und Insolvenzberatung, 19*(1), 5–11.

Exler, M. W., Situm, M., & Wanninger, A. (2017). Das Anforderungsprofil des CRO: Ergebnisse einer aktuellen Expertenbefragung im Vergleich mit Vorstudien. *Krisen-, Sanierungs- und Insolvenzberatung, 13*(3), 103–106.

Fang, H. C., Chrisman, J. J., & Holt, D. T. (2021). Strategic persistence in family business. *Entrepreneurship Theory and Practice, 45*(4), 931–950.

Flick, U. (2018). *An introduction to qualitative research*. London, UK: Sage Publications.

Giddens, A. (1984). *The constitution of society: Outline of a theory of structuration*. Berkeley: University of California Press.

Giddens, A. (1979). *Central problems in social theory: Action, structure and contradiction in social analysis*. Berkeley: University of California Press.

Giddens, A., (1976). *New rules of sociological method: A positive critique of interpretative sociologies*. Cambridge, MA: Polity Press.

Greenwood, R. & Suddaby, R. (2006). Institutional entrepreneurship in mature fields: The big five accounting firms. *The Academy of Management Journal, 49*(1), 27–48.

Hall, A., Melin, L., & Nordqvist, M. (2006). Understanding strategizing in the family business context. In: P. Z. Poutziouris, K. X. Smyrnios, & S. B. Klein (Eds.), *Handbook of research on family business* (pp. 253–268). Glos, UK: Edward Elgar.

Haugaard, M., (2002). *The constitution of power: A theoretical analysis of power, knowledge and structure*. New York, NY: Manchester University Press.

Ingram, A. E., Lewis, M. W., Barton, S., & Gartner, W. B., (2016). Paradoxes and innovation in family firms: The role of paradoxical thinking. *Entrepreneurship Theory and Practice, 40*(1), 161–176.

Jarzabkowski, P., Balogun, J. & Seidl, D., (2007). Strategizing: The challengees of a practice perspective. *Human Relations, 60*(1), 5–27.

Jarzabkowski, P., & Spee, A. P. (2009) Strategy-as-practice: A review and future directions for the field. *International Journal of Management Reviews, 11*(1), 69–95.

Jarzabkowski, P., Spee, A. P., & Smets, M., (2013). Material artifacts: Practices for doing strategy with „stuff". *European Management Journal, 31*(1), 41–54.

Kennedy, B. L., & Thornberg, R., (2018). Deduction, induction and abduction. In: U. Flick (Ed.), *The SAGE handbook of qualitative data collection* (pp. 49–64). London, UK: Sage Publications.

King, N., Horrocks, C., & Brooks, J. (2019). *Interviews in qualitative research*. London, UK: Sage Publications.

Langley, A. (1999). Strategies for theorizing from process data. *Academy of Management Review, 24*(4), 691–710.

Locke, K., Golden-Biddle, K., & Fellman, M. S. (2008). Perspective- making doubt generative: Rethinking the role of doubt in the research process. *Organization Science, 19*(6), 907–918.

McCracken, K. (2015). Best practice myths and trusted advisers. *Journal of Family Business Management, 5*(2), 130–139.

Mutch, A. (2014). Practice, substance and history: Reframing institutional logics. *Academy of Management Review, 43*(2), 242–258.

Nason, R., Mazzelli, A., & Carney, M. (2019). The ties that unbind: Socialization and business-owning family reference point shift. *Academy of Management Review, 44*(4), 846–870.

Nikolova, N., Möllering, G., & Reihlen, M. (2015). Trusting as a „leap of faith": Trust building practices in client-consultant relationships. *Scandinavian Journal of Management, 31*(2), 232–245.

Reeves, M., Levin, S., & Ueda, D. (2016). The biology of corporate survival: Natural ecosystems hold surprising lessons for business. *Harvard Business Review, 94*(1–2), 47–55.

Salvato, C., & Corbetta, G. (2013). Transitional leadership for advisors as a facilitator of successors` leadership construction. *Family Business Review, 26*(3), 235–255.

Schmutte, A. M. (2020). Digitale Transformation – Trends, Mythen und Konsequenzen für das Management. in: M. Harwardt, P. F.-J. Niemann, A. M. Schmutte, & A. Steuernagel (Eds.), *Führen und Managen in der digitalen Transformation: Trends, Best Practices und Herausforderungen* (pp. 35–66). Wiesbaden, Germany: Springer.

Situm, M., & Möllers, M. (2024). Der Einfluss von Innovationen auf die Resilienz von Unternehmen: Empirisch erhobene Ergebnisse zur Verbindung von Resilienz, Krisenmanagement und Innovation. *Krisen-, Sanierungs- und Insolvenzberatung*, *20*(6), 252–258.
Situm, M. (2021). Editorial: New challenges and opportunities in strategic decision making. *Corporate & Business Strategy Review*, *2*(1), 4–6.
Sloan, P., & Oliver, D. (2013). Building trust in mulit-stakeholder partnerships: Critical emotional incidents and practices of engagement. *Organization Studies*, *34*(6), 1835–1868.
Strike, V. M. (2013). The most trusted advisor and the subtle advice process in family firms. *Family Business Review*, *26*(3), 293–313.
Vaara, E., & Whittington, R. (2012). Strategy-as-practice: Taking social practices seriously. *The Academy of Management Annals*, *6*(1), 285–336.
Whittington, R. (2015). The massification of strategy. *British Journal of Management*, *26*(S1), S13–S16.

Juha Kansikas, Jaana Seikkula-Leino, Aino Leino, and Sophia Hornung

Employee Resilient Behavior and Its Leadership Prerequisites: Strategies for Founder Generation Family Firms

Abstract: This study, using an integrative review methodology, will focus on founder-generation family firms. The study results suggest that resilience, particularly in the form of pro-environmental employee behavior, needs more attention to increase our knowledge on the research agenda presented in this paper. In addition to the research agenda, we provide assumptions on how to effectively lead and manage resilience in a family business, thereby increasing ecological, sustainable, and financial value, offering a promising outlook for the future.

Keywords: Resilient behavior, Resilience, Founder generation, Entrepreneurial leadership, Family business, Integrative review

1 Introduction

This chapter aims to conduct an integrative literature review on employee pro-environmental behavior for coping with founder generation family firm resilience, crises and unexpected challenges and their outcomes in such an environment. Our approach to family business employee resilience is the adaptation of environmental aspects to employee decision-making to cope with business crises, as research is needed focusing on sustainability in family businesses (Jamil et al., 2025). Employee resilience skills increase survival in challenging business situations. Leadership prerequisites, which support – or hinder – employee resilience as pro-environmental behavior, create family business strategies to improve sustainable, ecological, and financial performance.

Earlier family business research has highlighted conceptual immatureness, which leads to the definition of family firms in multiple ways in current research (Minola et al., 2021). This chapter focuses on family entrepreneurship and literature related to small, entrepreneur-driven family firms. The current research literature refers to family firms, which are small- and medium-sized firms in which members of the same family are major shareholders and, therefore, in charge of decision-making (Villalonga & Amit, 2020). Transgenerational leadership is typical for family businesses, especially when two or more generations are involved in decision-making of some level (Jaskiewicz et al., 2015). Due to this, family ownership has some distinct characteristics in a business.

https://doi.org/10.1515/9783110790344-003

They include next generation and succession (Porfirio et al., 2020; Dorsch et al., 2023), values (Raitis et al., 2021; Amore & Miller, 2025; Picone et al. 2021), memories, experiences, and emotions (Humphrey et al., 2021), traditions of leadership (Suddaby & Jaskiewicz, 2020), women leadership (Ginalski, 2022; Calabro et al., 2024), long-lasting value creation mechanisms (Welsh et al., 2024) and the changing concept of a family in some parts of the world, leading to unmarried couples, divorced couples, and children of earlier spouses leading a same family business (Aldrich et al., 2021).

Family firms tend to be more CEO-focused than non-family firms. When they perform entrepreneurial actions, such as exploiting new opportunities for their business (de Massis et al., 2021), it is evident that leadership in family businesses is more focused on single or few decision makers. This reflects, among others, the context in which the CEO is a family member (Garcés-Galdeano et al., 2024). Founder centrality (Kelly et al., 2000) is a feature which is characteristic of entrepreneurial family firms. As founder-generation family firms offer a solid concept in the multitude of family business concepts (Daspit et al., 2021) and different types of family businesses (Chrisman et al., 2024), we focus on this chapter to contribute to leadership related to founder-owned and managed small and medium-sized family firms.

Founder-generation family firms are passive with corporate social responsibility, which makes studying pro-environmental behavior and resilience related to that even more needed (Dick et al., 2021). Subjective values, personal thinking, and governance mechanisms seem to influence on degree of activity in sustainable issues in founder generation family firm (Patuelli et al., 2022). Thus, our study contributes to the emerging field of family entrepreneurship (see Randerson, 2024) to understand resilience related to pro-environmental behavior in founder generation family firms.

Employee resilient behavior takes multiple forms in a small family business (Boers et al., 2025). According to Ones & Dilchert (2012b, 456), this employee pro-environmental behavior, also called green behavior, is defined as

> . . . scalable actions and behaviors that employees engage in that are linked with and contribute to or detract from environmental sustainability.

Earlier studies have seen leadership as a supportive element to employee pro-environmental behavior (Graves et al., 2013; Graves et al., 2019; Yukl, 2008). Consequently, in some circumstances, leadership can hinder employee resilience stemming from pro-environmental behavior. Thus, this paper aims to understand the opportunity- and growth-driven dynamics of founder-generation entrepreneurial leadership (Bagheri, 2017) as a two-edge resource for employee-resilient behavior.

Founder generation family firms are mostly small- and medium-sized firms, led by entrepreneurs, who reflect often in their daily business operations high degree of entrepreneurial leadership. As entrepreneurial leadership is about goal achievement and managing performance (Renko et al., 2015), it influences employee behavior in multiple ways. Recognizing and exploiting opportunities in entrepreneurial environments is typical for entrepreneurial leadership. Entrepreneurial family business leaders are defined according to behavioral characteristics that distinguish them from other leaders. Some typical characteristics of entrepreneurial leadership include risk-taking, proactiveness, innovativeness (Chen, 2007; Naldi et al., 2007), self-efficacy (Becherer et al., 2008), as well as opportunity recognition and exploitation (Shane & Venkataraman, 2000; Renko et al., 2015). Studies show that entrepreneurial leadership supports innovative organizational development, enhancing team creativity (Chen, 2007). Entrepreneurial outcomes take place through multiple sources. Early research suggests that an entrepreneur can be "born" with entrepreneurial personality traits but also be "made" through the influence of outside factors such as education or social interaction (Nielsen et al., 2017, p. 38).

Environmental behavior is part of the "environmental psychology" research area that describes the interactions between humans and their surroundings (Kollmuss & Agyeman, 2002, p. 240). Because environmental actions are highly dependent on individual factors such as the employee's tasks or the specific company, we differentiate between resilient behavior required as part of an employee's role within the organization and those behaviors that are voluntary and depend on the individual employee's attitude (Norton et al., 2015; Ones & Dilchert, 2012a).

2 Methodological Choices

In the study, we utilize an integrative review approach to assess, critique, and synthesize the literature on a research topic to enable theoretical frameworks and perspectives to emerge (Snyder, 2019; Torraco, 2005). We adopt the three main integrative review principles and divide them into five stages, in which we aim to contribute to the integrative review and create a new body of knowledge (see Table 1).

Table 1: Methodological choices of integrative review.

Stage	Purpose	Reference	Outcome
1 Increase of understanding	Aim of this stage is to provide the most cited articles on the topic which accumulate to the body of knowledge	Elsbach and van Knippenberg (2020); Alvesson and Sandberg (2020)	Review and comparison interpretatively between concepts and their meanings
2 Conclusions based on empirical articles	Aim of this stage is to conclude some of the relevant findings of the field of the study	Elsbach and van Knippenberg (2020); Alvesson and Sandberg (2020)	Future research topics

Table 1 (continued)

Stage	Purpose	Reference	Outcome
3 Validity and reliability	Aim of this stage is to evaluate validity and reliability of the study and its findings	Alvesson and Sanberg (2020)	Validity and reliability of data collection process, analysis, and contribution of the study are debated
4 Research agenda creation	Aim of this stage is to create future vision for the family business research	Kwon et al. (2020)	Research gaps, and future research questions are presented
5 Future research directions	Aim of this stage is to provide conceptual awareness of future research directions	Jolly et al. 2020; Cronin and George 2023	Future research streams, based on research topics, are presented as a part of the research agenda

According to Elsbach & van Knippenberg (2020), first, integrative review creates typically empirically based conclusions of the studied concepts and, second, will contribute toto the body of knowledge by new research suggestions and increasing understanding of still unstudied topics. Integrative review must be critical of the content and method (Alvesson & Sandberg, 2020). Careful analysis related to reliability and validity creates possibilities for critical assessment of the integrative review conducted. Third, according to Kwon et al. (2020), an integrative review typically creates a research agenda in which research gaps, future research topics, and possible research questions are presented. Thus, integrative review, first and foremost, serves to identify future research directions and even possible research gaps in which we do not have a sufficient body of knowledge yet (Jolly et al., 2020; Cronin & George, 2023).

Articles and book chapters previously described are included if they meet the criteria. The keywords used in Boolean searches on Google Scholar and the University of Turku library journal databases (including Web of Science, Ebsco, Scopus, Wiley, SAGE, ProQuest, Ebook Central, and Emerald) were the following:
- entrepreneurial leadership
- entrepreneurial leader
- founder generation
- family firm
- employee resilience
- pro-environmental behavior
- employee pro-environmental behavior.

The authors analyzed the articles deductively and inductively (Webster & Watson, 2002), and the results were agreed upon. Overall, we aim to address emerging topics such as pro-environmental behavior in the context of working life and entrepreneurial leadership. Thus, we aim to provide a new framework or way of thinking about an issue (Torraco, 2005). Therefore, we challenge and extend existing knowledge and provide family business strategies through an integrative review approach (Whetten, 1989).

3 Entrepreneurial Leadership in Founder Generation Family Firms

Leadership in founder-generation family firms is reflected by longevity in social capital and its relationships. As Ciravegna et al. (2020) have shown, many family firms do not leverage this social asset fully, which creates a need to invest resources in social relationship building and maintenance. Another example of resource usage and leverage are innovations in family firms, which need incentive mechanisms to activate employees to develop new solutions (Villani et al., 2023), and family commitment in case the founder generation is not involved in a business anymore (Dibrell et al., 2024). Thus, family traditions and past experiences influence on innovation processes of family firms (Erdogan et al., 2020). Family business governance mechanisms have an influence on the birth of innovations (Scholes et al., 2021).

At all levels, dysfunction in management and leadership can damage family firms, and internal and external influencers can create problems in finding good and functional practices (Kidwell et al., 2024). Family businesses contain opportunities for the birth of negative leadership characteristics such as nepotism and favouritism, but they also offer professional pathways to high-quality leadership based on performance and business logic (on psychology and family firms, see Sharma et al., 2020). Multiple existing studies indicate that other leadership theories, such as transformational leadership, have similar characteristics to entrepreneurial leadership (Renko et al., 2015; Cogliser & Brigham, 2004).

Transformational leadership consists of four components: 1) charismatic role modelling, 2) individualized consideration, 3) inspirational motivation, and 4) intellectual stimulation (Bass & Avolio, 1994, p. 27). Though entrepreneurial leadership differs from transformational leadership in the absence of individualized consideration (Renko et al., 2015), its focus on opportunity exploitation, and idea generation in co-creative processes (Lingo, 2020), the leadership styles share some mutual characteristics. As Kraus et al. (2018) suggest, family firms need both – individual processes done by themselves in management and a professional approach to their business development. Thus, family business leadership is often unique and subjectively driven by a founder of a family firm.

Renko et al. (2015) argue that entrepreneurial leaders play a crucial role as role models, influencing their subordinates' behavior and attitudes. By engaging in transformational leadership's intellectual stimulation, they encourage employees to rethink their working processes and recognize new opportunities. This not only fosters a dialogue among employees but also leads them to view their concerns about new implementations differently (Farahnak et al., 2020). Furthermore, entrepreneurial leaders motivate their subordinates, with their role modeling encouraging employees. This helps employees to activate their self-efficacy, and to adopt innovative behavior characteristics (Newman et al., 2018).

Substantial changes in corporations often demand adjustments in the organizational culture (Yukl, 2008), defined as employees' shared beliefs and values (Schein, 2010, p. 32). These beliefs and values can be communicated effectively through a leader's exemplary physical or psychological actions (Yukl, 2008; Schein, 2010). Bandura's (1988) social cognitive theory also highlights this role model behavior. Applied to family entrepreneurship, it states that an entrepreneurial leader's innovative actions and open encouragement to do so lead to similar competencies among employees. This aligns with Bagheri's (2017) findings, demonstrating that entrepreneurial leadership significantly positively impacts innovative behavior, opportunity recognition, and exploitation in the workplace. The literature also shows that management and coworkers can affect employees' normative beliefs by defining their values and getting personnel to accept them (Wiener, 1982; Ruepert et al., 2015).

One of the leadership characteristics of founder-generation family firms are succession processes. These include exit, transaction, family, and non-family transfer mechanisms in which passing the baton takes place. Succession is often in founder generation family firms a process of socializing next generation into intangible processes of business which are impossible to copy and to transfer as such (LeCounte, 2022). Enabling continuity and success among the next generation of family firm leaders is one of the main goals of succession and its leadership (Kandade et al., 2021; Istipliler et al., 2023).

Successful leadership in business needs long-term administrative mechanisms (Yukl, 2008; Nielsen et al., 2017), and family firms benefit in multiple ways from training leadership (Maharajh et al., 2024). With these mechanisms, entrepreneurial behavior can either be generated top-down or bottom-up (Burgelman, 1983; Nielsen et al., 2017). Combining both mechanisms is essential for successfully generating organizational and entrepreneurial behavior (Heinonen & Toivonen, 2008). Literature shows that different intervention mechanisms can influence employee beliefs directly and, from there on, their subsequent behavior (Ajzen, 2002, p. 2). These could consist of the previously mentioned administrative processes. Additionally, Renko et al. (2015, p. 69) argue that leaders' antecedents and positions in the organizational hierarchy also play a vital role in the success of entrepreneurial leadership.

4 Resilient Behavior and Its Characteristics

In the context of family businesses, especially their business families, family business characteristics like succession management, innovation processes, and suitable corporate governance mechanisms have been seen as a fundamental core of the resilience of a family business. (Calabro et al., 2021). This type of resilience reflects family business readiness to survive business crises or industry shocks. Naturally, good corporate governance also reflects family business capabilities that support employee-level pro-environmental resilient behavior. This type of resilience in an organization needs systems for its measurement, practices, and know-how to prepare family businesses to act when resilience is needed (see Beech et al., 2020).

It is natural that in founder-generation family firms, and in many other types of family firms, resilience is very much dependent on the individual decision-makers (Conz et al., 2020) and their closest companions, making resilient processes subjective and vulnerable. According to Yilmaz et al. (2024), family business resilience reflects values born and nurtured over a long-time horizon in family firms, often from one generation to another. As important as entrepreneur-level resilience is for a founder-generation family business, employee-level resilience is also needed to survive in a crisis, and therefore, family business human capital plays a vital role in the survival of a crisis (Santoro et al., 2021).

For family businesses, a typical mechanism to bolster resilience is social capital during crises. This includes support from business partners, colleagues, and other social relationships that provide guidance and resources for survival (Mzid et al., 2019; Mihotic et al., 2023). Just like social capital, human capital in terms of committed family members, employees and managers, and possible new recruitments, and financial capital in terms of survival, explain family business resilience economically (Gianiodis et al., 2022). Recovery and opportunity recognition in crisis, and in post-crisis environment is important feature for family business success (Salvato et al., 2020) just like organizational memory which allows long lasting family firms to consider how they have survived from the previous crisis (Czakon et al., 2023).

The influence of organizational culture on behavior has been extensively analyzed by Tudor et al. (2008). They noted the strong influence of organizational structure and culture on individual behavior. Further, research demonstrates that role model behavior and indicating openness to change among employees contributes to employee pro-environmental resilient behavior in organizations (Wesselink et al., 2017; Karp, 1996). Previous literature supports the notion that supervisory support for eco-initiatives in a company positively correlates with an employee's intention to promote eco-initiatives (Ramus & Steger, 2000). Ramus (2001) argues that managers' encouragement of innovation also leads to eco-innovations. Additionally, Green-Demers et al. (1997) state that providing programs that simplify environmental behavior will likely increase its occurrence.

As Robertson & Barling (2013) have shown, leaders' pro-environmental resilient behavior has a positive effect on the voluntary green behavior of their subordinates. Multiple studies have implemented Ajzen's Theory of Planned Behavior (see Figure 1) to predict pro-environmental resilient behavior in the workplace (e.g., Groot & Steg, 2007; Greaves et al., 2013). Additionally, the model is studied in the literature in the field of entrepreneurship (Rueda et al., 2015). A core element in the "Theory of Planned Behavior" is the intention to perform a given behavior, which is influenced by three attributes (Ajzen, 1991, pp. 181–188). Intentions are vital to one's motivation to perform a behavior. All in all, a stronger intention is more likely to lead to an action by an individual. The first attribute influencing the intention is the attitude towards the behavior. This is defined as how positively or negatively an individual views an action. The second factor is subjective norms, which refer to the anticipated social constraint to act or not to act in a certain way. The third attribute is PBC, which describes how complex or straightforward a particular behavior is predicted. This is comparable to Bandura's self-efficacy theory (Ajzen, 1991, pp. 181–188; Bandura, 1977, p. 193), according to which believing oneself capable of completing an action leads to a positive outcome.

Each behavioral attribute is influenced by a specific belief (Ajzen, 1991). Behavioral beliefs affect attitude and are foremost beliefs about the outcomes of an action. Normative beliefs influence subjective norms and are determined by the degree of social acceptance of a behavior. They are closely associated with the formation of organizational cultures (Rosseau, 1990). Control beliefs signify beliefs about existing factors that could turn a specific behavior on or off, setting the parameters for perceived behavioral control (Ajzen, 1991, p. 196).

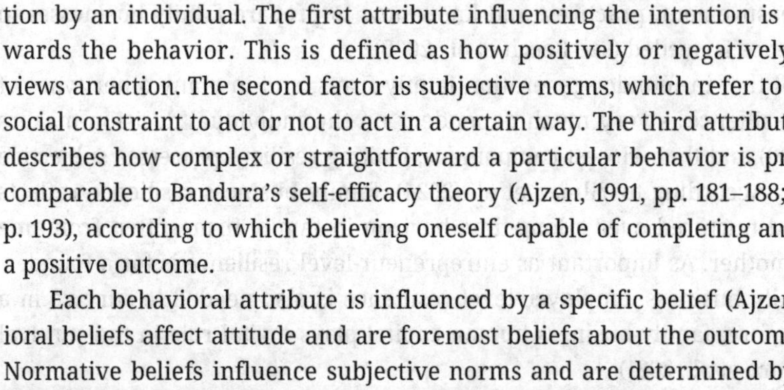

Figure 1: Simplified display of the theory of planned behavior.
Source: Own illustration based on Ajzen (2002, 1)

By applying the employee pro-environmental behavior, we can identify that people intend to perform green behavior when the three following variables align:

1. Employees have a positive attitude towards sustainability
2. Their surroundings, which include colleagues and superiors, expect and support green behavior
3. The employees believe they have sufficient control to perform the behavior.

Greaves et al. (2013) found that all three elements of Planned Behavior constructs significantly influence pro-environmental intentions in the workplace. Using several examples, they examined attitude and subjective norms as the main predictors of pro-environmental resilient behavior, while perceived behavioral control had a comparatively small influence.

5 Theory of Planned Behavior and Employee Resilient Behavior

This chapter delves into the influence of entrepreneurial leadership on the Theory of Planned Behavior constructs attitude, social norm, and perceived behavioral control, and its overall impact on employee pro-environmental behavior. Research on transformational leadership has established a positive link between intellectual stimulation and a positive mindset toward change among employees (Farahnak et al., 2020). This connection is also evident in entrepreneurial leadership (Renko et al., 2015), where the encouragement of employees to voice their concerns about new implementations leads to a change in their attitude towards these matters (Farahnak et al., 2020). This openness to change is crucial for the implementation of pro-environmental resilient behavior. With environmental responsibility being a relatively new issue in organizations, employees may be grappling with new policies and a changing environment. Therefore, to start acting pro-environmentally at work, employees need to have a positive attitude towards different ways of working. This has also been confirmed by Karp (1996), who states that openness is a strong indicator of employee green behavior. Asserting that entrepreneurial leaders are positively influencing employees' attitude towards change through intellectual stimulation (Renko et al., 2015), we can discern a positive influence of entrepreneurial leadership behavior on employees' attitude and therefore their intention to act pro-environmentally.

In addition, research suggests that employees who value the environment are more likely to act pro-environmentally (Ruepert et al., 2015). However, even with solid personal norms, employees often feel inhibited from acting upon them when there are perceived barriers to the behavior (Ruepert et al., 2015, p. 65). Leadership is needed to facilitate the employees' ability to implement their pro-environmental values by creating a supportive work context. Providing programs that simplify environmental behavior will likely increase their occurrence (Green-Demers et al., 1997). For instance, people are more likely to recycle when the proper bins are available on-site. Entrepreneurial leaders have been found to work persistently to secure the resources the employee needs to be innovative and to offer ideas for improvement and creative solutions (Renko et al., 2015). This should, therefore, include resources and support to encourage pro-environmental actions. Entrepreneurial leaders can increase employee pro-environmental resilient behavior by providing programs that facilitate sustainable behavior and support employees in being innovative in sustainable contexts (Bagheri & Harrison, 2020).

Furthermore, this paper's literature review underscores a positive relationship between entrepreneurial leadership behavior and the normative beliefs of employees. As noted by Wiener (1982), normative pressures significantly impact employee behavior. Consequently, the thoughts and acceptance of co-workers regarding an individual's green behavior significantly influence their decision to act pro-environmentally (Ruepert et al., 2015). Literature shows management can influence employees' normative beliefs by clearly defining their values (Wiener 1982). Personnel will then learn to accept them and work accordingly. When it comes to entrepreneurial leaders, values such as innovation, proactiveness, opportunity recognition, and exploitation are clearly defined (Chen, 2007; Naldi et al., 2007; Shane & Venkataraman, 2000). By sharing these values with employees, an innovative organizational culture that is intrinsically linked to normative beliefs in the workplace (Rosseau, 1990) is created (Chen, 2007). Further, Tudor, Barr, and Gilgs (2008) identified a controlling influence of organizational structure and culture on individual behavior. Based on these results, we expect employees to be more innovative and open to change when entrepreneurial social norms are established. Comparing these results to research on employee pro-environmental resilient behavior, we can identify openness to change as a significant contributor to green behavior (Karp, 1996). Likewise, research shows that innovativeness and opportunity recognition are directly linked to innovations in the ecological context (Ramus, 2001). Family influences positively on innovativeness especially when family is very committed or not committed at all into the project (Hatak et al. 2016). Subsequently, entrepreneurial leadership behavior positively impacts employee pro-environmental resilient behavior by creating social norms. However, it is also argued that leaders' pro-environmental resilient behavior is essential in encouraging ecological actions among employees and should be considered (Robertson & Barling, 2013).

Lastly, our study shows that entrepreneurial leaders' self-efficacy influences employees' control beliefs, which is further positively correlated with employee pro-environmental resilient behavior. Self-efficacy is linked to control beliefs among subordinates (Ajzen, 1991; Bandura, 1977) and is a typical characteristic of entrepreneurial leadership (Becherer et al., 2008). In addition, an entrepreneurial leader also practices role modelling to pass on behavioral characteristics to their employees (Renko et al., 2015). By combining these, it can be confirmed that an entrepreneurial leader's self-efficacy leads to similar competencies among employees (Bandura, 1988). According to the Theory of Planned Behavior, people perform a behavior if they are confident in their ability to execute it (Ajzen, 1991). With increased self-efficacy copied from their leaders, employees gain the confidence to perform pro-environmental actions. By these means, it can be confirmed that entrepreneurial leaders act as role models for employee self-efficacy, which is further positively correlated with employee pro-environmental resilient behavior. This result shows that entrepreneurial leaders raise employees' perceived behavioral control and, therefore, their intention to act pro-environmentally. However, Greaves, Zibarras, and Stride (2013) argue that perceived behavioral control, stemming from control beliefs, only has little influence on the pro-environmental intentions of employees compared to the other elements in the Theory of Planned Behavior.

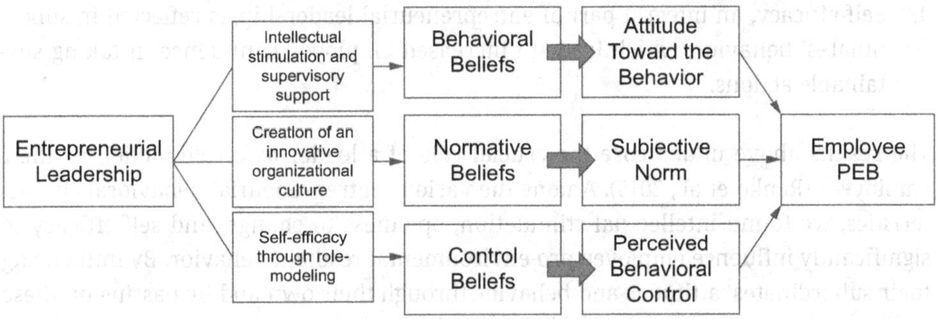

Figure 2: Family business entrepreneurial leadership influences on employee pro-environmental resilient behavior.
Source: Own illustration

6 Discussion

Our findings give valuable insights into what resilient behavioral attributes family business leaders should adopt and how to use them to promote green actions and initiatives among employees. This guides leader seeking new business strategies to move towards more sustainable workplaces. We recommend that entrepreneurial leaders display behavioral attributes such as self-efficacy, intellectual stimulation, opportunity recognition, and exploitation since we found these to impact employee resilient behavior. Given that employees copy the values of their leaders and act accordingly (Bandura, 1988), leaders must use their function as role models by incorporating these attributes into their behavior.

We would also like to highlight the importance of implementing pro-environmental leadership in founder generation family firms. Providing a pro-environmental work climate is essential for increasing employee resiliency (Hicklenton, 2019) and should, therefore, be combined with entrepreneurial leadership to maximize employee motivation. Our analysis confirms that an entrepreneurial leader holds significant influence over the beliefs and actions of their employees, which in turn impacts their pro-environmental resilient behavior (see Figure 2):

1. An entrepreneurial leader's intellectually stimulating behavior positively influences employee attitudes toward possible organizational changes, empowering them to take new actions to support the environment.
2. Entrepreneurial leadership supports employees in acting according to their attitudes towards pro-environmental resilient behavior.
3. Entrepreneurial leaders create innovative organizations by establishing entrepreneurial social norms such as innovation, proactiveness, opportunity recognition and exploitation. This stimulates normative beliefs about innovation, eco-innovations, and openness toward change.
4. Self-efficacy, an integral part of entrepreneurial leadership, is reflected in subordinates' behavior, which leads to increased employee confidence in taking sustainable actions.

The results above underscore the crucial role of a leader as a role model for their employees (Renko et al., 2015). Among the various entrepreneurial behavioral characteristics, we found intellectual stimulation, openness to change, and self-efficacy to significantly influence employee pro-environmental resilient behavior. By influencing their subordinates' attitudes and behavior through their own and by passing on these attributes, leaders can play a significant role in employees' pro-environmental efforts. Entrepreneurial leadership is about recognizing and exploiting opportunities (Renko et al., 2015; Shane & Venkataraman, 2000) and, therefore, generating entrepreneurial behavior on all organizational levels (Ireland et al., 2003).

The research has shown that these values allow entrepreneurial leadership to positively influence employee pro-environmental resilient behavior. Exploiting opportunities allows employees to make decisions and act autonomously within the organization, enabling them to develop individual ideas to promote sustainability within a company. These behaviors are voluntary pro-environmental resilient behaviors that are not part of the employee's job or task (Norton et al., 2015; Ones & Dilchert, 2012a). Because the actions are not required, employees solely participate in them by following their entrepreneurial leaders' values due to their function as role models. This explains why role model behavior is essential in this paper. Additionally, the nature of pro-environmental resilient behavior in the workplace largely depends on many factors, such as the employees' occupation, the use of technology, or organizational procedures (Boiral, 2015). Therefore, predicting how entrepreneurial leadership and role modelling influence specific employees in different companies is difficult.

This process is positive, but we must not overlook the potential for failure of leadership in promoting employee resilience. Thus, the paper provides a scenario in which entrepreneurial leadership creates failure in employee resilience. The paper will also contain strategic options for family business leaders to support employee resilience. This paper's first overview of leadership's influence on resilient behavior led us to recommend future studies. We strongly urge researchers to further explore leadership attributes and their impact on employee resilience through an empirical study. A significant shortcoming in the literature is a lack of research on practical implications and concrete administrative mechanisms that leaders can implement to strengthen employee resilience. Addressing these deficiencies is not just recommended but crucial for future research to reinforce employee resilience and help organizations meet their sustainability goals and move towards a greener future.

7 Conclusion

The research agenda of founder-generation family firm resilience from the perspective of pro-environmental employee behavior contains multiple research gaps (see Table 2). For the research agenda, we have focused on identifying research gaps related to founder-generation family firms and their entrepreneurial leadership, which influences the pro-environmental behavior of employees. Thus, supporting, controlling and measuring resilience in the form of pro-environmental behavior are identified as distinct features of founder-generation family firms; social capital and succession are also part of the research agenda.

Table 2: Research agenda.

Research gaps	Future research topics	Future research questions	References
Social capital as a mechanism to influence on resilience in a founder generation family firm	Social capital and entrepreneurial leadership Social capital and resilience from the perspective of pro-environmental behavior	How, and why social capital influences on pro-environmental resilience in founder generation family firms?	Ciravegna et al. (2020)
Succession and pro-environmental behavior	Succession and resilience from the perspective of pro-environmental behavior	How to increase organizational pro-environmental resilience in succession processes?	LeCounte (2022); Kandade et al. (2021); Istipliler et al. (2024)
Pro-environmental behavior creation top-down or bottom-up	Pro-environmental behavior supporting systems	How to create from founder perspective and from employee perspective pro-environmentally friendly working place?	Burgelman (1983); Nielsen et al. (2017)

Table 2 (continued)

Research gaps	Future research topics	Future research questions	References
Pro-environmental behavior as an outcome of innovative organizational culture	Pro-environmental behavior support systems	How to create an innovative organizational culture by entrepreneurial leadership in a founder generation family firm?	Renko et al. (2015); Ruepert et al. (2015)
Pro-environmental behavior	Pro-environmental behavior support systems	How to benefit in pro-environmental behavior creation employee self-efficacy and role modeling in a founder generation family firm?	Renko et al. (2015); Robertson and Barling (2013);
Pro-environmental behavior	Pro-environmental behavior control systems	How to create measurement systems and rewarding mechanisms related to pro-environmental behavior in a founder generation family firm?	Ajzen (1991); Bandura (1977); Chen (2007); Naldi et al. (2007); Shane and Venkataraman (2000); Rosseau (1990)

Leading a founder-generation family firm toward the pro-environmental behavior of employees increases opportunities for multiple types of value creation. Both financial, ecological, and sustainable values are promoted. First and foremost, a triple-value strategy is needed in founder-generation family firms to create profitable, ecological, and sustainable business value for society, customers, and themselves.

Increasing family firm resilience in these topics requires a strategic plan that might contain elements of goal setting, execution, measurement of goal achievement, renewal, and exit phases. This type of evaluation strategy helps founder-generation family firms create efficient intangible knowledge on sustainable business processes. Thus, founder-generation family firms benefit from fine-tuning their processes and becoming better competitors in the sustainable body of knowledge.

The founder generation family firm needs entrepreneurial leaders who create role models that inspire employees to pro-environmental behavior. Together with leading by doing incentives, it helps employees change their behavior. The specific and tailored rewarding strategy helps the founder generation family firm to influence not just employees but also managers, corporate board, and executives. As initiatives which promote pro-environmental behavior are rewarded, employees change their behavior to produce more qualified ideas and solutions to support ecological, sustainable, and financial value in a family firm.

Rewarding does not mean only monetary benefits as financial rewarding mechanisms. Non-financial rewarding mechanisms are more durable and long-lasting than financial ones. This means public recognition and thanks for good ideas in a family firm and publicly increasing participation in pro-environmentally friendly activities. Measuring pro-environmental behavior in family firms increases their capacity to handle crises related to them and to increase resilience in times of struggle.

Pro-environmental behavior not only enhances the sustainable capabilities of family firms but also fosters a culture of innovation and problem-solving. This, in turn, creates a reservoir of innovative ideas and solutions, paving the way for exciting growth opportunities. Founder-generation family firms that leverage the technology, staff knowledge, values, and blueprints they have developed over the long term can craft a future strategy with a new vision. They can pioneer products and services designed for markets that increasingly value sustainability.

It is evident that most of the current and future growth companies not just commercialize sustainable solutions, but create core competencies on more sustainable consumption, and manufacturing processes. These processes need agility to make decisions and to be creative and innovative by combining new types of technology and business vision into sustainable solutions. Thus, pro-environmental resilience is not just about crisis solutions but also about building a brighter and more innovative future for the business.

References

Ajzen, I. (1991) The theory of planned behavior. *Organizational Behavior and Human Decision Processes*, *50*(2), 179–211.

Ajzen, I. (2002) *Behavioral interventions based on the theory of planned behavior*, available at: https://people.umass.edu/aizen/pdf/TheoryofPlannedBehavior.intervention.pdf, accessed on June 14, 2020.

Aldrich, H. E., Brumana, M., Campopiano, G., & Minola, T. (2021). Embedded but not asleep: Entrepreneurship and family business research in the 21st century. *Journal of Family Business Strategy*, *12*(1), 100390.

Alvesson, M., & Sandberg, J. (2020). The problematizing review: A counterpoint to Elsbach and Van Knippenberg's argument for integrative reviews. *Journal of Management Studies*, *57*(6), 1290–1304.

Amore, M. D., & Miller, D. (2025). The role of culture in family firms. *Small Business Economics*, *64*(2), 261–278.

Bagheri, A. (2017). The impact of entrepreneurial leadership on innovation work behavior and opportunity recognition in high-technology SMEs. *Journal of High Technology Management Research*, *28*(2), 159–166.

Bagheri, A., & Harrison, C. (2020). Entrepreneurial leadership measurement: a multi-dimensional construct. *Journal of Small Business and Enterprise Development*, *27*(4), 659–679.

Bandura, A. (1977) Self-efficacy: Toward a unifying theory of behavioral change. *Psychological Review*, *84*(2), 191–215.

Bandura, A. (1988) Organisational applications of social cognitive theory. *Australian Journal of Management*, *13*(2), 275–302.

Bass B. M., & Avolio, B. J. (1994). *Improving organizational effectiveness through transformational leadership*. Thousand Oaks, CA: Sage Publications.

Becherer, R. C., Mendenhall, M., & Eickhoff, K. F. (2008) Separated at birth: An inquiry on the conceptual independence of the entrepreneurship and the leadership constructs. *New England Journal of Entrepreneurship*, *11*(2), 13–27.

Beech, N., Devins, D., Gold, J., & Beech, S. (2020). In the family way: an exploration of family business resilience. *International Journal of Organizational Analysis*, *28*(1), 160–182.

Boers, B., Billström, A., & Brozović, D. (2025). Entrepreneurial resilience (ER) and family business: a perspective article. *Journal of Family Business Management*, *15*(1), 3–9.

Boiral, O., Paillé, P., & Raineri, N. (2015). The nature of employees' pro-environmental behaviors. in: J. L. Robertson & J. Barling (Eds.), *The psychology of green organizations* (pp. 12–32), New York, NY: Oxford University Press.

Burgelman, R. A. (1983). Corporate entrepreneurship and strategic management: Insights from a process study. *Management Science*, *29*(12), 1349–1364.

Calabrò, A., Conti, E., & Masè, S. (2024). Trapped in a "golden cage"! The legitimation of women leadership in family business. *Journal of Family Business Strategy*, *15*(2), 100569.

Calabrò, A., Frank, H., Minichilli, A., & Suess-Reyes, J. (2021). Business families in times of crises: The backbone of family firm resilience and continuity. *Journal of Family Business Strategy*, *12*(2), 100442.

Chen, M.-H. (2007). Entrepreneurial leadership and new ventures: Creativity in entrepreneurial teams. *Creativity and Innovation Management*, *16*(3), 239–249.

Chrisman, J. J., Fang, H., Vismara, S., & Wu, Z. (2024). New insights on economic theories of the family firm. *Small Business Economics*, *63*(2), 697–711.

Ciravegna, L., Kano, L., Rattalino, F., & Verbeke, A. (2020). Corporate diplomacy and family firm longevity. *Entrepreneurship Theory and Practice*, *44*(1), 109–133.

Cogliser, C. C.; Brigham, K. H. (2004). The intersection of leadership and entrepreneurship: Mutual lessons to be learned. *The Leadership Quarterly*, *15*(6), 771–779.

Conz, E., Lamb, P. W., & De Massis, A. (2020). Practicing resilience in family firms: An investigation through phenomenography. *Journal of Family Business Strategy*, *11*(2), 100355.

Cronin, M. A., & George, E. (2023). The why and how of the integrative review. *Organizational research methods*, *26*(1), 168–192.

Czakon, W., Hajdas, M., & Radomska, J. (2023). Playing the wild cards: Antecedents of family firm resilience. *Journal of Family Business Strategy*, *14*(1), 100484.

Daspit, J. J., Chrisman, J. J., Ashton, T., & Evangelopoulos, N. (2021). Family firm heterogeneity: A definition, common themes, scholarly progress, and directions forward. *Family Business Review*, *34*(3), 296–322.

De Groot, J.; Steg, L. (2007). General beliefs and the theory of planned behavior: The role of environmental concerns in the THEORY OF PLANNED BEHAVIOR. *Journal of Applied Social Psychology*, *37*(8), 1817–1836.

De Massis, A., Eddleston, K.A. and Rovelli, P. (2021). Entrepreneurial by design: How organizational design affects family and non-family firms' opportunity exploitation. *Journal of Management Studies*, *58*(1), 27–62.

Dibrell, C., Gamble, J. R., Clinton, E., & Sherlock, C. (2024). Family firm innovativeness: an investigation of family governance, commitment, and generation involvement. Entrepreneurship & Regional Development, 1–22. https://doi.org/10.1080/08985626.2024.2338171

Dick, M., Wagner, E., & Pernsteiner, H. (2021). Founder-controlled family firms, overconfidence, and corporate social responsibility engagement: Evidence from survey data. *Family Business Review*, *34*(1), 71–92.

Dorsch, T., Jaskiewicz, P., Combs, J. G., & Wulf, T. (2023). Uncertainty around transgenerational Control: Implications for innovation prior to succession. *Family Business Review*, *36*(4), 402–425.

Erdogan, I., Rondi, E., & De Massis, A. (2020). Managing the tradition and innovation paradox in family firms: A family imprinting perspective. *Entrepreneurship Theory and Practice*, *44*(1), 20–54.

Elsbach, K. D., & van Knippenberg, D. (2020). Creating high-impact literature reviews: An argument for 'integrative reviews'. *Journal of Management Studies*, *57*(6), 1277–1289.

Farahnak, L. R., Ehrhart, M. G., Torres, E. M., & Aarons, G. A. (2020). The influence of transformational leadership and leader attitudes on subordinate attitudes and implementation success. *Journal of Leadership and Organizational Studies*, *27*(1), 98–111.

Garcés-Galdeano, L., Kotlar, J., Caicedo-Leitón, A.L., Larraza-Kintana, M., & Frattini, F. (2024). Absorptive capacity in family firms: exploring the role of the CEO. *International Journal of Entrepreneurial Behavior & Research*, *30*(6), 1349–1371.

Gianiodis, P., Lee, S. H., Zhao, H., Foo, M. D., & Audretsch, D. (2022). Lessons on small business resilience. *Journal of Small Business Management*, *60*(5), 1029–1040.

Ginalski, S. (2022). How women broke into the old boys' corporate network in Switzerland. *Business History*, *66*(8), 2137–2158.

Graves, L. M., Sarkis, J., & Gold, N. (2019). Employee pro-environmental behavior in Russia: The roles of top management commitment, managerial leadership, and employee motives. *Resources, Conservation & Recycling*, *140*, 54–64.

Graves, L. M., Sarkis, J., & Zhu, Q. (2013). How transformational leadership and employee motivation combine to predict employee pro-environmental behaviors in China. *Journal of Environmental Psychology*, *35*, 81–91.

Greaves, M., Zibarras, L. D., & Stride, C. (2013). Using the theory of planned behavior to explore environmental behavioral intentions in the workplace. *Journal of Environmental Psychology*, *34*, 109–120.

Green-Demers, I., Pelletier, L. G., & Ménard, S. (1997). The Impact of Behavioral Difficulty on the Saliency of the Association Between Self-Determined Motivation and Environmental Behaviors. *Canadian Journal of Behavioral Science*, *29*(3), 157–166.

Hatak, I., Kautonen, T., Fink, M., & Kansikas, J. (2016). Innovativeness and family-firm performance: The moderating effect of family commitment. *Technological Forecasting and social Change*, *102*, 120–131.

Heinonen, J., & Toivonen, J. (2008). Corporate entrepreneurs or silent followers? *Leadership and Organization Development Journal*, *29*(7), 583–599.

Hicklenton, C., Hine, D. W., & Loi, N. M. (2019). Can work climate foster pro-environmental behavior inside and outside of the workplace? *PLOS ONE*, *14*(10), 1–13.

Humphrey, R. H., Massis, A. D., Picone, P. M., Tang, Y., & Piccolo, R. F. (2021). The Psychological Foundations of Management in Family Firms: Emotions, Memories, and Experiences. *Family Business Review*, *34*(2), 122–131.

Ireland, R. D., Hitt M. A., & Sirmon D. G. (2003). A model of strategic entrepreneurship: the construct and its dimensions. *Journal of Management*, *29*(6), 963–989.

Istipliler, B., Ahrens, J. P., Hauer, A., Steininger, D., & Woywode, M. (2023). Heroes of the Green Room – How able successors revitalize and reinvent family firms. *Journal of Small Business Management*, *62*(3), 1604–1651.

Jamil, M., Stephens, S., & Md Fadzil, A.F. (2025). Sustainability in family business settings: a strategic entrepreneurship perspective. *Journal of Family Business Management*, *15*(1), 29–47.

Jaskiewicz, P., Combs, J. G., & Rau, S. B. (2015). Entrepreneurial legacy: Toward a theory of how some family firms nurture transgenerational entrepreneurship. *Journal of Business Venturing*, *30*(1), 29–49.

Jolly, P. M., Kong, D. T., & Kim, K. Y. (2020). Social support at work: An integrative review. *Journal of Organizational Behavior*, *42*(2), 229–251.

Kandade, K., Samara, G., Parada, M. J., & Dawson, A. (2021). From family successors to successful business leaders: A qualitative study of how high-quality relationships develop in family businesses. *Journal of Family Business Strategy*, *12*(2), 100334.

Karp, D. G. (1996). Values and their effect on pro-environmental behavior. *Environment and Behavior, 28*(1), 111–133.
Kelly, L. M., Athanassiou, N., & Crittenden, W. F. (2000). Founder centrality and strategic behavior in the family-owned firm. *Entrepreneurship Theory and Practice, 25*(2), 27–42.
Kidwell, R. E., Eddleston, K. A., Kidwell, L. A., Cater, J. J., & Howard, E. (2024). Families and their firms behaving badly: A review of dysfunctional behavior in family businesses. *Family Business Review, 37*(1), 89–129.
Kollmuss A., & Agyeman J. (2002). Mind the Gap: Why do people act environmentally and what are the barriers to pro-environmental behavior? *Environmental Education Research, 8*(3), 239–260.
Kraus, S., Kallmuenzer, A., Stieger, D., Peters, M., & Calabrò, A. (2018). Entrepreneurial paths to family firm performance. *Journal of Business Research, 88*, 382–387.
Kwon, S.-W., Rondi, E., Levin, D. Z., De Massis, A., & Brass, D. J. (2020). Network Brokerage: An Integrative Review and Future Research Agenda. *Journal of Management, 46*(6), 1092–1120.
LeCounte, J. F. (2022). Founder-CEOs: Succession planning for the success, growth, and legacy of family firms. *Journal of Small Business Management, 60*(3), 616–633.
Lingo, E. L. (2020). Entrepreneurial leadership as creative brokering: The process and practice of co-creating and advancing opportunity. *Journal of Management Studies, 57*(5), 962–1001.
Maharajh, R., Dhliwayo, S., & Chebo, A. K. (2024). The influence of family dynamics on business performance: does effective leadership matter? *Journal of Family Business Management, 14*(3), 515–533.
Mihotić, L., Raynard, M., & Sinčić Ćorić, D. (2023). Bouncing forward or bouncing back? How family firms enact resilience in times of crisis. *Journal of Family Business Management, 13*(1), 68–86.
Minola, T., Kammerlander, N., Kellermanns, F. W., & Hoy, F. (2021). Corporate entrepreneurship and family business: Learning across domains. *Journal of Management Studies, 58*(1), 1–26.
Mzid, I., Khachlouf, N. & Soparnot, R. (2019). How does family capital influence the resilience of family firms? *Journal of International Entrepreneurship 17*(2), 249–277.
Naldi, L., Nordqvist, M., Sjöberg, K., & Wiklund, J. (2007). Entrepreneurial orientation, risk-taking, and performance in family firms. *Family Business Review, 20*(1), 33–47.
Newman, A., Tse, H. H. M., Schwarz, G., & Nielsen, I. (2018). The effects of employees' creative self-efficacy on innovative behavior: The role of entrepreneurial leadership. *Journal of Business Research, 89*, 1–9.
Nielsen, S. L., Klyver, K., Evald, M. R., & Bager, T. (2017). *Entrepreneurship in theory and practice*. Cheltenham: Edward Elgar Publishing Limited.
Norton, T. A., Parker, S. L., Zacher, H., & Ashkanasy, N. M. (2015). Employee green behavior: A theoretical framework, multilevel review, and future research agenda. *Organization & Environment, 28*(1), 103–125.
Ones, D. S., & Dilchert, S. (2012a). Environmental sustainability at work: A call to action. *Society for Industrial and Organizational Psychology, 5*(4), 444–466.
Ones, D. S., & Dilchert, S. (2012b). Employee green behaviors, in: S. E. Jackson, D. S. Ones & S. Dilchert S. (Eds.), *The SIOP professional practice series: Managing human resources for environmental sustainability* (pp. 85–116), San Francisco, CA: Jossey-Bass.
Patuelli, A., Carungu, J., & Lattanzi, N. (2022). Drivers and nuances of sustainable development goals: Transcending corporate social responsibility in family firms. *Journal of Cleaner Production, 373*, 133723.
Picone, P. M., De Massis, A., Tang, Y., & Piccolo, R. F. (2021). The psychological foundations of management in family firms: Values, biases, and heuristics. *Family Business Review, 34*(1), 12–32.
Porfírio, J. A., Felício, J. A., & Carrilho, T. (2020). Family business succession: Analysis of the drivers of success based on entrepreneurship theory. *Journal of Business Research, 115*, 250–257.
Raitis, J., Sasaki, I., & Kotlar, J. (2021). System-spanning values work and entrepreneurial growth in family firms. *Journal of Management Studies, 58*(1), 104–134.

Ramus, C. A. (2001). Organizational support for employees: encouraging creative ideas for environmental sustainability. *California Management Review, 43*(3), 85–105.

Ramus, C. A., & Steger, U. (2000). The roles of supervisory support behaviors and environmental policy in employee "eco initiatives" at leading-edge European companies. *Academy of Management Journal, 43*(4), 605–626.

Randerson, K. (2024). Family entrepreneurship: a perspective article. *Journal of Family Business Management, 14*(3), 431–436.

Renko, M., El Tarabishy, A, Carsrud, A. L., & Brännback, M. (2015). Understanding and measuring entrepreneurial leadership style. *Journal of Small Business Management, 53*(1), 54–74.

Robertson, J. L., & Barling, J. (2013). Greening organizations through leaders' influence on employees' pro-environmental behaviors. *Journal of Organizational Behavior, 34*(2), 176–194.

Rosseau, D. M. (1990). Normative beliefs in fund-raising organizations: linking culture to organizational performance and individual responses. *Group & Organization Studies, 15*(4), 448–460.

Rueda, S., Moriano, J. A., & Liñán, F. (2015). Validating a theory of planned behavior questionnaire to measure entrepreneurial intentions. in: A. Fayolle, P. Kyrö & F. Liñán (Eds.), *Developing, shaping and growing entrepreneurship* (pp. 60–78), Cheltenham: Edward Elgar Publishing Limited.

Ruepert A., Keizer K., Steg L., Maricchiolo F., Carrus G., Dumitru A., Mira R. G., Stancu A., & Moza D. (2015). Environmental considerations in the organizational context: A pathway to pro-environmental behavior at work. *Energy Research & Social Science, 17*, 59–70.

Salvato, C., Sargiacomo, M., Amore, M. D., & Minichilli, A. (2020). Natural disasters as a source of entrepreneurial opportunity: Family business resilience after an earthquake. *Strategic Entrepreneurship Journal, 14*(4), 594–615.

Santoro, G., Messeni-Petruzzelli, A., & Del Giudice, M. (2021). Searching for resilience: the impact of employee-level and entrepreneur-level resilience on firm performance in small family firms. *Small Business Economics, 57*(1), 455–471.

Schein, E. H. (2010). *Organizational culture and leadership*. San Francisco: Jossey-Bass.

Scholes, L., Hughes, M., Wright, M., De Massis, A., & Kotlar, J. (2021). Family management and family guardianship: Governance effects on family firm innovation strategy. *Journal of Family Business Strategy, 12*(4), 100389.

Shane, S., & Venkataraman, S. (2000). The promise of entrepreneurship as a field of research. *The Academy of Management Review, 25*(1), 217–226.

Sharma, P., Chrisman, J. J., Chua, J. H., & Steier, L. P. (2020). Family firm behavior from a psychological perspective. *Entrepreneurship Theory and Practice, 44*(1), 3–19.

Snyder, H. (2019). Literature review as a research methodology: An overview and guidelines. *Journal of Business Research, 104*, 333–339.

Suddaby, R., & Jaskiewicz, P. (2020). Managing traditions: A critical capability for family business success. *Family Business Review, 33*(3), 234–243.

Torraco, R.J. (2005). Writing integrative literature reviews: Guidelines and examples. *Human Resource Development Review, 4*(3), 356–367.

Tudor, T. L., Barr, S. W., & Gilg, A. W. (2008). A novel conceptual framework for examining environmental behavior in large organizations: A case study of the Cornwall National Health Service (NHS) in the United Kingdom. *Environment and Behavior, 40*(3), 426–450.

Villalonga, B., & Amit, R. (2020). Family ownership. *Oxford Review of Economic Policy, 36*(2), 241–257.

Villani, E., Linder, C., De Massis, A., & Eddleston, K. A. (2023). Employee incentives and family firm innovation: A configurational approach. *Journal of Management, 50*(5), 1797–1835.

Webster, J., & Watson, R. T. (2002). Analyzing the past to prepare for the future: Writing a literature review. *MIS Quarterly, 26*(2), xiii–xxiii.

Welsh, D. H. B., Llanos-Contreras, O., & Hebles, M. R. (2024). Effectuation and strategic evolution for sustainable longevity: the case of a 19th-generation family firm. *International Journal of Entrepreneurial Behavior & Research*, *30*(4), 834–855.

Wesselink, R., Blok, V., & Ringersma, J. (2017). Pro-environmental behavior in the workplace and the role of managers and organisation, *Journal of Cleaner Production*, *168*, 1679–1687.

Whetten, D.A. (1989). What constitutes a theoretical contribution? *Academy Management Review*, *14*(4), 490–495.

Wiener, Y. (1982). Commitment in organizations: A normative view, *Academy of Management Review*, *7*(3), 418–428.

Yilmaz, Y., Raetze, S., Groote, J. de, & Kammerlander, N. (2024). Resilience in family businesses: A systematic literature review. *Family Business Review*, *37*(1), 60–88.

Yukl, G. (2008). *Leadership in organizations*. New Jersey: Pearson Prentice Hall.

Ante Vuletić

The Impact of Family Ownership on SME Resilience: A Three-Circle Model Analysis

Abstract: Family-owned enterprises represent a vital component of the global economy, distinguished by unique governance structures and resilience mechanisms. This study explores the influence of family ownership on business resilience in small and medium-sized enterprises (SMEs), using the Three-Circle Model as a conceptual framework. Based on data from 80 family-owned enterprises, the analysis investigates the relationships among family participation, succession planning, and the integration of professional management in relation to organizational resilience. The findings indicate that family ownership ($r = 0.67$, $p < 0.01$) and succession planning ($r = 0.54$, $p < 0.05$) significantly enhance resilience, while professional management shows a moderate positive effect ($\beta = 0.20$, $p = 0.10$). These results offer practical implications for family enterprises aiming to balance familial governance with professional expertise.

Keywords: Family business, SME resilience, Three-Circle Model, Succession planning, Professional management

1 Introduction

Family-owned enterprises represent a cornerstone of the global economy, generating approximately 70–90% of global GDP (Anderson & Reeb, 2003; Zahra et al., 2008). These organizations exhibit unique characteristics in their governance and management approaches (Berrone et al., 2010; Sharma, 2004), which significantly influence their resilience and adaptability (Wu et al., 2017). The distinctive nature of family businesses – combining familial values with commercial imperatives – creates unique challenges and opportunities in fostering organizational resilience.

Family-owned enterprises constitute a crucial segment of the global economy, characterized by their distinctive governance structures, management approaches, and resilience strategies. These organizations integrate familial values, long-term orientation, and a strong sense of heritage, often implementing governance frameworks that set them apart from non-family entities. While these characteristics promote stability and continuity, they also present specific challenges, particularly regarding adaptability and succession planning.

The global relevance of family-owned enterprises cannot be overstated.

These businesses contribute approximately 70–90% of global GDP annually and represent an estimated 85% of all business start-ups worldwide. Furthermore, they account for nearly two-thirds of all enterprises and provide employment for 50–80%

https://doi.org/10.1515/9783110790344-004

of the workforce in most countries. Their widespread presence and economic contributions underscore the necessity of understanding their internal dynamics, particularly in relation to resilience and sustainability.

Despite their economic importance, family-owned small and medium-sized enterprises (SMEs) face distinctive challenges that may influence their capacity for resilience in times of disruption. This study seeks to explore how family ownership affects SME resilience by examining a set of interrelated factors. Specifically, the research aims to:

1. Assess the extent of family participation in both ownership and managerial roles, and its corresponding impact on resilience outcomes.
2. Evaluate the effectiveness and robustness of succession planning processes within family enterprises.
3. Investigate the role of deeply embedded family values in shaping strategic and operational business decisions.
4. Examine the degree to which professional management practices are adopted and integrated alongside traditional family-based governance mechanisms.

The investigation is grounded in a multi-theoretical framework that captures the complexity and multidimensionality of family-owned businesses. The primary lens through which the study is conducted is the Three-Circle Model, which conceptualizes family businesses as the intersection of three overlapping systems: family, ownership, and business. This model provides a comprehensive foundation for understanding how the interplay of these systems shapes organizational behavior and outcomes. Complementing this framework, Stewardship Theory is employed to explain how family members often exhibit intrinsic motivation to act in the best interests of the firm, prioritizing collective goals over individual gain.

In contrast, Agency Theory is used to highlight potential conflicts of interest that may arise between family owners and non-family professional managers, particularly in contexts where control and accountability mechanisms are underdeveloped. Finally, Systems Theory provides a holistic perspective on the interdependence of the various subsystems within the family business, emphasizing how their interactions contribute to, or detract from, organizational resilience. Together, these theoretical perspectives facilitate a nuanced understanding of the mechanisms through which family involvement influences SME resilience, offering valuable insights for both academic inquiry and practical application.

2 Literature Review

The theoretical understanding of family businesses has evolved through several distinct phases. The foundational work of Jensen & Meckling (1976) established a basic framework for analyzing ownership–management relationships through the lens of Agency

Theory. This was followed by significant theoretical advancements in the 1990s, most notably the development of the Three-Circle Model by Tagiuri & Davis (1996), which fundamentally reshaped the conceptualization of family business dynamics.

Contemporary research has extended these foundational theories by incorporating more complex elements of family business operations. As Fernández-Roca & Gutiérrez Hidalgo (2021) observe, modern family businesses operate within intricate networks of relationships that transcend the traditional owner–manager dichotomy.

The Three-Circle Model remains a cornerstone for understanding the unique structure of family businesses, identifying three overlapping systems: family, ownership, and business (Tagiuri & Davis, 1996). At the same time, Agency Theory continues to provide valuable insights into the distinct challenges and advantages encountered by family enterprises (Jensen & Meckling, 1976). Recent studies have expanded this perspective by exploring how family relationships influence and reshape traditional agency dynamics (Berrone et al., 2010). Empirical evidence suggests that family businesses often incur lower agency costs due to a stronger alignment of interests between owners and managers (Anderson & Reeb, 2003).

Stewardship Theory, as articulated by Davis et al. (1997), offers an alternative to the traditionally dominant Agency Theory by emphasizing the intrinsic motivation of individuals to act in the best interests of the organization. Within the context of family businesses, stewardship behaviors are frequently observed and are shaped by several factors, including a strong emotional investment in the firm, a long-term orientation, concerns regarding family reputation, and objectives related to the intergenerational transfer of wealth. These dimensions foster a culture of commitment and responsibility, contributing significantly to organizational stability and resilience.

Empirical research has identified several key structural elements that enhance the resilience of family-owned enterprises. One such element is the ownership structure. Recent studies have demonstrated that the concentration of family ownership plays a pivotal role in shaping resilience capabilities. Wu et al. (2017) provide compelling evidence that higher levels of family ownership are positively correlated with increased resilience ($r = 0.67$, $p < 0.01$). Furthermore, family-controlled boards have been shown to exhibit superior crisis response capabilities, while concentrated ownership structures facilitate faster and more cohesive decision-making processes during periods of uncertainty.

Another critical structural component is the governance mechanism. Effective governance frameworks within family firms are instrumental in fostering resilience (Bammens et al., 2008). Research findings suggest that family councils enhance intra-organizational communication and support collaborative decision-making. Additionally, the inclusion of professional board members introduces external perspectives that can improve strategic agility and responsiveness. Hybrid governance models – those that integrate both family and non-family elements – have been shown to outperform purely familial or purely professional structures in terms of organizational resilience and adaptability.

Succession planning represents a further determinant of long-term resilience in family firms. As Sharma (2004) highlights, the presence of formal succession plans is positively associated with improved firm performance. Table 1 demonstrates the significant impact of succession planning across multiple dimensions of business resilience, showing substantial differences in performance stability, crisis recovery speed, and stakeholder confidence between firms with and without formal succession plans. Moreover, the active involvement of next-generation family members contributes to the development of organizational capabilities and the continuity of core values and strategic vision. Clear and well-structured succession processes reduce uncertainty, foster leadership legitimacy, and support the sustained resilience of the enterprise across generations.

Table 1: Impact of Succession Planning on Business Resilience.

Aspect	With Succession Plan	Without Succession Plan	Statistical Significance
Performance Stability	High ($\mu = 4.2$)	Moderate ($\mu = 3.1$)	$p < 0.01$
Crisis Recovery	Rapid (87%)	Delayed (45%)	$p < 0.05$
Stakeholder Confidence	Strong (82%)	Weak (34%)	$p < 0.01$

The integration of professional management into family businesses represents a multifaceted and often delicate challenge (Henderson & Fredrickson, 2001). While the adoption of professional managerial practices can yield significant organizational benefits, it also introduces complexities related to the firm's familial character and culture. Recent research has highlighted several advantages associated with professionalization, including enhanced strategic planning capabilities, improved operational efficiency, and increased access to external networks and resources. These benefits can strengthen the firm's competitive position and foster long-term sustainability.

However, the professionalization process is not without its challenges. The introduction of external managers can lead to tensions stemming from potential misalignment with core family values. Communication barriers may emerge between family and non-family members, particularly when informal governance structures dominate. Additionally, concerns about the potential erosion of family control can hinder the effective implementation of professional management practices. These dynamics underscore the need for careful navigation of the professionalization process to ensure alignment with the family's strategic and cultural objectives.

Cultural factors also play a critical role in shaping the resilience of family-owned enterprises. As noted by Zahra et al. (2008), family business resilience is deeply embedded in cultural foundations that influence behavior, decision-making, and long-term orientation. Recent findings by Yilmaz et al. (2024) emphasize two central cultural dimensions that contribute to organizational resilience.

The first is value transmission, which refers to the intergenerational transfer of core business principles, the preservation of family traditions, and the integration of familial values into everyday business practices. This transmission reinforces continuity and a sense of purpose across generations, providing a stable foundation during periods of disruption or change. The second dimension is organizational identity, which has been shown to correlate positively with resilience outcomes ($r = 0.58$, $p < 0.01$). A strong family business identity is characterized by a shared vision among family members, a cohesive organizational culture, and high levels of employee loyalty. These elements collectively enhance the firm's ability to withstand external shocks, adapt to evolving environments, and maintain internal cohesion under pressure.

Finally, financial resilience in family businesses operates differently from that in non-family enterprises. As Anderson & Reeb (2003) suggest, the financial behavior of family firms is often influenced by long-term priorities and conservative risk profiles. Table 2 illustrates these distinct financial characteristics, comparing family businesses with non-family enterprises across investment horizon, risk tolerance, and capital structure, demonstrating how these differences contribute to enhanced resilience. These firms tend to prioritize capital preservation, prudent investment, and sustained growth over short-term gains, which can confer a degree of stability in times of economic uncertainty.

Table 2: Financial Resilience Comparison.

Aspect	Family Businesses	Non-Family Businesses	Impact on Resilience
Investment Horizon	Long-term (>5 years)	Short-term (1–3 years)	Positive ($\beta = 0.42$)
Risk Tolerance	Moderate	High	Mixed ($\beta = 0.18$)
Capital Structure	Conservative	Aggressive	Positive ($\beta = 0.35$)

3 Research Model and Hypotheses

Based on the theoretical framework and the reviewed literature, the following hypotheses are proposed:

H1: Family ownership concentration positively influences SME resilience.
H2: Professional management integration positively influences SME resilience.
H3: The interaction between family ownership and professional management positively influences SME resilience.

Figure 1 presents the conceptual research model, illustrating the relationships between family ownership, professional management integration, governance mechanisms, adaptability, and business resilience within the Three-Circle Model framework.

The analysis reveals complex relationships between family ownership, management structures, and organizational resilience. Table 3 presents the multiple regression results, demonstrating the significant predictive relationships between the independent variables and SME resilience ($R^2 = 0.65$, Adjusted $R^2 = 0.63$). The data indicate that family ownership significantly enhances business resilience, with correlation analysis showing a strong positive relationship ($r = 0.67$, $p < 0.01$). This finding supports Anderson & Reeb's (2003) assertions regarding the unique advantages of family ownership structures, while extending the understanding of how these advantages contribute to resilience capabilities.

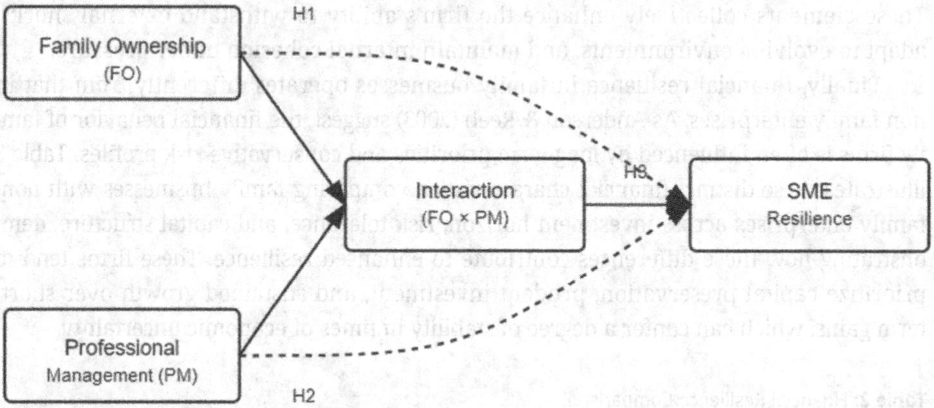

Figure 1: Research model.

Table 3: Multiple Regression Results.

Variable	β	SE	t	p-value	VIF
Constant	1.25	0.45	2.78	0.01	–
Family Ownership	0.45	0.12	3.75	<0.01	1.42
Succession Planning	0.30	0.14	2.14	0.03	1.35
Professional Management	0.20	0.11	1.82	0.10	1.28
FO×PM Interaction	0.25	0.13	1.92	0.05	1.31

Note: $R^2 = 0.65$; Adjusted $R^2 = 0.63$; $F(4,75) = 24.8$, $p < 0.01$

Table 4: Structural Equation Model Results.

Path	Estimate (β)	SE	CR	P-value
FO → GOV	0.45	0.06	7.50	<0.001
SP → GOV	0.38	0.07	5.43	<0.001
PM → GOV	0.32	0.08	4.00	<0.01
GOV → ADAP	0.41	0.06	6.83	<0.001
ADAP → RES	0.52	0.05	10.40	<0.001
RES → PERF	0.48	0.06	8.00	<0.001

Model Fit Indices: $\chi^2 = 245.32$ (df = 124, $p < 0.001$); CFI = 0.942; TLI = 0.935; RMSEA = 0.058 (90% CI: 0.047–0.069); SRMR = 0.046

The SEM analysis reveals several significant pathways through which family ownership influences business resilience. The model demonstrates a good fit with the data across all major indices. Family ownership exhibits a strong direct effect on governance quality ($\beta = 0.45$, $p < 0.001$), which subsequently influences adaptability ($\beta = 0.41$, $p < 0.001$). The pathway from adaptability to resilience is particularly strong ($\beta = 0.52$, $p < 0.001$), supporting the theoretical framework that emphasizes the mediating role of organizational adaptability in fostering resilience.

The relationship between family ownership and resilience is especially pronounced in enterprises with established succession planning. Regression analysis indicates that succession planning has a significant positive effect on resilience ($\beta = 0.30$, $p < 0.05$), reinforcing Sharma's (2004) findings regarding the importance of structured leadership transitions. This effect appears more substantial in mature businesses, where formal succession planning processes have been developed over time. The data show that firms with structured succession plans report consistently higher resilience scores (mean difference = 0.85, $p < 0.01$) compared to those without such plans.

Professional management integration emerges as a critical moderating factor. While it demonstrates a moderate direct effect on resilience ($\beta = 0.20$, $p < 0.10$), its influence becomes most significant when considered alongside family ownership structures. This finding extends the work of Wu et al. (2017), illustrating how professional expertise can complement family leadership without undermining core family values.

The structural equation modeling further reveals that governance mechanisms significantly mediate the relationship between family ownership and resilience (indirect effect = 0.23, $p < 0.05$). This mediation is most pronounced in organizations that have successfully integrated professional management while maintaining strong family involvement, supporting Berrone et al.'s (2010) conclusions on the importance of balanced governance structures.

To evaluate the theoretical framework comprehensively, structural equation modeling was employed. The analysis confirms complex interrelationships among family ownership, governance mechanisms, and organizational outcomes. Table 4 presents the comprehensive structural equation model results, including standardized path coefficients and significance levels for all hypothesized relationships. The model demonstrates excellent fit with the empirical data (CFI = 0.942, TLI = 0.935, RMSEA = 0.058, SRMR = 0.046), providing strong support for the proposed framework.

The SEM analysis reveals several critical pathways through which family ownership influences business resilience. Family ownership demonstrates a strong direct effect on governance quality ($\beta = 0.45$, $p < 0.001$), supporting Berrone et al.'s (2010) assertions regarding the importance of family-influenced governance structures. This relationship is further reinforced by significant positive effects from succession planning ($\beta = 0.38$, $p < 0.001$) and professional management integration ($\beta = 0.32$, $p < 0.01$).

Governance quality, in turn, has a substantial positive effect on organizational adaptability ($\beta = 0.41$, $p < 0.001$), which subsequently influences resilience ($\beta = 0.52$, $p < 0.001$). This sequence of relationships aligns with Wu et al.'s (2017) findings on the

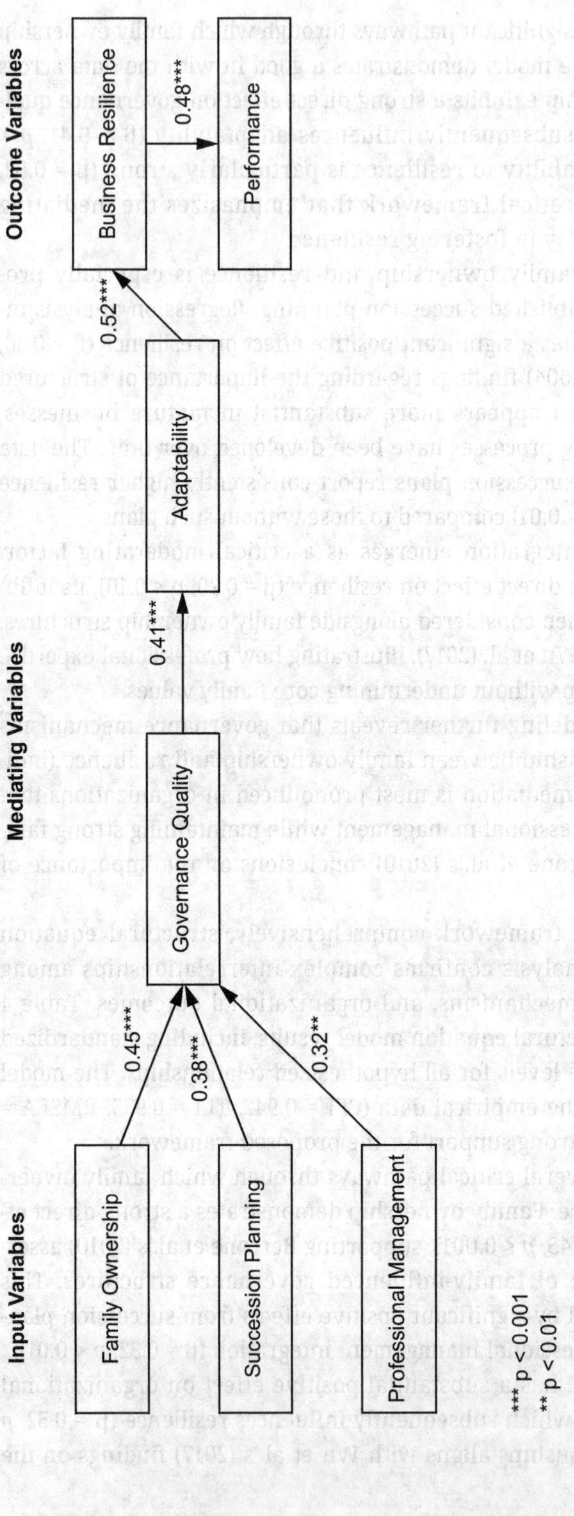

Figure 2: Structural Equation Model of Family Business Resilience.

role of governance mechanisms in fostering adaptive capabilities, while extending the understanding of how these capabilities contribute to organizational resilience.

The SEM results provide strong support for the theoretical framework, revealing nuanced relationships among key variables. The robust path coefficient from family ownership to governance quality (β = 0.45) suggests that family involvement fosters distinctive governance capabilities, consistent with Tagiuri & Davis's (1996) Three-Circle Model. At the same time, the significant contribution of professional management (β = 0.32) indicates that external expertise complements – rather than undermines – family-based advantages.

The mediating role of adaptability emerges as particularly important. The strong path coefficient between adaptability and resilience (β = 0.52) supports Zahra et al.'s (2008) argument on the importance of strategic flexibility in family firms, while offering quantitative validation of this relationship. This finding helps to explain why some family businesses exhibit superior resilience despite facing comparable external challenges.

These results carry important implications for both theory and practice. The model suggests that family businesses can enhance their resilience by developing governance structures that balance family influence with professional expertise. This extends Henderson & Fredrickson's (2001) work on organizational adaptation and offers actionable guidance for family business leaders seeking to strengthen long-term resilience.

4 Summary

The structural equation modeling (SEM) results provide compelling evidence for the complex mechanisms through which family ownership influences business resilience. The significant path coefficients in the model (Figure 2) demonstrate that the relationship between family ownership and resilience operates through multiple, interconnected channels, supporting and extending prior theoretical frameworks (Tagiuri & Davis, 1996; Davis et al., 1997).

The strong direct effect of family ownership on governance quality (β = 0.45, $p < 0.001$) suggests that family involvement fosters distinctive governance capabilities. This finding aligns with the work of Anderson & Reeb (2003), while offering quantitative evidence of the specific mechanisms involved. Notably, the model indicates that this relationship is enhanced – rather than diminished – by the integration of professional management (β = 0.32, $p < 0.01$), suggesting a complementary rather than competitive dynamic between family and professional leadership.

The mediating role of adaptability emerges as particularly significant. The substantial path coefficients from governance quality to adaptability (β = 0.41, $p < 0.001$), and from adaptability to resilience (β = 0.52, $p < 0.001$), reveal a clear chain of influence. These findings support Zahra et al.'s (2008) theoretical propositions and provide empirical validation for the pathways through which family businesses build resilience capabilities.

The SEM results extend existing theory in several meaningful ways. First, they offer empirical support for the integrated nature of family business systems as proposed by the Three-Circle Model (Tagiuri & Davis, 1996). The significant path coefficients linking family ownership, governance, and performance outcomes ($\beta = 0.48$, $p < 0.001$) demonstrate how these systems interact to foster organizational resilience. For practitioners, the findings highlight concrete strategies to enhance resilience in family firms. Specifically, the strong relationship between governance quality and adaptability ($\beta = 0.41$) suggests that family businesses should prioritize the development of robust governance structures that balance family influence with professional expertise. This supports the recommendations of Berrone et al. (2010) while offering quantitative insights for practical implementation.

The SEM results also provide robust evidence for the interrelationships among family ownership, governance mechanisms, and organizational resilience. The excellent model fit indices (CFI = 0.942, TLI = 0.935) indicate that the proposed theoretical framework effectively captures the essential components of these dynamics and offers a solid foundation for future research. Future studies should investigate the temporal dynamics of these relationships, particularly how they evolve through generational transitions. The strong path coefficient between succession planning and governance quality ($\beta = 0.38$) highlights this as a promising area for longitudinal analysis. Additionally, the findings suggest several areas warranting further investigation: the role of environmental factors in moderating the identified relationships, the impact of digital transformation on resilience mechanisms in family businesses, and cross-cultural variations in the effectiveness of governance approaches.

This study presents several limitations that should be considered. First, the sample size of 80 SMEs may limit the generalizability of the findings across different regions, cultures, or industries. Expanding the sample in future research could enhance external validity. Second, the cross-sectional design restricts causal inferences. Longitudinal studies are recommended to better capture how resilience develops over time, particularly during generational transitions. Third, the study focused primarily on internal factors. Future research should incorporate external influences – such as market conditions or regulatory environments – to provide a more comprehensive view of SME resilience.

Finally, while the Three-Circle Model provided a useful framework, future studies could explore in greater depth the dynamic interactions between family, business, and ownership systems, particularly in the context of digital transformation and sustainability.

References

Anderson, R. C., & Reeb, D. M. (2003). Founding-family ownership and firm performance: Evidence from the S&P 500. Journal of Finance, 58(3), 1301–1328. https://doi.org/10.1111/1540-6261.00567

Bammens, Y., Voordeckers, W., & Van Gils, A. (2008). Boards of directors in family firms: A generational perspective. Small Business Economics, 31(2), 163–180. https://doi.org/10.1007/s11187-007-9087-5

Berrone, P., Cruz, C., Gomez-Mejia, L. R., & Larraza-Kintana, M. (2010). Socioemotional wealth and corporate responses to institutional pressures: Do family-controlled firms pollute less? Administrative Science Quarterly, 55(1), 82–113. https://doi.org/10.2189/asqu.2010.55.1.82

Chang, S. J. (2011). Sony vs Samsung: The inside story of the electronics giants' battle for global supremacy. John Wiley & Sons.

Davis, J. H., Schoorman, F. D., & Donaldson, L. (1997). Toward a stewardship theory of management. Academy of Management Review, 22(1), 20–47. https://doi.org/10.5465/amr.1997.9707180258

Davis, P. S., & Harveston, P. D. (1998). The influence of family on the family business succession process: A multi-generational perspective. Entrepreneurship Theory and Practice, 22(3), 31–53. https://doi.org/10.1177/104225879802200302

Delzaher, D., Kira, M., & Rasha, E. (2018). The influence of organizational determinants on employee resilience in family businesses. Journal of Family Business Strategy, 9(2), 115–125. https://doi.org/10.1016/j.jfbs.2018.03.001

Fernández-Roca, F. J., & Gutiérrez Hidalgo, F. (2021). Understanding the family business system: Elements and interconnections. Family Business Review, 34(2), 185–203. https://doi.org/10.1177/0894486520927289

Gersick, K. E., Davis, J. A., Hampton, M. M., & Lansberg, I. (1997). Generation to generation: Life cycles of the family business. Harvard Business School Press.

Habbershon, T. G., & Williams, M. L. (1999). A resource-based framework for assessing the strategic advantages of family firms. Family Business Review, 12(1), 1–25. https://doi.org/10.1111/j.1741-6248.1999.00001.x

Henderson, A. D., & Fredrickson, J. W. (2001). Top management team coordination needs and the CEO pay gap: A competitive test of economic and behavioral views. Academy of Management Journal, 44(1), 96–117. https://doi.org/10.5465/3069339

Jensen, M. C., & Meckling, W. H. (1976). Theory of the firm: Managerial behavior, agency costs and ownership structure. Journal of Financial Economics, 3(4), 305–360. https://doi.org/10.1016/0304-405X(76)90026-X

Lansberg, I. (1999). Succeeding generations: Realizing the dream of families in business. Harvard Business School Press.

Sharma, P. (2004). An overview of the field of family business studies: Current status and directions for the future. Family Business Review, 17(1), 1–36. https://doi.org/10.1111/j.1741-6248.2004.00001.x

Stewart, J. B. (2019, May 23). The fall of the Hertz family empire. The New York Times. https://www.nytimes.com/2019/05/23/business/hertz-family-business.html

Stone, B. (2014). The everything store: Jeff Bezos and the age of Amazon. Little, Brown and Company.

Tagiuri, R., & Davis, J. (1996). Bivalent attributes of the family firm. Family Business Review, 9(2), 199–208. https://doi.org/10.1111/j.1741-6248.1996.00199.x

Wiegmann, R. (2020). The Schwarz Group: A strategic analysis of Europe's largest retail conglomerate. Business Insider Deutschland.

Wu, S., Levitas, E., & Priem, R. L. (2017). CEO tenure and company invention under differing levels of technological dynamism. Academy of Management Journal, 48(5), 859–873. https://doi.org/10.5465/amj.2005.18803927

Yilmaz, K., Karpuzoglu, S., & Ertan, M. (2024). A systematic literature review on resilience in family businesses. Journal of Family Business Strategy, 15(1), 100–117. https://doi.org/10.1016/j.jfbs.2023.100352

Zahra, S. A., Hayton, J. C., & Salvato, C. (2008). Family firms' commitment to continuity, strategic flexibility, and performance. Family Business Review, 21(3), 292–308. https://doi.org/10.1177/08944865080210030601

Sascha Frohwerk, Carsten Kruppe and Holger Wassermann

Implications of Company Succession on Resilience of Small and Medium Size Companies

Abstract: Small and medium-sized enterprises represent a significant economic factor. Their continued existence is often closely tied to the owner, as ownership and management are typically unified. As a result, the succession process plays a crucial role in ensuring long-term business continuity. To assess a company's resilience, this article utilizes the Creditreform Rating creditworthiness index. An analysis of all successions supported by a guarantee bank in Germany over the past ten years identifies key factors that contribute to strengthening resilience. One notable finding is the particular relevance of the successor's age, which – consistent with existing literature – is primarily associated with greater experience. To further explore this aspect, a survey was conducted among 200 successors, focusing on both existing and missing knowledge. While overall experience was rated positively, retrospective insights highlighted a desire for stronger competencies in management, personnel leadership, and legal fundamentals. These results offer valuable implications: they suggest how potential successors can enhance their preparation and how succession processes might be more effectively supported.

Keywords: Succession, Knowledge, SME, Resilience, Performance

1 Introduction

Small and medium-sized enterprises (SMEs) form the backbone of many economies worldwide, particularly in Germany, where they are known as the *Mittelstand*. These companies account for more than 99% of all businesses (Haunschild & Wolter, 2010) and employ 55% of the workforce (Statistisches Bundesamt, 2024). While SMEs are generally defined by revenue and number of employees, the term *Mittelstand* – or family firms – refers to enterprises characterized by the unity of ownership and management. There is considerable overlap between the two definitions. Given their substantial economic importance, research into the factors that influence SME longevity and success is essential.

Acknowledgement: The authors would like to thank the VDB and especially Stephan Jansen as well as Dr. Benjamin Mohr from Creditreform Rating AG for their long term cooperation on this project.

https://doi.org/10.1515/9783110790344-005

Company succession represents a critical juncture for SMEs, often determining their long-term viability and resilience. Studies have shown that failed successions can result in significant job losses and economic disruption (Hauser et al., 2010). In SMEs, management and ownership are typically concentrated in a single individual, giving that person a decisive influence on the company's success. A change in ownership, therefore, presents a sensitive and complex challenge that requires careful preparation.

German SMEs face unique challenges in succession planning. An aging population and demographic shifts have resulted in a shortage of potential successors (Kay & Suprinovič, 2013), while a highly regulated environment may discourage prospective acquirers. To better understand which factors are most relevant for successful, especially non-family, successions, empirical evidence is needed. However, detailed data in this area remain scarce. This paper analyzes loan data from German guarantee banks related to company successions over a ten-year period. To gain deeper insights, the analysis is supplemented with survey responses from successors. Finally, conclusions are drawn regarding the implications for the organizational resilience of SMEs.

2 Literature Review

2.1 Definitions

Succession in SMEs typically refers to the transfer of ownership and/or management from one generation to the next, often within a family context (Handler, 1994). It is a complex process involving multiple stakeholders and can span several years. Organizational resilience is defined as a company's ability to anticipate, prepare for, respond to, and adapt to incremental change and sudden disruptions (Denyer, 2017). For SMEs, resilience is particularly crucial given their vulnerability to market fluctuations and resource constraints.

2.2 Positive and Negative Impacts of Company Succession on Resilience

Several studies have found that well-planned successions can enhance SME resilience.

- **Improved adaptability:** Successors often bring fresh perspectives and new skills, enabling companies to better adapt to changing market conditions (Cabrera-Suárez et al., 2018).
- **Enhanced innovation:** New leadership can drive innovation, helping SMEs stay competitive (Hauck & Prügl, 2015). Studies highlight the importance of innovation and technology adoption for SME resilience (Zimmermann, 2017).
- **Strengthened stakeholder relationships:** Successful transitions can reinforce relationships with employees, customers, and suppliers (De Massis et al., 2016).

However, the literature also highlights several ways in which succession can undermine SME resilience:

- **Loss of tacit knowledge:** The departure of experienced leaders can result in the loss of valuable implicit knowledge (Steier, 2001).
- **Disrupted organizational culture:** Leadership changes can destabilize company culture, potentially affecting employee morale and productivity (Kets de Vries, 1993).
- **Financial strain:** Succession-related costs and potential conflicts can strain SME resources (Molly et al., 2010).

2.3 Factors Influencing Succession's Impact on Resilience

The literature indicates three main factors that determine how a succession influences a company's resilience:

- **Succession Planning:** Multiple studies emphasize the importance of comprehensive succession planning in fostering resilience (Le Breton-Miller et al., 2004; Sharma et al., 2003). Well-planned successions tend to result in smoother transitions and better post-succession performance.
- **Successor Preparation:** The literature consistently highlights the significance of successor preparation. Nordqvist et al. (2013) found that successors who were properly trained and integrated into the business prior to taking over were more likely to maintain or improve company resilience.
- **Family Dynamics:** In family-owned SMEs, family dynamics play a crucial role in succession outcomes. Harmonious family relationships and clear communication have been linked to more resilient post-succession companies (Eddleston et al., 2013).

2.4 Research Gaps

While the existing literature provides valuable insights, several areas warrant further investigation.

- **Long-term impacts:** Most studies focus on short-term succession outcomes. Longitudinal research examining the long-term effects of succession on SME resilience is needed.
- **Non-family successions:** The majority of research focuses on family businesses. More studies on non-family SME successions could provide a broader understanding of succession dynamics.
- **Industry-specific factors:** Research exploring how industry-specific factors influence the relationship between succession and resilience could yield valuable insights.

- **Resilience metrics:** Development of standardized metrics for measuring SME resilience before, during, and after succession would enhance comparability across studies.
- **External factors:** Further research on how external factors (e.g., economic conditions, technological changes) interact with succession processes to affect SME resilience is needed.

2.5 Contribution

To address some of the previously mentioned research gaps, the study analyzes a comprehensive dataset spanning ten years. The data covers all company successions in Germany that were supported by a guarantee bank, which were typically non-family successions. To place these successions in context, industry-specific and region-specific external data were incorporated. Additionally, survey data from successors were used to gain deeper insight into their level of preparedness and to identify key obstacles to successful succession. Finally, the findings were used to draw conclusions about the implications of these factors for organizational resilience.

3 Data & Method

3.1 Dataset

The study is based on data from the 16 German guarantee banks for the years 2014 to 2023 and includes master data on the transferred companies, such as sector, number of employees at the time of succession, and district. Key balance sheet figures – such as revenues, costs, fixed assets, and profit prior to the takeover – are available for most companies. For some, this information is also available for the years before the handover. Additional data on financing, including guaranteed and other loans, is also included. This dataset was enriched by Creditreform Rating AG with information on the previous owner and the company's creditworthiness (credit rating index).

The dataset also contains information on the individuals taking over the companies, including age, gender, marital status, and district. Publicly available data was added for sectors and districts to allow analysis of factors such as regional centrality, unemployment rate, and sectoral development. All data is anonymized to prevent identification of specific companies or individuals. In total, information is available on 10,245 companies and 12,329 successors. Creditreform Rating was able to supplement data on 3,008 predecessors. As is standard in such analyses, the dataset was cleaned for errors and outliers, although some fields contain missing values (Burns & Burns, 2008, pp. 113–115; Jamshidian, 2009, pp. 114–117).

For financial ratios, the amount of usable data is reduced due to a typical two-year lag in the availability of annual reports. Because many comparisons are made between values two years before and two years after the takeover, only six of the ten years effectively remain for financial analysis. After data cleaning, a dataset of 903 companies was extracted. The difference in the credit rating index two years after compared to two years before the succession is used as the target variable.

3.2 Measuring Resilience

The concept of resilience as 'the ability of an organization to anticipate, prepare for, respond and adapt to incremental change and sudden disruptions in order to survive and prosper.' (Denyer, 2017) with its four dimensions preventative control, mindful action, performance optimization and adaptive innovation contains many aspects that can hardly be represented in a single key figure. If we limit ourselves primarily to the quantitatively measurable dimensions that can be captured by company characteristics, entrepreneurs and accounting, we remain with profit (or EBIT / EBITDA) and revenue. These two metrics have a couple of shortcomings.

Revenue only indicates whether the company's products and services have been sold. They do not contain any information on whether the costs of manufacturing a product could be covered. This statement is contained in profit figures such as EBIT or EBITDA. However, these profit figures are not entirely advantageous either. For example, EBIT and EBITDA do not include the costs of financing, which are likely to be considerable in the event of a company takeover.

If there is an exceptionally high need for investment shortly after the takeover, depreciation and amortization will be above average and thus reduce EBIT considerably more than before the takeover. EBITDA, on the other hand, does not include depreciation and amortization, which means that even less can be said about cost coverage. For these reasons, none of the key figures alone is meaningful enough, but rather a combination of different key figures is useful to make a statement about the financial stability of a company, which is the basis for resilience.

Another option is to use an existing index that has been developed in a specific direction. The Creditreform Rating AG's creditworthiness index is an obvious choice due to the data available and its orientation. It is intended to provide information on creditworthiness and is based on several dimensions (see Figure 1)

The creditworthiness index evaluates a company's solvency and financial stability – key components of resilience. It combines several financial indicators into a composite measure that serves as a proxy for solvency. The index is based on a wide range of financial ratios, payment histories, and other economic factors that enable a well-founded assessment. Its standardized format allows for comparisons between companies, facilitating an evaluation of resilience within the industry context. A poor credit rating can act as an early warning signal for financial instability and, therefore,

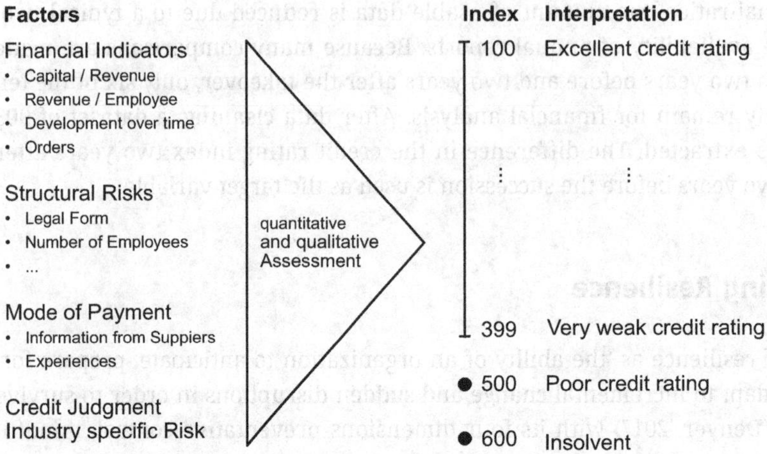

Figure 1: Construction of the creditworthiness index.

lower resilience. In addition to financial metrics, qualitative aspects such as company management and market position – both relevant to resilience – are also considered.

Despite its advantages as a resilience indicator, the creditworthiness index has limitations. It primarily focuses on financial aspects, while resilience also depends on factors like innovation capacity, corporate culture, and crisis management. Moreover, the index reflects current creditworthiness but does not reliably capture long-term adaptability or innovative potential. External influences – such as geopolitical risks or supply chain disruptions – also affect resilience but are not fully reflected in the index. In some cases, companies provide their own financial data, which may lack objectivity or be outdated, potentially affecting the index's validity. Another limitation is that, while the key components of the index are known, the exact weighting and evaluation of qualitative factors are not publicly disclosed. Overall, the Creditreform Creditworthiness Index offers a practical and measurable proxy for resilience, particularly valuable for long-term analysis.

3.3 Methods

Several methods were used to address the research questions. As little empirical data was available on the topic of succession, the analysis first provided an overview of the succession landscape in Germany using descriptive statistics. Based on this foundation, relevant factors were identified through linear regression models. Since resilience, as previously described, could not be reduced to a single key figure, a survey of successors was conducted in a third step to gain deeper insights.

4 Findings from the Quantitative Study

4.1 Descriptive Statistics Compared to Other Studies

Companies

The dataset includes just over 10,000 companies that changed ownership between 2014 and 2023. As shown in Figure 2, one third of these belong to the skilled crafts sector, followed by retail, the liberal professions, services, and the hospitality industry. Over the long term, the share of skilled crafts increased, while the proportion of liberal professions declined. The retail sector showed particularly strong fluctuations, especially during the COVID years. The average number of employees across all companies is 21, though this figure varies significantly between sectors.

Industry	2014 – 2023	Count	Share	Mean Workforce
Craft	247 – 373	3.356	33	21
Retail	144 – 152	1.558	15	14
Free Professions	120 – 99	1.142	11	12
Service Industry	90 – 125	1.129	11	25
Hotels & Restaurants	78 – 88	1.002	10	16
Industry	44 – 65	730	7	40
Other Industries	25 – 46	461	5	32
Wholesale & f. Trade	24 – 21	277	3	23
Transport	14 – 21	229	2	41
Horticulture	5 – 8	94	1	24
Agriculture & Fishing	2 – 7	68	1	5
Information Industry	4 – 3	39	0	18

Tabelle: Sascha Frohwerk • Quelle: Verband Deutscher Bürgschaftsbanken • Erstellt mit Datawrapper

Figure 2: Shares of industries in the dataset.

Throughout the entire observation period, the number of cases per year varied only slightly, ranging from 923 in 2014 to 1,111 in 2021. The vast majority of companies are located in very central (40%) or central areas (37%). Only 19% are situated in peripheral locations, and just 4% in very peripheral areas.

Predecessors and Successors

The average age of transferees remained stable at around 38 years. However, transferors have gradually become older over time, with a noticeable decline in the proportion of those handing over before the age of 60. The lower age quantile increased from 55 to 59 years between 2014 and 2023. This trend is partly driven by demographic changes, but it may also indicate increasing difficulty in finding a successor in a timely manner.

The proportion of female successors remained relatively constant over the entire period at 22%, which is below the overall proportion of female managers, estimated at around 30%. There are notable differences across sectors: the construction industry has the lowest share of female successors at 5%, while the highest is found in other services at 56%. A comparison between the share of female employees and female successors by sector also reveals striking disparities. For example, in the education sector, 72% of the workforce is female, but only 32% of successors are women. In contrast, the health and social work sector has 77% female employees and 53% female successors.

Financial Development

While a detailed financial analysis of the succession phase is not the focus of this article, a brief overview is provided here. As previously mentioned, revenue development is a more suitable measure of succession continuity than profit figures. This is because costs often include depreciation and amortization of new investments made after the takeover, and they are generally more controllable by the successor. Revenue, by contrast, reflects the ability to successfully position products or services in the market. Since family businesses typically rely heavily on the owner, this becomes a critical factor.

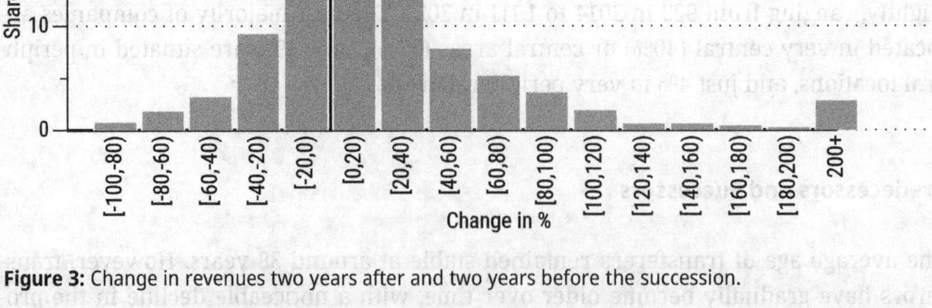

Figure 3: Change in revenues two years after and two years before the succession.

Figure 3 illustrates the change in revenues before and after succession. Overall, 67% of the companies were able to increase their sales, while 33% experienced a decline. It should be noted that inflation is not accounted for in this analysis; however, inflation rates in Germany during the period in question were relatively low. Despite this, the overall trend can be considered a positive development.

4.2 Regression Analyses

As described above, if the creditworthiness index could serve as an indicator of resilience, the question still arose as to whether the absolute value after the handover should be considered, or rather the change before and after the handover. Arguments could easily be made in favor of both approaches. Since the focus of this study was on company succession, it was initially logical to examine the change in the index. This provided insight into whether the new owner made the company more resilient or whether the succession had a negative impact on its crisis resistance. This allowed for an assessment of which circumstances or characteristics of the successor or the company contributed to resilience.

However, this approach posed a challenge: if a company already had a low (i.e. favorable) creditworthiness index before the handover, the successor might not have been able to improve it further, or there might not have been a need for improvement at all. This consideration supported the use of the absolute post-succession value. Nevertheless, since the study aimed to measure the effect of succession itself – and thus to filter out industry- or region-specific influences on company performance – the change in the index was used.

The selection of independent variables depended on data availability and was divided into three groups. First, company-related data such as sector, legal form, and number of employees were considered. Second, location-related variables such as district, federal state, population density, centrality, unemployment rate, the number of small and medium-sized enterprises, and regional growth were included. Third, characteristics of the successor(s), including age, gender, marital status, and the number of individuals taking over the company jointly, were examined. For the previous owner, only age was known.

When conducting the regressions, the nature of the dependent variable – the creditworthiness index – had to be taken into account. It was a continuous variable ranging from 100 to 400, with discrete values of 500 (poor creditworthiness) and 600 (insolvency). Two strategies were considered for handling this: either excluding the values 500 and 600 or converting the index into categorical values. Both approaches had advantages and disadvantages. The first allowed for more precise measurement of small changes but excluded problematic cases. The second retained all values, including 500 and 600, but required the creation of meaningful categories.

In this study, the change in the index was used as an indicator of the extent to which the successor had a positive or negative impact on the company's resilience. This approach also had the advantage that certain components of the index, such as sector and company size, could still be used as explanatory variables, as they did not change as a result of succession. The values 500 and 600 were excluded to allow for the measurement of smaller, more nuanced changes.

Table 1 summarizes the two linear regression models. The first includes all available variables, with coefficients for non-significant classes (province, industry, legal form) omitted for readability. In the second model, insignificant variables were excluded entirely. Industry and province were also left out, as they were mostly insignificant, and because the dataset was highly unbalanced with respect to province.

Table 1: Regression results.

Variable	Variable	Model 1	Model 2
	Intercept	−5.133e+03*	−5.544e+03*
	Index -2	−5.682e-01***	−5.375e-01***
	Year of succession	2.644e+00*	2.836e+00*
Company	Industry: Services	1.988e+01**	
	Crafts	1.019e+01*	
	Transport	2.317e+01**	
	Size 10–49	−8.918e+00***	−6.542e+00**
	Size 50–249	−1.478e+01**	−9.995e+00*
	Legal form	not significant	
Region	Province: HamburgHessen	−1.626e+01**	
	Schleswig-Holstein	1.440e+01**	
	others (separately)	1.574e+01*	
		not significant	
	Urbanity index	5.592e+00	
	Growth index	−2.472e+00	
	Centrality index	1.030e+00	
	Unemployment rate	8.756e-02	
	Change unem. rate	3.361e+00	
Successor	Team size	−1.035e+00	
	Avg. Age	−5.402e-01***	−5.467e-01***
	In relationship	1.161e+00	
	Share women	1.209e+00	
Predecessor	Age	−4.172e-01***	−2.647e-01*
Adjusted R^2		0.3308	0.2975

*Significances: *** = 1 percent; ** = 5 percent; * = 10 percent*

When interpreting the results of the linear regressions, it became evident that the index two years prior to the succession and the age of the successor were highly significant. A negative coefficient indicated a reduction in the index and, therefore, an improvement in creditworthiness. This implied that if the index was already low two years before the succession, it was easier to reduce it further. Additionally, older successors proved to be more effective than younger ones in lowering the index.

4.3 Conclusions

Using a detailed dataset of more than 10 000 successions already the descriptive statistics produced valuable insights. Concerning company performance, we see a tendency to higher revenues two years after the succession compared to two years before the succession. Nevertheless, revenues are only one part of company resilience. Therefore, we decided to use the creditworthiness index provided by Creditreform Rating AG for the regressions. These show one important result: the most important factor to decrease the index (and hence to improve resilience) is the age of the successor. In our interpretation that is due to higher experience. To find out more about this aspect, a questionnaire was sent out to successors. The results are described in the next section.

5 Insights from the Survey

Additionally, questionnaire data were used to explore the skills, experience, and knowledge of successors at the time of the company takeover. The questionnaire covered a broad range of potential issues surrounding company succession. Most questions employed a five-point Likert scale. To assess the competencies of the successor, the focus was placed on questions concerning their personal knowledge – specifically, what they knew at the time of the takeover and what they believed they should have known. This allowed for a comparison between the time of succession and the time of the survey.

The survey targeted largely the same population as the main dataset. It was distributed to 1,710 successors in the federal state of Baden-Württemberg who took over companies between 2013 and 2021, representing a regional subset of the broader dataset. From this group, 111 valid responses were received, with 79 relating to successions that occurred between 2014 and 2018. Most respondents were male and married or partnered. In the majority of cases, successors were external candidates rather than family members, although many had worked for the company beforehand. Among respondents, 17% were women -slightly below the share observed in the broader Baden-Württemberg dataset. Seven out of ten had a university or master's degree. Most were aged between 40 and 44, with an average age just under 46. Gender-based differences in mean values and distributions were negligible.

Most successors acquired a company stake of 90% or more. At the time of the takeover, 63% of the companies were classified as micro-enterprises with fewer than 10 employees. By the time of the survey, this figure had declined to 50%. Regarding business development, revenues were mostly between 100% and 124% of the takeover level, and EBIT had generally increased by €0–199k. Overall, respondents reported stable and positive development two years after the takeover.

The most important motivations for taking over a company were securing a livelihood, a sense of personal connection to the business, and the desire for self-employment – particularly among respondents under 40. Family expectations and preventing external takeovers were less commonly cited, indicating that intrinsic motivations played the dominant role in the decision to succeed. Successors were also asked about the challenges they faced during the takeover. Using a five-point Likert scale, most challenges were rated as fairly significant. The least challenging areas were related to technology and sales. Overall, functions tied directly to the core product or service – such as production and sales – were perceived as less challenging than administrative tasks like finance, legal matters, and organizational issues.

Respondents were also asked to assess the importance of workforce-related aspects, both at the time of succession and from today's perspective. Working atmosphere, employee retention, and the availability of skilled workers were seen as the three most important workforce factors – both then and now. Notably, the perceived importance of all workforce aspects increased considerably over time. Successors further evaluated the knowledge and skills of their workforce at the time of the takeover. Technical, methodological, personal, and social competencies were generally rated as good. However, other competencies – such as network management, personnel management experience, business knowledge, interaction with public authorities, IT skills, and legal knowledge – received more ambivalent ratings. Interestingly, younger successors (under 40) rated workforce competencies in personnel management, legal knowledge, and IT significantly higher than their older counterparts. With a focus on the successor as an individual, respondents were asked to assess their own knowledge, experience, and skills at the time of the takeover, as well as what those competencies ideally should have been. According to self-assessments, competency levels were generally high, ranging from 3.0 to 4.4 on a five-point scale at the time of the takeover, and increasing to 3.6 to 4.4 at the time of the survey. This indicates that only a slight skills gap was perceived in hindsight.

To better understand this gap, responses were analyzed in more detail. Regardless of age, business knowledge, personnel management experience, and legal knowledge were consistently identified as competencies that should have been more developed at the time of the takeover. Networking, interaction with public authorities, and social skills were also rated as more important in retrospect than initially perceived. Conversely, self-competence, technical and methodological skills, and IT knowledge were considered sufficient at the time of succession and remained similarly valued afterward (see Figure 4).

In general, all knowledge and skill areas were considered somewhat insufficient in retrospect. The most significant gaps – found in business knowledge, personnel management, and legal knowledge -were concentrated in traditional administrative disciplines. It appeared that younger successors evaluated their own personnel man-

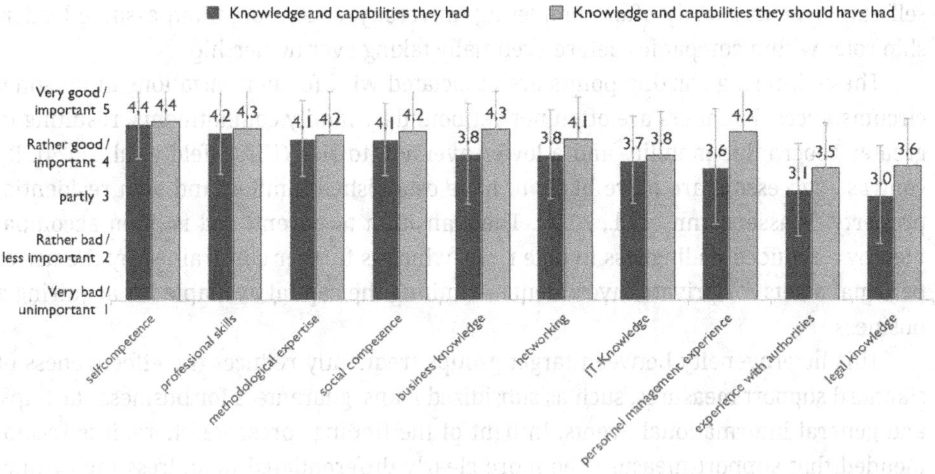

Figure 4: Knowledge, experience, and skills of successors.

agement and legal knowledge in direct comparison to their employees' competencies. The pronounced difference between the successors' self-assessment and their positive assessment of staff capabilities suggests that these may have been the areas where successors learned the most after the takeover. Interestingly, IT knowledge did not emerge as a major concern for the majority of respondents.

6 Implications for the Resilience of SMEs

The present finding – that a higher age of successors has a positive effect on company resilience – may have several important implications. It suggests the need for a more targeted approach to addressing the diverse profiles of business successors. Tailored support and preparation strategies could be developed to meet the specific needs of different age groups, enhancing the overall success and stability of business transitions.

6.1 More Targeted Approach to Different Groups of Entrepreneurs

To date, the term business start-up has been used – particularly by policymakers and funding institutions – as a broad label encompassing both the creation of a new business and the acquisition of an existing one. However, existing research has highlighted a notable age discrepancy between founders and successors: founders tend to be younger than successors. These differences can largely be attributed to the distinct life phases in which each group typically finds themselves. While many founders pursue self-employment shortly after completing university, successors often assume leadership roles within companies before eventually taking over ownership.

These differing starting points are associated with further variations in personal circumstances. Founders are often not yet bound by family commitments, resulting in greater geographic mobility and a lower aversion to risk (Hirschfeld et al., 2024). By contrast, successors are more likely to have established families and own residential property (Wassermann et al., 2024). The transition to parenthood is often accompanied by a reduced willingness to take risks, which is further constrained by the use of personal assets for private investments – limiting the capital available for acquiring a business.

This heterogeneity between target groups frequently reduces the effectiveness of standard support measures, such as subsidized loans, guarantees for business start-ups, and general informational events. In light of the findings presented here, it is recommended that support measures be more clearly differentiated to address the distinct needs of founders and successors across various age groups. Doing so could encourage a greater number of experienced professionals over the age of 40 to consider business succession. Targeted support for this demographic may not only increase the success rate of successions but also strengthen the resilience of companies by placing them in the hands of seasoned individuals.

6.2 Family and External Succession

These findings also prompt reflection on the perceived advantages of internal succession, which is often favored by those handing over a business. Research shows that younger successors are more frequently found in intra-family successions (Otten-Pappas & Jäkel-Wurzer, 2017). For many transferors, passing the business on to their own descendants represents an opportunity to preserve their life's work within the family (Garnitz et al., 2023). This approach is often driven by the intention to retain wealth in the family and by the implicit belief that a successor who has long been associated with the business will maintain its existing philosophy and values. This presumed continuity in management is commonly regarded as a strength that fosters resilience.

However, the strong correlation observed between the successor's age and company resilience may suggest that family affiliation plays a smaller role than often assumed. If the desire for intra-family succession results in a relatively young and potentially less experienced individual assuming responsibility, this may even have counterproductive effects. In this context, the present findings could serve as an impetus to assess the suitability of potential successors based on qualifications and experience, rather than family ties alone. This may involve considering long-term employees or external candidates more seriously.

At the same time, the findings can be interpreted as a call not to assign full responsibility to family successors too early, but rather to prepare them over a longer period. Thorough preparation is widely discussed in the literature and is consistently identified as a key success factor (e.g., Hülsbeck et al., 2016). However, extended preparation phases are not without risk, as they may lead to frustration and result in potential successors leaving the company. One possible solution, supported by numerous scholars, is to encourage potential successors to gain experience in external organizations before assuming leadership of the family business. This approach combines professional development with continuity and may ultimately enhance resilience.

6.3 The Role of Buy-and-build Concepts in Business Succession

Due to the existing succession gap, buy-and-build schemes are increasingly being discussed as a potential solution to ensure the continuity of businesses that are unable to secure individual successors (Scheuplein, 2021). Available evidence suggests that these models can not only increase the number of successful business transfers but also enhance the resilience of companies. In such schemes, the management of individual enterprises is no longer primarily carried out by independent entrepreneurs but by employed managers. This helps to circumvent common challenges such as limited motivation for self-employment and difficulties in securing financing, while still ensuring that experienced professionals are placed in leadership roles. As shareholding models are often used to increase managerial commitment to the business, buy-and-build schemes can be viewed as a form of intrapreneurship – and thus as a contemporary evolution in the practice of business succession.

7 Conclusions

7.1 Summary

This study aimed to provide insights into how corporate succession influences the resilience of companies and how that resilience can be strengthened. Since organizational resilience is a broad and not entirely quantifiable concept, a suitable indicator was first required for quantitative analysis. The Creditreform Rating creditworthiness index was selected, as it incorporates various indicators and thus offers a relatively comprehensive basis. Using this index, a quantitative analysis was conducted, covering approximately 10,000 successions over a ten-year period. Descriptive statistics were used to identify key characteristics of business successions.

Given the limited availability of statistical data in this area, such findings are valuable for deepening the understanding of succession dynamics. A linear regression was then performed on a subset of nearly 1,000 companies to identify which factors influence the development of the creditworthiness index. In addition to the initial index level, the successor's age emerged as a particularly significant factor, suggesting that experience plays a crucial role in successful transitions.

Complementary to this, a questionnaire was used to investigate how successors assessed their own knowledge at the time of the takeover and to identify areas where knowledge was lacking. Overall, the level of knowledge at the time of succession was rated as relatively good. In hindsight, however, respondents reported deficits in business knowledge, personnel management, and legal matters.

As a result, support measures for successors should differ from those designed for founders. Successors are typically in a different stage of life and therefore face distinct challenges. They also bring a different level of experience and expertise, which calls for more targeted training and development programs. An alternative approach could involve buy-and-build concepts, where companies are managed by experienced professionals.

7.2 Discussion

The insight that knowledge and experience are key success factors in business takeovers aligns well with existing literature. Venter et al. (2005) analyzed 332 questionnaires completed by successors in South Africa and concluded that the level of preparation of the successor has a measurable impact on company performance following succession. This finding is also supported by Nordqvist et al. (2013) – based on an extensive literature review – who emphasized the importance of training.

By combining the findings from the empirical data analysis and the survey of successors from Baden-Württemberg, it becomes clear that the resilience of companies can be enhanced through targeted training of potential successors. Focusing on business knowledge, personnel management experience, and legal knowledge promises the greatest benefit. Notably, younger successors rated their workforce's skills in personnel management and legal knowledge significantly higher – suggesting that these areas are especially important for older acquirers, who may not perceive the same level of competence within their teams and therefore require stronger personal expertise in these fields.

7.3 Limitations and Suggestions for Further Research

Although the study yielded valuable insights, certain methodological and data-related limitations must be acknowledged. First, the creditworthiness index, used as an indicator of resilience, warrants further discussion (see Section 3.2). Future research could incorporate alternative concepts or measures of resilience to provide a more comprehensive assessment. Additionally, the regression models explain only a portion of the variance in the index. It would be worthwhile to investigate which factors – beyond those captured in the current dataset – significantly influence changes in the index.

Second, the data from the German guarantee banks primarily reflect more challenging successions, particularly non-family ones. This introduces a degree of bias into the dataset. A comparative analysis with broader industry or regional data could help assess the extent and impact of this bias. Future research should also emphasize long-term analyses, as some effects – according to Wenneberg et al. (2011) – may only materialize over time. Another area of interest is the role of knowledge and experience in successful succession. Here, qualitative research could prove particularly valuable in identifying the specific types of knowledge that were present and where gaps existed.

References

Burns, R. B., & Burns, R. A. (2008). *Business research methods and statistics using SPSS*. London, UK: Sage Publications.

Cabrera-Suárez, M. K., García-Almeida, D. J., & De Saá-Pérez, P. (2018). A Dynamic Network Model of the Successor's Knowledge Construction from the Resource- and Knowledge-Based View of the Family Firm. *Family Business Review*, *31*(2), 178–197.

De Massis, A., Frattini, F., Kotlar, J., Petruzzelli, A. M., & Wright, M. (2016). Innovation Through Tradition: Lessons From Innovative Family Businesses and Directions for Future Research. *Academy of Management Perspectives*, *30*(1), 93–116.

Denyer, D. (2017). *Organizational resilience*. UK: BSI and Cranfield University.

Eddleston, K. A., Kellermanns, F. W., Floyd, S. W., Crittenden, V. L., & Crittenden, W. F. (2013). Planning for growth: Life stage differences in family firms. *Entrepreneurship Theory and Practice*, *37*(5), 1177–1202.

Garnitz, J., von Maltzan, A., & Müller, J. (2023). Nachfolge-Monitoring deutscher Familienunternehmen: Eine empirische Analyse auf Datenbasis der Datenbank FamData. *ifo Schnelldienst 12/2023, 76. Jg*. https://www.ifo.de/DocDL/sd-2023-12-garnitz-maltzan-mueller-unternehmensnachfolge-famdata.pdf

Handler, W. C. (1994). Succession in family business: A review of the research. *Family Business Review*, *7*(2), 133–157.

Hauck, J., & Prügl, R. (2015). Innovation activities during intra-family leadership succession in family firms: An empirical study from a socioemotional wealth perspective. *Journal of Family Business Strategy*, *6*(2), 104–118.

Haunschild, L., & Wolter, H.-J. (2010). *Volkswirtschaftliche Bedeutung von Familien- und Frauenunternehmen*. IfM-Materialien.

Hauser, H.-E., Kay, R., & Boerger, S. (2010). *Unternehmensnachfolgen in Deutschland 2010 bis 2014: Schätzung mit weiterentwickeltem Verfahren*. IfM-Materialien.

Hirschfeld, A., Kollmann, T., Gilde, J., Valke, V., & Ansorge, M. (2024). *Deutscher Startup Monitor 2024*. Bundesverband Deutsche Startups e.V.

Hülsbeck, M., Klinken, P., & Jansen, T. (2016). Persönliche Kompetenzen in der Nachfolge – Eine Studie des Wittener Instituts für Familienunternehmen in Kooperation mit der Banque de Luxembourg. *WIFU Wittener Institut für Familienunternehmen*. https://www.wifu.de/download/3997/

Jamshidian, M. (2009). Strategies for analysis of incomplete data. In: M. Hardy & A. Bryman (Eds.), *The handbook of data analysis* (pp. 113–130). London, UK: Sage Publications.

Kay, R., & Suprinovic, O. (2013). Unternehmensnachfolgen in Deutschland 2014–2018, *Daten und Fakten Nr. 11*. IfM Bonn.

Kets de Vries, M. F. (1993). The dynamics of family controlled firms: The good and the bad news. *Organizational Dynamics*, *21*(3), 59–71.

Le Breton-Miller, I., Miller, D., & Steier, L. P. (2004). Toward an integrative model of effective FOB succession. *Entrepreneurship Theory and Practice*, *28*(4), 305–328.

Molly, V., Laveren, E., & Deloof, M. (2010). Family Business Succession and Its Impact on Financial Structure and Performance. *Family Business Review*, *23*(2), 131–147.

Nordqvist, M., Wennberg, K., Bau', M., & Hellerstedt, K. (2013). An entrepreneurial process perspective on succession in family firms. *Small Business Economics*, *40*(4), 1087–1122.

Otten-Pappas, D. & Jäkel-Wurzer, D. (2017). Weibliche Nachfolge: Ausnahme oder Regelfall? Eine Studie zur aktuellen Situation im generationenwechsel Deutscher Familienunternehmen. *WIFU Wittener Institut für Familienunternehmen*. https://www.nachfolgeworkshop.de/wp-content/uploads/2017/09/WIFU-Studie-Weibliche-Nachfolge-2017.pdf

Scheuplein, C. (2021). Private Equity Monitor: Die Aktivität von Private-Equity-gesellschaften in Deutschland von 2012 bis 2018 in der Gesamtschau. *Study 467. Hans-Böckler-Stiftung*. https://www.imu-boeckler.de/fpdf/HBS-008194/p_study_hbs_467.pdf

Sharma, P., Chrisman, J. J., & Chua, J. H. (2003). Succession planning as planned behavior: Some empirical results. *Family Business Review*, *16*(1), 1–15.

Statistisches Bundesamt. (2024). *55 % in kleinen und mittleren Unternehmen tätig*. https://www.destatis.de/DE/Themen/Branchen-Unternehmen/Unternehmen/Kleine-Unternehmen-Mittlere-Unternehmen/aktuell-beschaeftigte.html

Steier, L. (2001). Next-generation entrepreneurs and succession: An exploratory study of modes and means of managing social capital. *Family Business Review*, *14*(3), 259–276.

Venter, E., Boshoff, C., & Maas, G. (2005). The Influence of Successor-Related Factors on the Succession Process in Small and Medium-Sized Family Businesses. *Family Business Review*, *18*(4), 283–303.

Wassermann, H., Frohwerk, S., Kruppe, C. (2024). Nachfolgemonitor 2023. *Schriftenreihe Nachfolgemonitor, Band 7*. https://bit.ly/nachfolgemonitor2023

Wennberg, K., Wiklund, J., Hellerstedt, K., & Nordqvist, M. (2011). Implications of intra-family and external ownership transfer of family firms: short-term and long-term performance differences. *Strategic Entrepreneurship Journal*, *5*(4), 352–372. https://doi.org/10.1002/sej.118

Zimmermann, V. (2017). Success factors of high-growth enterprises. *KFW Research: Focus on Economics*, *177*(1), 1–5.

Sophia Maier, Julia Riepl, Markus Kathan and Michael Kuttner

Passing the Torch: Perceived Risks and Opportunities in Family Business Succession

Abstract: Based on a qualitative case study of a traditional Austrian family business, we investigate which risks and opportunities arise from the succession. Our results indicate that risks are due to emotional ties to the family business, inadequate know-how transfer, family-internal conflicts, and the inability to hand over the company. Opportunities are seen in the integration of external consultants, the involvement of employees, the existence of an emergency plan and a structured succession plan, and an early transfer of know-how and innovation combined with tradition. Concerning gender, the risks are seen primarily in a possible lack of acceptance of the female successor and the reconciliation of family and career. In particular, the increased social competence, the avoidance of power struggles, and the increased conscientiousness were mentioned as opportunities due the gender of the successors. The conclusions drawn from the results have numerous implications for future research (e.g., cross-country and cross-industry comparisons) and corporate practice (e.g., a guide for succession, necessity of structured succession planning).

Keywords: Family Business, Gender, Qualitative Study, Risks and Opportunities, Succession

1 Introduction

A succession is a decisive event within the life cycle of a family business (Koropp et al., 2013; Neubauer, 2003; Ramón, 2021; Vassiliadis & Vassiliadis, 2014) because it influences the family business's continued existence, value, and performance (Diwisch et al., 2009; Rumanko et al., 2021). Succession transfers the family business from a previous entrepreneur to one or more entrepreneurs or a new generation (Boyd et al., 2014; DeTienne, 2010; Nordqvist et al., 2013). Moreover, succession in family businesses is a complex (DeTienne, 2010; Neubauer, 2003; Nordqvist et al., 2013) and lengthy process (DeTienne, 2010; Rumanko et al., 2021). It is characterized by risks associated with succession, such as psychological and emotional challenges (Alayo et al., 2016; de Massis et al., 2008), the complexity of the transfer process (Ahrens et al., 2015; Alayo et al., 2016; de Massis et al., 2008), and compliance with national regulations (de Massis et al., 2008; Koropp et al., 2013; Sharma & Rao, 2000). However, in addition to the succession risks, there are also opportunities, for instance, family-specific opportunities (Astrachan & Jaskiewicz, 2008; Berrone et al., 2012; Fendri & Nguyen, 2019), innovation promotion (Cabrera-Suárez

https://doi.org/10.1515/9783110790344-006

et al., 2001; Fendri & Nguyen, 2019; Rumanko et al., 2021; Yuan, 2019) and female successors as an opportunity (Ahrens et al., 2015; Constantinidis & Cornet, 2008; Kalm & Gómez-Mejía, 2016).

Only a small proportion of family businesses continue to exist after a succession (Boyd et al., 2014; Cucculelli & Micucci, 2008; Fendri & Nguyen, 2019; Luan et al., 2018; Ungerer & Mienie, 2018) due to the complexity of the process and the multidimensionality of family businesses (Nelson & Constantinidis, 2017; Ramón, 2021). In family businesses, the separation of ownership and management is often unclear (Sund et al., 2010). Furthermore, risks are frequently found in the family structures and not directly in the business itself (Neubauer, 2003; Nordqvist et al., 2013; Ramón, 2021; Sharma & Rao, 2000). However, succession has an impact on key areas of the family business (Neubauer, 2003; Nordqvist et al., 2013), such as the financial situation, the valuation of the business, the distribution of ownership, and tax aspects (Nordqvist et al., 2013; Ramón, 2021).

Various risks, including psychological and emotional aspects, such as the decision favoring a potential successor, can be considered in succession (Vassiliadis & Vassiliadis, 2014). However, this decision is also linked to the complexity of the transfer process and the lack of experience of the potential successor (Alayo et al., 2016; Fendri & Nguyen, 2019; Sharma & Rao, 2000; Vassiliadis & Vassiliadis, 2014). All potential male and female successors in the corporate family should be considered, with first-born male offspring traditionally being favored (Ahrens et al., 2015; Lefebvre & Lefebvre, 2016; Nelson & Constantinidis, 2017; Powell, 2018; Rumanko et al., 2021; Vera & Dean, 2005). Succession within the family occurs significantly more frequently if the predecessor has a son, even if female successors have higher competencies (Ahrens et al., 2015; Lefebvre & Lefebvre, 2016). There is also a risk that successors are favored as managers in family businesses, even if they are less competent than external managers and do not have the necessary qualifications (Lee et al., 2003; Liu et al., 2015; Neubauer, 2003).

The emotional attachment of the incumbent entrepreneur, but especially of the founder, can lead to a reduced willingness to promote succession (Ramón, 2021; Rumanko et al., 2021; Vassiliadis & Vassiliadis, 2014). In the face of unforeseen events, such as divorce or the sudden death of the entrepreneur, succession planning must be initiated promptly to be able to react appropriately (Alayo et al., 2016; de Massis et al., 2008; Liu et al., 2015; Ramón, 2021; Rumanko et al., 2021). Before such unexpected events occur, preparedness measures should be taken, such as documenting the contact details of tax advisors and the location of the will (Liu et al., 2015). In Austria, around half of business successions within the family are usually carried out as a gift. Therefore, half of the family businesses are transferred before the entrepreneur's death (Neubauer, 2003). Furthermore, know-how transfer often occurs too late or insufficiently (Rumanko et al., 2021). Thus, successors often have little know-how of the market and the business partners of the family business, making succession more difficult (Lefebvre & Lefebvre, 2016).

Moreover, risks lie in the potential lack of acceptance of the successor by internal and external stakeholders (e.g., employees, business partners) (Neubauer, 2003). Additionally, succession risks can stem from national laws, such as company regulations or taxation, as well as from administrative formalities (Vassiliadis & Vassiliadis, 2014). However, these risks are usually financial in nature (de Massis et al., 2008; Sharma & Rao, 2000; Vassiliadis & Vassiliadis, 2014). The succession of family businesses can result in high transaction costs, such as inheritance and gift taxes and restructuring costs, which can hinder succession and restrict future business growth (Koropp et al., 2013). Changes in legal form and the transfer of assets can also be fraught with risk (Vassiliadis & Vassiliadis, 2014).

Apart from these succession risks, the successor can contribute innovative ideas to the company through external work experience, such as internships outside the family business (Alayo et al., 2016; Fendri & Nguyen, 2019; Rumanko et al., 2021). The comprehensive consideration of all potential successors can be seen as an opportunity, as this can expand the possible circle of successors (Ahrens et al., 2015; Constantinidis & Cornet, 2008). By considering both male and female successors in succession, organizations can be enriched by new perspectives and experiences, leading to improved decision-making, innovative solutions, and increased adaptability to changing market conditions (Constantinidis & Cornet, 2008; Yuan, 2019). The takeover by a female successor can ensure continuity and the long-term success of the company, with female successors often demonstrating a high level of responsibility for the business family and corporate culture (Constantinidis & Cornet, 2008; Kalm & Gómez-Mejía, 2016). Furthermore, female successors contribute significantly to the preservation of family values and a responsible orientation of the company (e.g., social responsibility, sustainability), which can have a positive impact on the company's performance, image, and reputation (Astrachan & Jaskiewicz, 2008; Berrone et al., 2012; Constantinidis & Cornet, 2008; Kalm & Gómez-Mejía, 2016).

Further research is needed, particularly about integrating the entrepreneurial perspective into the succession planning process (Nordqvist et al., 2013; Yuan, 2019). Research on succession focuses primarily on the success of the succession itself (Cabrera-Suárez et al., 2001) and has so far paid little attention to succession risks and opportunities (de Massis et al., 2008; Yuan, 2019). Moreover, there is little research on gender in the succession of family businesses (Bang et al., 2023; Kubíček & Machek, 2019; Sharma, 2004; Stewart & Hitt, 2012). To close this research gap, we investigate the following research questions: *What succession risks and opportunities arise within the case family business? Does gender play a role as a succession risk or opportunity?*

This study analyzes the succession risks and opportunities within a case family business. Moreover, this study intends to generate valuable insights for developing practical guidelines for successful succession in family businesses. Findings stem from a family business that has already completed a successful succession and is currently undergoing a second succession. This opens unique opportunities, as not only past but also current insights into the influence of the corporate family on succession are gained. By interviewing the current managing directors, the potential successors, and different internal and external stakeholders, an in-depth analysis of the complex relationships and dynamics within the case family business is offered.

2 Family Businesses, Succession, Risks and Opportunities

Family businesses form the backbone of economies worldwide (Kraus et al., 2012; Rosado-Serrano & Navarro-García, 2019; Rumanko et al., 2021). However, there is no common definition for the term "family business" (Kraus et al., 2012; Steiger et al., 2015). One frequently used definition is that of Chua et al. (1999, p. 25), who define family business as *"(. . .) a business governed and/or managed with the intention to shape and pursue the vision of the business held by a dominant coalition controlled by members of the same family or a small number of families in a manner that is potentially sustainable across generations of the family or families."* The definition underlines the close connection between the corporate family and the business and emphasizes the dual role of owner and decision-maker. Furthermore, the definition indicates that family businesses differ significantly from non-family businesses due to different characteristics and dynamics (Berrone et al., 2012; Chua et al., 1999; Nieto et al., 2015).

However, succession is a time-lasting process that sometimes takes several years (DeTienne, 2010; Fendri & Nguyen, 2019; Neubauer, 2003; Nordqvist et al., 2013; Rumanko et al., 2021). Accordingly, succession and succession planning are highly relevant within family businesses (DeTienne, 2010; Fendri & Nguyen, 2019; Liu et al., 2015). Following Nordqvist et al. (2013), succession can be divided into four phases: (1) pre-succession, (2) planning succession, (3) managing succession, and (4) post-succession. The pre-succession phase focuses on questions that precede the succession, for instance, the willingness of family members to take over the business (Nordqvist et al., 2013), the recruitment of family members for the succession (Steier & Miller, 2010), and the owner's willingness to hand over the company (Nordqvist et al., 2013). The planning phase aims to ensure an orderly transition. It requires time, the support of external advisors, the corporate family's involvement, and the willingness to resolve interpersonal conflicts (Ghee et al., 2015; Nordqvist et al., 2013). In the third phase, the succession plan is implemented, and the formal ownership and know-how, as well as social networks, are successively transferred to the successor (Lefebvre & Lefebvre, 2016; Nordqvist et al., 2013; Rumanko et al., 2021). The post-succession phase is characterized by consolidating activities aimed at ensuring the long-term success of the succession (Nordqvist et al., 2013; Steier & Miller, 2010).

As mentioned, succession is associated with several risks and opportunities. In particular, emotional risks arise during succession, with the corporate family often facing challenges (Vassiliadis & Vassiliadis, 2014), especially when deciding on a potential successor. Previously, first-born male successors were frequently preferred (Ahrens et al., 2015; Lefebvre & Lefebvre, 2016; Nelson & Constantinidis, 2017). Moreover, family businesses are usually dominated by traditional role expectations (Ahrens et al., 2015), and female successors are confronted with conflicts between family obligations and professional demands (Vera & Dean, 2005). To maintain the family business within the family (Chua et al., 1999; Fendri & Nguyen, 2019), own successors are often preferred for succession, even if they are less competent and do not have the necessary qualifications (Lee et al., 2003; Liu et al., 2015; Neubauer, 2003).

Other risks are, for example, a lack of acceptance by stakeholders (e.g., employees, business partners) (Neubauer, 2003), which can arise due to change processes within the succession (e.g., strategic orientation, corporate culture) (Fendri & Nguyen, 2019). However, unplanned risks influencing succession, such as the entrepreneur's death, illness, and divorce, should also be mentioned (Alayo et al., 2016; Liu et al., 2015; Ramón, 2021; Rumanko et al., 2021). Risks can also arise from national laws (e.g., company law, tax law) (Vassiliadis & Vassiliadis, 2014). For example, succession can be associated with high transaction costs, such as inheritance and gift taxes, which can restrict the future development of the family business (Koropp et al., 2013). These costs can hinder succession and limit the future growth of the business (Koropp et al., 2013; Vassiliadis & Vassiliadis, 2014).

However, succession is also associated with opportunities. In addition to opportunities that arise from the individual characteristics of the successor (e.g., leadership skills) (Pyromalis & Vozikis, 2009; Sharma et al., 2001; Sharma & Rao, 2000), several family-specific opportunities result from the know-how and ability of the successor to acquire this specific know-how (Sharma & Rao, 2000; Rumanko et al., 2021). For instance, the willingness to transfer know-how to the next generation represents an advantage over non-family businesses (Rumanko et al. 2021), and the transfer of know-how and socio-emotional wealth[1] provides an opportunity to ensure the long-term survival of the family business (Fendri & Nguyen, 2019; Makó et al., 2016; Tatoglu et al., 2008).

Integrating a successor early can develop their leadership skills (de Massis et al., 2008; Fendri & Nguyen, 2019; Rumanko et al., 2021). Increased loyalty and trust within family businesses can also be seen as an opportunity (Berrone et al., 2012; Kellermanns et al., 2012), especially as the chances of a successful succession increase (Fendri & Nguyen, 2019; Tatoglu et al., 2008). Family successors tend to be more loyal to the company than external managers (Berrone et al., 2010; Berrone et al., 2012). A further opportunity for succession is the combination of experience and new impulses, whereby existing concepts and thought patterns can be broken up, and new perspectives can be developed, which leads to innovation and thus strengthens future competitiveness (Fendri & Nguyen, 2019; Rumanko et al., 2021; Yuan, 2019).

1 See Gómez-Mejía et al. (2007), Cennamo et al. (2012), Kalm & Gómez-Mejía (2016), and Berrone et al. (2012) for more information on socioemotional wealth.

The involvement of female successors and the avoidance of excluding them can generate significant opportunities in succession (Ahrens et al., 2015; Constantinidis & Cornet, 2008). This increases the chance of selecting the most suitable candidates for the management position (Constantinidis & Cornet, 2008). Furthermore, women often play a key role in preserving family values and the sustainable orientation of the company (Ahrens et al., 2015).

3 Methods

Within our study, we refer to a qualitative research design, namely a case study design, which offers the opportunity to view complex phenomena in their context and to adopt critical and reflective perspectives (Eriksson & Kovalainen, 2015; Gustafsson, 2017). A case study is characterized by a detailed and comprehensive data collection (Baskarada, 2014; Creswell & Poth, 2016), which provides an in-depth understanding of the object of investigation (Creswell & Poth, 2016; Gustafsson, 2017).

The case company was founded in 1967 in Salzburg, Austria, as a carpentry managed by the founder and his wife. The family business was gradually expanded to include a sawmill, a timber store, and a joinery until it was handed over to the founder's two daughters in 2000. However, the founder continued to work in the family business until he died in 2010 (first succession). The company has been run by the family's second generation, the founder's daughters, for 14 years. In 2024, the timber construction company employs approx. 140 employees. Nowadays, the services of the family business include planning, timber construction, carpentry, joinery, furniture, interior design, and building and project management. The sawmill and the timber store no longer exist. The family business is currently being handed over to the three successors (third generation) of the founder's two daughters (second generation) within the current succession.

The primary data collection was carried out through interviews and company visits. The interviews were conducted in German and translated into English without changing their meaning. Eight people were interviewed in total: the current managing directors (the founder's daughters, second generation), the two male successors (third generation), two employees in management positions, and the bank and management consultants as external stakeholders. The third successor (female, third generation) was not interviewed because she is involved in the study as an author. The interviews were conducted in the first half of 2024 and transcribed on time. Table 1 illustrates the descriptive data of the interview participants. Additionally, the company's homepage, social media sites, and annual reports were analyzed as part of the secondary data collection.

All data were analyzed using Thomas's (2006) qualitative inductive approach. This inductive approach is characterized by the fact that the categories are only formed during the analysis. Through repeated reading, the original data material is

Table 1: Descriptive data of the interview participants.

	Family-internal interview participants			
	Managing directors (2nd generation)		***Successors (3rd generation)***	
Current position	Managing Director A	Managing Director B	Successor A	Successor B
Responsibilities	Accounting and human resources	Technical area, marketing, and sales	Planning and building management	Planning and sales
Gender	Female	Female	Male	Male
	Family-external interview participants			
	Internal stakeholders		***External stakeholders***	
Current position	Head of Purchasing and Inventory Management	Head of Construction Management	Bank Consultant	Management Consultant
Since	1983	1990	1999	2010

reduced and brought to a general level of abstraction. The evaluation was carried out with the utmost care. Ambiguities were discussed between the authors until a consensus was reached. The results of the case study are presented in the next chapter.

4 Results

During the first succession, the emotional attachment of the founder to the family business is perceived as a significant risk by all interview participants. As a result, even at an advanced age, the founder found it challenging to disengage emotionally from the family business (Management Consultant, Managing Director A, Head of Purchasing and Inventory Management). During succession, conflicts arose between the founder and his daughters simply because of who made decisions (Managing Directors A & B). Although the family business had already been transferred formally to the successors in 2000, the company founder still had the last word in many decisions until he died in 2010 (Managing Directors A & B), which meant that the successors were unable to find their place in the company for a long time (Management Consultant). In addition to conflicts in the business family, this also resulted in employee insecurity (Management Consultant, Managing Directors A & B).

In the context of the current succession, the successors expressed conflicting concerns. The two successors (A & B) mentioned that the current succession had begun even though their education (e.g., study program) had not yet been completed and they had not worked in the company. The early withdrawal of the current owners and the fact that the education had not yet been completed led to concerns about an inadequate transfer of internal company know-how (e.g., internal process know-how) (Successors A & B).

Another frequently mentioned risk within the current succession is the joint takeover by three successors (e.g., Bank Consultant, Head of Construction Management, Managing Director B). With three successors, there is a risk that two successors will join forces against the third (Managing Director B). Unequal company share distribution is another risk within the corporate family. However, this fear is perceived as a potential risk exclusively by the successors (A & B). Due to the numerical size of the successors in the current succession, the unequal distribution of company shares would occur due to the legal succession, whereby particular reference is made to equal opportunities and fairness, as the statement of successor A exemplifies: *"Everyone should do their best, and then you should also have the same number of shares because otherwise, it would be unfair."*

The family ties and frequent private contacts have led to conflicts in the past (Managing Director B). In the case family business, the third sister of the two current owners (second generation) had to be paid off in the first succession, which led to significant financial challenges and further conflicts within the family and the family business (Managing Directors A & B). Other financial risks (e.g., reorganization costs) were not identified (Managing Director B, Successors A & B).

Another frequently mentioned succession risk was the death of the company founder (e.g., Bank Consultant, Head of Purchasing and Inventory Management, Managing Directors A & B). Due to the aforementioned emotional attachment to the family business, the founder of the family business was perceived as the head of the company until the day of his sudden death. Accordingly, the first succession was very slow, and with the death of the company founder, his daughters had to take over all company activities immediately (Managing Directors A & B). The absence of the founder was then seen as just as much of a risk as the inability of the founder to hand over the company to his successors (Management Consultant). The death of the company founder also led to a loss of trust among stakeholders since the founder represented the family business externally and internally (Managing Directors A & B). The statement of the management consultant can be used as an example: *"Now there are two women at the top of the company who (. . .) never held the leadership role. How should it continue now? What happens now? Who decides now? Who will give us the instructions we are used to?"* In particular, competing companies were initially very skeptical about the new managing directors (Managing Director B, Head of Purchasing and Inventory Management). The loss of trust in regular customers would be fatal for the family business (Head of Construction Management). The employees had to get used to the new way of working and the new female managing directors (Head of Construction Management). However, doubts about the new female leaders were never addressed directly (Managing Director B).

Within the first succession, additional risks arose due to the gender of the two female successors. The founder of the family business was concerned that managing the family business would be too much of a challenge for two women and sought, albeit in vain, male support for his two daughters (Managing Director B). The founder believed that his daughters first had to prove themselves within the company and earn the respect of the employees (Managing Director B, Head of Purchasing and Inventory Management). Another risk is reconciling family and career, as Managing Director A explains: *"If you have children, there is often not much time left for the company. That is certainly something that men did not have to struggle with in my day. They had wives at home to take care of the children."* The founder's second daughter (Managing Director B) was not confronted with that challenge since her partner took on the task of raising their children (Successor B). Table 2 summarizes the identified succession risks.

Table 2: Overview of the identified succession risks.

Identified Succession Risks		
Emotional attachment to the family business	*Missing or inadequate know-how transfer*	*Joint takeover of several successors*
Family-internal conflicts	*Payoff of a family member*	*Death*
Inability to hand over the company	*Loss of stakeholder trust*	*Lack of acceptance of female successors*
Reconciling family and career		

However, succession also involves several potential opportunities. In particular, integrating an external consultant is often perceived as an opportunity in the past and the current succession (e.g., Managing Directors A & B, Successors A & B). Without external support, one can be trapped in daily business (Managing Director B). External consultants are often used for financial and tax advice, reviewing contracts, reorganizing, taking on a new corporate structure, and facilitating discussions between the generations of owners and successors (Bank Consultant, Management Consultant, Managing Directors A & B). The interviewees consistently mentioned the tasks taken on by external consultants as an opportunity in the succession (e.g., Managing Directors A & B, Successors A & B).

The involvement of employees in the succession is also seen as an opportunity. In the past succession, a further management hierarchy was established in the family business for the first time as a link between the managing directors and the employees (e.g., Head of Construction Management, Head of Purchasing and Inventory Management). The management team consists of employees responsible for the family business since the founder's death (Management Consultant, Successor A). The new management hierarchy has led to greater transparency in the family business, more quickly accepted decisions, and increased employee trust (Management Consultant, Managing Director A). In particular, this management hierarchy has absorbed the unease caused by the founder's death (Management Consultant).

An emergency plan is also highlighted as an opportunity in the past succession. The emergency plan, which consisted of contracts, wills, and the early transfer of assets and company shares, enabled the company to continue as usual after the sudden death of the founder (Managing Directors A & B). In the case of the current company succession, an emergency plan was also in place. This stipulates that, in the event of the death of the two female owners, selected employees will take over the company's management until the successor generation is old enough to take over the management. An early transfer of assets has also already taken place and is still seen as a first opportunity (Managing Directors A & B, Successors A & B).

Furthermore, a structured succession plan is seen as an opportunity to successfully organize the succession (e.g., Head of Construction Management, Head of Purchasing and Inventory Management, Managing Directors A & B). In the first succession, a structured succession plan was drawn up with the help of an external consultant (Managing Director A). Thanks to the planning, the successors could gradually take over more responsibility from the founder, and no unexpected costs arose (Managing Directors A & B). In the context of the current succession, there is an even more detailed succession plan (Managing Director B), which is perceived positively, as the statement from the bank consultant exemplifies: *"I get a certain insight and know that the three successors have been coached for years and included in decisions. This sets the course for the future. It is not common for successors to be prepared so well, meticulously, and long-term."* Furthermore, the transfer of know-how is seen as an opportunity. In the context of the first succession, the founder was willing to pass on know-how (Management Consultant, Managing Directors A & B), which was valuable for the founder's daughters (Managing Director A).

Family-specific opportunities are often seen as a possibility for gaining experience and getting to know the different stakeholders (Managing Directors A & B). Within the first succession, Managing Director A was involved in the family business very early on, which means that she knows all employees, customs, processes, and procedures within the family business very well. The involvement of the current successors is also viewed positively and as an opportunity (Bank Consultant, Successors A & B). In particular, the integration of successors in business policy decisions is emphasized as an opportunity (Successor A). After the death of the company founder, the employees were perceived as highly supportive. While customers and suppliers completely trusted the family business, the competitors were skeptical about the female successors (Head of Construction Management, Head of Purchasing and Inventory Management, Managing Director A). However, this skepticism on the part of the competition led to increased cooperation and greater cohesion among the employees

(Managing Director B). In the current succession, there are no concerns regarding stakeholder acceptance (Successors A & B).

The integration of several successors is perceived as an opportunity in the past and the current succession. Due to the greater number of successors, work areas can be divided, and there is an opportunity to advise on decisions (e.g., Managing Directors A & B, Successors A & B). Dividing up the work areas makes it possible to specialize and share responsibility as well as the time burden (Bank Consultant, Managing Director A & B). The current owners were described as opposites, which proved advantageous in decision-making (Head of Construction Management, Management Consultant), as the Management Consultant states: *"The two owners have been ingenious opposites over the years. While one was innovative and wanted to push the company forward, was very future-oriented and progressive about corporate development and the associated financial expenditure, the other was very reflective and had an overview of the financial possibilities."*

In particular, the changes in the corporate structure that go hand in hand with succession are seen as an opportunity. For example, the newly introduced hierarchy level led to increased employee acceptance, and decisions are made based on employees' many years of experience, which positively affects the quality of those decisions (e.g., Head of Construction Management, Head of Purchasing and Inventory Management). The involvement of employees is considered essential for today's success (Head of Purchasing and Inventory Management, Managing Director A). Furthermore, the successor's economic use of resources led to improved financial performance after the first succession. Departments were optimized, and uneconomical areas were sold (e.g., sawmill), which would have been unthinkable for the founder of the family business (Bank Consultant, Managing Director B).

However, new ideas from the successor generation and breaking existing, outdated thought patterns are opportunities. The following statement from the Management Consultant illustrates the combination of innovation and tradition as an advantage of family-internal succession: *"New ideas can be thought of and implemented, and new things can be achieved. To consolidate this, the connection to the old is needed. Therefore, I see a great opportunity for family businesses to create something new without losing touch with their roots. It's about anchoring the new in the old."*

Potential opportunities also arise from the gender of the successor generation. For example, reference is made to the increased social competence of women, the avoidance of power struggles, and increased conscientiousness (e.g., Bank Consultant, Head of Purchasing and Inventory Management, Managing Director A). Managing Directors A and B have ensured employees enjoy working in the family business (Management Consultant). The preparation of the current company succession, with consultants and with the introduction of a meeting culture, proves the extremely high level of competence of Managing Directors A & B and would undoubtedly have happened differently in a male-dominated company (Bank Consultant). Managing Directors A & B have distinguished themselves by consciously never entering into a power struggle with an employee by changing the corporate structure, as evidenced by the Management Consultant's statement: *"They did not compete with their male colleagues, and conversely, the managers saw no reason to compete with their female managing directors."* Table 3 illustrates an overview of the identified succession opportunities.

Table 3: Overview of the identified succession opportunities.

Identified Succession Opportunities		
Integration of external consultants	*Involvement of employees*	*Existence of an emergency plan*
Existence of a structured succession plan	*Early know-how transfer*	*Involvement of the successors at an early stage*
Joint takeover of several successors	*Changes in the corporate structure*	*New ideas and breaking with thought patterns*
Combination of innovation and tradition	*Increased social competence of female successors*	*Increased conscientiousness of female successors*

5 Discussion and Summary

Our results indicate several succession risks and opportunities have arisen within the Austrian case company. One frequently mentioned succession risk is emotional attachment. Founders often possess a high degree of emotional attachment to the business (Vassiliadis & Vassiliadis, 2014), which can lead to conflicts between the handing over and taking over generations regarding the distribution of power and decision-making (Lefebvre & Lefebvre, 2016), which was also shown in our case family business. Further succession risks refer to an insufficient or missing know-how transfer, also discussed in academic literature (Makó et al., 2016; Lefebvre & Lefebvre, 2016; Makó et al., 2016; Rumanko et al., 2021). Moreover, other risks include the inability to hand over the business, a lack of stakeholder acceptance, unplanned risks such as the death of a family member, and family-internal conflicts. Family-internal conflicts often arise within the corporate family regarding power distribution and decision-making responsibility (Lefebvre & Lefebvre, 2016). Usually, a succession risk also represents an opportunity, as with the joint succession of several successors. On the one hand, there is an increased risk of conflicts due to different opinions. On the other hand, a succession by several successors makes it possible to focus on the core competencies of each family member.

However, the study also reveals several potential succession opportunities. For instance, the integration of external consultants, the involvement of employees, an early know-how transfer, and the early involvement of the successor within the family business are some opportunities that come with succession. Involving successors at an early stage helps to gradually develop their leadership skills (de Massis et al., 2008; Fendri & Nguyen, 2019; Rumanko et al., 2021). Another opportunity that arises from succession is innovation. For instance, succession offers an opportunity to implement new ideas and break away from existing, outdated thought patterns. Family businesses can combine innovation with tradition, one of the main strengths. Through innovation, family businesses ensure their future competitiveness while focusing on traditional, proven values that have been part of the family business for a long time. Other authors have also mentioned strengthening future competitiveness through innovation (Fendri & Nguyen, 2019; Rumanko et al., 2021; Yuan, 2019).

Regarding the role of gender in the context of succession risks and opportunities, the results show that in the case family business during the first succession, there was a particular fear that various stakeholders would not accept the female successors. Furthermore, the reconciliation of family and career is perceived as a risk, especially if the person in question has taken on a leadership position and has yet to establish themselves in that role. Nevertheless, succession by female successors also offers opportunities. The results show that female successors possess greater social skills, avoid power struggles with employees, and exhibit increased conscientiousness. However, considering female successors can generate opportunities in the context of succession (Ahrens et al., 2015; Constantinidis & Cornet, 2008), and the chance of selecting the most suitable candidate for the management position increases (Constantinidis & Cornet, 2008).

The present study highlights that there are still many different research possibilities concerning succession risk and opportunities. Future research could use quantitative studies to confirm or refute the obtained results. Furthermore, future research could consider other contextual factors (e.g., company size, national culture, industry) to examine their influence on the nature of succession risks and opportunities. A comparison between family-internal and family-external successors could also yield interesting results. There is also a need for further research on gender. One of the difficulties here is determining the extent to which individual factors can be attributed to personality or gender. The long-term effects, such as performance development after a company succession, offer further research potential and could reveal interesting differences between male and female successors.

The study also has implications for corporate practice. The results can guide family entrepreneurs to gain insights into succession risks and opportunities. Through know-how and awareness, risks can be identified and avoided early, and potential opportunities can be exploited to a greater extent. Furthermore, the study promotes an understanding of the interplay between the corporate family and the family business, which determines the uniqueness of this business category. The study underscores the necessity of having a contingency plan for a company succession to avoid jeopardizing the continued existence of the family business in the event of unforeseen incidents (e.g., death). Structured succession planning promotes smooth succession and sets a time frame for the handover, creating transparency for both the transferor and the successor about tasks and responsibilities. A succession also offers room for innovation. The successor contributes new perspectives and ideas on the business and breaks down existing, often outdated thought patterns, thus ensuring the future viability and competitiveness of the family business.

Nevertheless, this study is also subject to limitations. Qualitative research is not suitable for deriving generalizations. The results are only valid in the specific research context (e.g., industry, country). Furthermore, qualitative research is subject to a certain degree of subjectivity. For example, the interview participants may have presented the family business in a better light. Although the data analysis was carried out carefully, other researchers could draw different conclusions. Another limitation associated with the first author is that she is herself a successor in the family business under consideration, and accordingly, a subjective perspective could also be present here. In general, many of these succession risks and opportunities must be considered individually, and other companies may show further or different succession risks and opportunities. However, this should not diminish the value of the results but rather provide suggestions for future research.

References

Ahrens, J. P., Landmann, A., & Woywode, M. (2015). Gender preferences in the CEO successions of family firms: Family characteristics and human capital of the successor. *Journal of Family Business Strategy, 6*(2), 86–103.

Alayo, M., Jainaga, T., Maseda, A., & Arzubiaga, A. (2016). Critical factors for successful succession of family firms. *European Journal of Economics, Finance and Administrative Sciences, 85*(6), 90–103.

Astrachan, J. H., & Jaskiewicz, P. (2008). Emotional returns and emotional costs in privately held family businesses: Advancing traditional business valuation. *Family Business Review, 21*(2), 139–149.

Bang, N. P., Ray, S., & Kumar, S. (2023). Women in family business research—What we know and what we should know? *Journal of Business Research, 164*(September 2023), 113990.

Baskarada, S. (2014). Qualitative case study guidelines. *The Qualitative Report, 19*(40), 1–25.

Berrone, P., Cruz, C., Gómez-Mejía, L. R., & Larraza-Kintana, M. (2010). Socioemotional wealth and corporate responses to institutional pressures: Do family-controlled firms pollute less? *Administrative Science Quarterly, 55*(1), 82–113.

Berrone, P., Cruz, C., & Gómez-Mejía, L. R. (2012). Socioemotional wealth in family firms: Theoretical dimensions, assessment approaches, and agenda for future research. *Family Business Review, 25*(3), 258–279.

Boyd, B., Botero, I. C., & Fediuk, T. A. (2014). Incumbent decisions about succession transitions in family firms: A conceptual model. *International Journal of Financial Studies, 2*(4), 335–358.

Cabrera-Suárez, K., De Saá-Pérez, P., & García-Almeida, D. (2001). The succession process from a resource- and knowledge-based view of the family firm. *Family Business Review, 14*(1), 37–46.

Cennamo, C., Berrone, P., Cruz, C., & Gómez-Mejía, L. R. (2012). Socioemotional wealth and proactive stakeholder engagement: Why family-controlled firms care more about their stakeholders. *Entrepreneurship Theory and Practice, 36*(6), 1153–1173.

Chua, J. H., Chrisman, J. J., & Sharma, P. (1999). Defining the family business by behavior. *Entrepreneurship Theory and Practice, 23*(4), 19–39.

Constantinidis, C., & Cornet, A. (2008). *Daughters taking over the family business: A gender analysis.* In ISBE Conference 2008 Proceedings.

Creswell, J. W., & Poth, C. N. (2016). *Qualitative inquiry and research design: Choosing among five approaches.* Sage publications.

Cucculelli, M., & Micucci, G. (2008). Family succession and firm performance: Evidence from Italian family firms. *Journal of Corporate Finance, 14*(1), 17–31.

De Massis, A., Chua, J. H., & Chrisman, J. J. (2008). Factors preventing intra-family succession. *Family Business Review, 21*(2), 183–199.

DeTienne, D. R. (2010). Entrepreneurial exit as a critical component of the entrepreneurial process: Theoretical development. *Journal of Business Venturing, 25*(2), 203–215.

Diwisch, D. S., Voithofer, P., & Weiss, C. R. (2009). Succession and firm growth: Results from a non-parametric matching approach. *Small Business Economics, 32*, 45–56.

Eriksson, P., & Kovalainen, A. (2015*). Qualitative methods in business research: A practical guide to social research.* Sage publications.

Fendri, C., & Nguyen, P. (2019). Secrets of succession: how one family business reached the ninth generation. *Journal of Business Strategy, 40*(5), 12–20.

Ghee, W. Y., Ibrahim, M. D., & Abdul-Halim, H. (2015). Family business succession planning: Unleashing the key factors of business performance. *Asian Academy of Management Journal, 20*(2), 103–126.

Gómez-Mejía, L. R., Haynes, K. T., Núñez-Nickel, M., Jacobson, K. J., & Moyano-Fuentes, J. (2007). Socioemotional wealth and business risks in family-controlled firms: Evidence from Spanish olive oil mills. *Administrative Science Quarterly, 52*(1), 106–137.

Gustafsson, J. (2017). *Single case studies vs. multiple case studies: A comparative study.* https://www.diva-portal.org/smash/get/diva2:1064378/FULLTEXT01.pdf (accessed on January 3, 2025)

Kalm, M., & Gómez-Mejía, L. R. (2016). Socioemotional wealth preservation in family firms. *Revista de Administração (São Paulo), 51*, 409–411.

Kellermanns, F. W., Eddleston, K. A., & Zellweger, T. M. (2012). Article commentary: Extending the socioemotional wealth perspective: A look at the dark side. *Entrepreneurship Theory and Practice, 36*(6), 1175–1182.

Koropp, C., Grichnik, D., & Gygax, A. F. (2013). Succession financing in family firms. *Small Business Economics, 41*, 315–334.

Kraus, S., Pohjola, M., & Koponen, A. (2012). Innovation in family firms: an empirical analysis linking organizational and managerial innovation to corporate success. *Review of Managerial Science, 6*, 265–286.

Kubíček, A., & Machek, O. (2019). Gender-related factors in family business succession: a systematic literature review. *Review of Managerial Science, 13*(5), 963–1002.

Lee, K. S., Lim, G. H., & Lim, W. S. (2003). Family business succession: Appropriation risk and choice of successor. *Academy of Management Review, 28*(4), 657–666.

Lefebvre, M. R., & Lefebvre, V. (2016). Anticipating intergenerational management transfer of family firms: A typology of next generation's future leadership projections. *Futures, 75*, 66–82.

Liu, C., Eubanks, D. L., & Chater, N. (2015). The weakness of strong ties: Sampling bias, social ties, and nepotism in family business succession. *The Leadership Quarterly, 26*(3), 419–435.

Luan, C. J., Chen, Y. Y., Huang, H. Y., & Wang, K. S. (2018). CEO succession decision in family businesses–A corporate governance perspective. *Asia Pacific Management Review, 23*(2), 130–136.

Makó, C., Csizmadia, P., & Heidrich, B. (2016). Succession in the family business: Need to transfer the 'Socio-Emotional Wealth'(SEW). *Vezetéstudomány-Budapest Management Review, 47*(11), 16–28.

Nelson, T., & Constantinidis, C. (2017). Sex and gender in family business succession research: A review and forward agenda from a social construction perspective. *Family Business Review, 30*(3), 219–241.

Neubauer, H. (2003). The dynamics of succession in family businesses in western European countries. *Family Business Review*, *16*(4), 269–281.

Nieto, M. J., Santamaria, L., & Fernandez, Z. (2015). Understanding the innovation behavior of family firms. *Journal of Small Business Management*, *53*(2), 382–399.

Nordqvist, M., Wennberg, K., Bau', M., & Hellerstedt, K. (2013). An entrepreneurial process perspective on succession in family firms. *Small Business Economics*, *40*, 1087–1122.

Powell, G. N. (2018). Family science and the work-family interface: An interview with Gary Powell and Jeffrey Greenhaus. *Human Resource Management Review*, *28*(1), 98–102.

Pyromalis, V. D., & Vozikis, G. S. (2009). Mapping the successful succession process in family firms: Evidence from Greece. *International Entrepreneurship and Management Journal*, *5*, 439–460.

Ramón, J. F. C. (2021). Succession in the family business: the great challenge for the family. *European Journal of Family Business*, *11*(1), 64–70.

Rosado-Serrano, A., & Navarro-García, A. (2019). Family business in transition economies: an exploratory study of private business. *European Journal of Family Business*, *9*(1), 39–53.

Rumanko, B., Lušňáková, Z., Moravanská, M., & Šajbidorová, M. (2021). Succession as a risk process in the survival of a family business—Case of Slovakia. *Journal of Risk and Financial Management*, *14*(10), 458.

Sharma, P. (2004). An overview of the field of family business studies: Current status and directions for the future. *Family Business Review*, *17*(1), 1–36.

Sharma, P., Chrisman, J. J., Pablo, A. L., & Chua, J. H. (2001). Determinants of initial satisfaction with the succession process in family firms: A conceptual model. *Entrepreneurship Theory and Practice*, *25*(3), 17–36.

Sharma, P., & Srinivas Rao, A. (2000). Successor attributes in Indian and Canadian family firms: A comparative study. *Family Business Review*, *13*(4), 313–330.

Steier, L. P., & Miller, D. (2010). Pre-and post-succession governance philosophies in entrepreneurial family firms. *Journal of Family Business Strategy*, *1*(3), 145–154.

Steiger, T., Duller, C., & Hiebl, M. R. (2015). No consensus in sight: an analysis of ten years of family business definitions in empirical research studies. *Journal of Enterprising Culture*, *23*(01), 25–62.

Stewart, A., & Hitt, M. A. (2012). Why can't a family business be more like a nonfamily business? Modes of professionalization in family firms. *Family Business Review*, *25*(1), 58–86.

Sund, L. G., Almlof, H., & Haag, K. (2010). Divorce and death in the family firm-A business law perspective. *European Business Law Review*, *21*(2), 101–118.

Tatoglu, E., Kula, V., & Glaister, K. W. (2008). Succession planning in family-owned businesses: Evidence from Turkey. *International Small Business Journal*, *26*(2), 155–180.

Thomas, D. R. (2006). A general inductive approach for analyzing qualitative evaluation data. *American Journal of Evaluation*, *27*(2), 237–246.

Ungerer, M., & Mienie, C. (2018). A family business success map to enhance the sustainability of a multi-generational family business. *International Journal of Family Business and Management Studies*, *2*(1), 1–13.

Vassiliadis, S., & Vassiliadis, A. (2014). The Greek family businesses and the succession problem. *Procedia Economics and Finance*, *9*, 242–247.

Vera, C. F., & Dean, M. A. (2005). An examination of the challenges daughters face in family business succession. *Family Business Review*, *18*(4), 321–345.

Yuan, X. (2019). A review of succession and innovation in family business. *American Journal of Industrial and Business Management*, *9*(4), 974.

Petter Gottschalk

Convenience Study of Criminal Deviance in the Entrepreneurial Family Business: Husband as Lawyer and Wife as Accountant in the Law Firm

Abstract: This case study from Norway addresses criminal entrepreneurship in a family business. A lawyer in his own law firm admitted to embezzlement of funds on client bank accounts and had to go to prison for several years. The lawyer's wife presented herself as a victim of the husband's wrongdoing. However, one police investigator found it interesting that the wife had been the accountant in the husband's law firm. The investigation revealed that the wife as an accountant had handled many of the financial transactions ordered by the husband as an attorney. A state prosecutor decided to charge the wife with money laundering of the funds that the husband had embezzled. She was convicted to prison in district court. At the time of writing this case study, she has appealed the verdict.

Keywords: Interim CEO (CRO, advisor), Family firms, Strategy-as-Practices, Trust and emotions, Strategizing

1 Introduction

This chapter presents the case of a wife who was accused of following her husband in crime. He had already been convicted in a Norwegian court when she was prosecuted. He was a successful lawyer who embezzled client funds to buy expensive real estate. She was the accountant and assistant in the husband's law firm where she allegedly manipulated accounting figures to make transactions seem legal.

This chapter starts by reviewing the general literature on leader and follower in crime. The theory of convenience is introduced by its structural model to identify convenience propositions that seem to be particularly prominent in the role of follower in financial crime. Then the general literature on focal concerns for women is reviewed. Again, the structural model for convenience is used to identify convenience propositions that seem to be particularly prominent for female focal concerns in financial crime.

Next, the case of the prosecuted wife as the accountant and assistant is introduced in several steps in this chapter. Firstly, we review how she has been portrayed in a book and in the media. Secondly, we interpret how she is portrayed in the indictment from the serious fraud office. Thirdly, we attended the trial where the wife was

https://doi.org/10.1515/9783110790344-007

the defendant and analyze our records from the courtroom. Finally, the verdict was released from the court that is again analyzed by application of convenience theory to the presentation of the defendant in the sentence document.

The purpose of this chapter is to study shifting convenience propositions by addressing the following research question: What convenience propositions dominate depending on perspectives regarding a woman as follower in white-collar crime in the family busiess? This research is important, as it illustrates the application of convenience theory to different offender perspectives. The theory of convenience is an emerging theoretical explanation of the white-collar crime phenomenon first introduced by Gottschalk (2017) and later expanded by Gottschalk (2023) while in the meantime been applied by several scholars including Braaten & Vaughn (2021) and Saad et al. (2022a, 2022b).

While the convenience triangle of motive, opportunity, and willingness has similarities to the traditional fraud triangle (Cressey, 1972; Murphy & Free, 2015), there are significant differences. In convenience theory, crime is a choice among alternatives, the crime scene is the organizational setting, and the opportunity structure changes over time. Rashidian & Archie (2025, p. 6608) reflected on convenience theory when discussing the embezzlement scheme of lawyer Tom Girardi in the United States:

> Convenience theory posits that white-collar crime results from the perceived convenience of engaging in criminal behavior, encompassing motive, opportunity, and willingness. In Girardi's case, this theory illuminates how his position as a trusted attorney created both the motive (financial gain) and opportunity (access to client funds) for embezzlement, while his willingness was likely influenced by his evaluation of risks and rewards.

The seemingly successful lawyer in Norway in the current case study might resemble Girardi. In the case study, the husband as a lawyer and leader of the company was convicted to prison for more than five years after having embezzled money on client accounts (Asting & Gottschalk, 2023). A few years later, the wife as his follower and the only accountant in the law firm was charged with laundering the money that her husband had embezzled.

2 Convenience Propositions for Crime Followers

White-collar criminals can either be leaders in crime or adapt to the role of followers in such crime. The difference between leaders and followers might be found in motives, opportunities, and willingness for deviant behavior. For example, leaders may tend to commit crime based on the motive of greed by wanting more all the time, while followers tend to find themselves in a less assertive position who trail behind someone else into criminal activities, possibly due to the lack of strength and independence. This makes followers seem like passive participants who are weaker than the leaders, and who are unable to stand up to the leaders to prevent crime.

Deviant actions by followers can be the consequence of obedience (Baird & Zelin, 2009), where obedience is a voluntary or not so voluntary behavior among followers to obey their leaders to do what leaders wants them to do. Obedience is not so voluntary in cases of abusive supervision, where subordinates perceive that supervisors engage in a sustained display of hostile verbal and non-verbal behaviors (Mawritz et al., 2017).

Individuals with high social status in privileged positions sometimes use language that people simply do not understand. Executives and others in the elite may use language that followers not necessarily understand – however nevertheless they trust executive messages (Ferraro et al., 2015). Language is a window into organizational culture (Srivastava & Goldberg, 2017), where offender language can cause obedience among followers (Mawritz et al., 2017). As the wife as a follower said in court: "He has always been so convincing"; "He always had a convincing reason and explanation".

An example of offender language is aggressive humor that refers to a specific style of humor aimed at teasing or ridiculing. It may include sarcasm humorously to convey disapproving information to followers. Aggressive humor may signal to followers that the accepted social norm of being respectful towards others is not important. It signals that violating norm of human decency is acceptable. The leader humor perspective suggests that leader sense of humor is positively associated with followers' perceived acceptability of norm violations.

Aggressive leader humor might cause fear among subordinates that prevent them from intervening or in any visible way reacting when the deviant leader is into wrongdoing and misconduct (Dion, 2020, p. 1032):

> Machiavelli asserted that wise leaders want to be liked and feared by people. They can be benevolent toward their friends and cruel toward their enemies. People harm others either by fear or by hatred. An excess of fear is always better than an excess of love, since it allows the leader to keep his power and influence. The leader could lose power and influence if people do not fear his cruelty. However, people's fear must be accompanied by an absence of hatred. The balance between fear and love could allow the leader to safeguard his political stability.

Followers may perceive innocence that can be justified by peer pressure, where the offender claims that the offense had to take place because a person with authority had told the offender to do so (Gao & Zhang, 2019). Figure 1 illustrates the main convenience propositions for followers in financial crime as suggested by the above referenced literature. Being a follower is at the individual level characterized more by strain than by greed. The follower has no particular status but may have access to resources to commit crime on behalf of the leader. It is favorable to the follower to conceal wrongdoing if there is chaos from lack of oversight and guardianship. In the willingness dimension, the follower learns from the leader and has a perception of innocence from obedience that both justifies own actions and neutralizes potential guilt feelings.

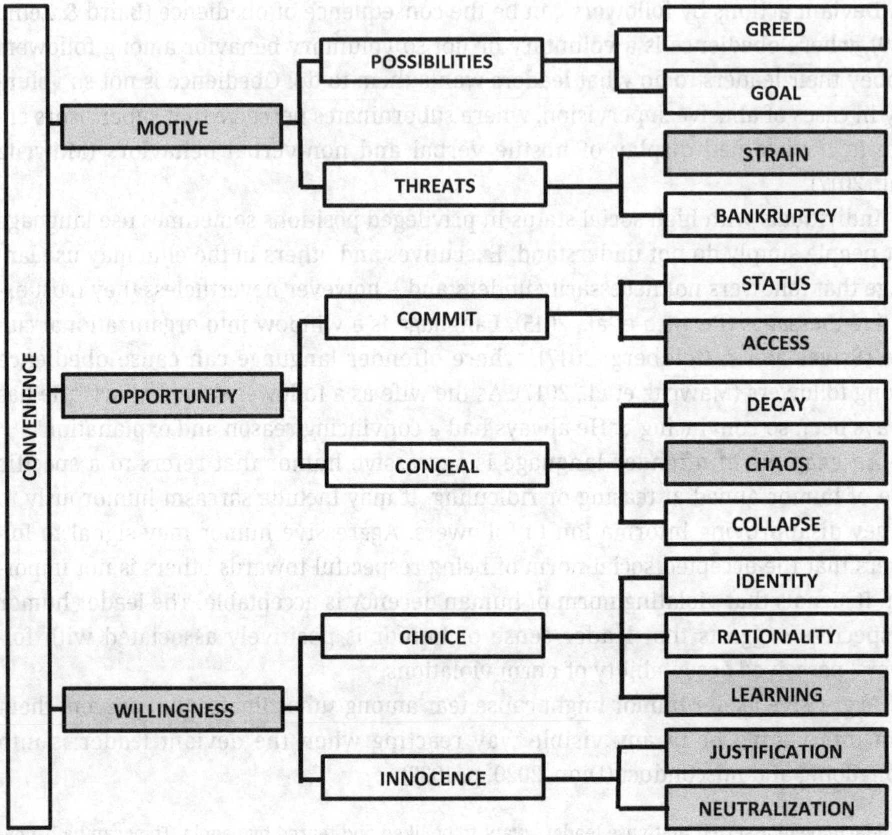

Figure 1: Convenience propositions for followers in financial crime.

3 Convenience Propositions for Women Offenders

The convenience of committing financial crime might vary depending on gender. Men might find crime more or less convenient compared to women. When Sutherland introduced the concept of white-collar crime in 1939, gender roles were significantly different than what we experience today. At that time, women lacked the organizational opportunities to engage in criminal activities, as such actions typically necessitated holding higher positions within a company or independent professional positions associated with respectability. It was mostly the man in the household who enjoyed employment to commit both legitimate as well as illegitimate actions.

Since then, there has been an increased focus on gender equality. Yet in our perspective of convenience propositions, women convenience in financial crime may differ from male convenience in financial crime, i.e., out of the fourteen convenience propositions in the theory, some may be more relevant for women while others may be more relevant for men. The difference can be explored by the concept of gendered focal concerns, which argues that women have different focal concerns compared to men even when there is gender equality (Gupta et al., 2023).

Women committing white-collar crime is sometimes referred to as pink-collar crime. The focal concerns address gender differences in interests and priorities. The paradigm of gendered focal concern contends that women socialize into accepting nurturing role obligations that emphasize the importance of social relationships and communalistic orientations towards others. Through the assimilation of these obligations, women develop identities as caregivers (Steffensmeier et al., 2013). Agnew (2014) introduced the motive of social concern and crime, where there is a desire to help others, and thus moving beyond the assumption of simple self-interest. When Klenowski et al. (2011, p. 58) interviewed twenty convicted pink-collar offenders, "the most common way that females framed their actions was to show that their ultimate goals were to provide support and aid to those for which they cared", for example:

> Well, what really happened is my two daughters when they were three and five years old in 1990, they were sexually abused by their father, and I aligned myself with somebody that was able to pay my legal bills to fight for custody and to fight for justice in that regard so I guess I'm here because of what I did and I should be here but I don't think I should be here because of my motive. I feel like I was only doing what I had to do as a mother.

Furthermore, as argued by Holtfreter (2015), strain might vary with gender. For example, there are suggestions that gender differences exist in the types of strain experienced, as well as in the reactions to particular strains. Females may respond to strain with depression and anxiety (Brands & Mehra, 2019), while males may respond with negative emotions in the form of anger aggression. In the opportunity dimension of convenience theory, women are less likely to be suspected of crime. A typical employer will seldom suspect female employees of misconduct and crime as compared to male suspects. Lack of suspicion leads to lack of crime signal detection (Szalma & Hancock, 2013). Gottschalk (2022) assumed in the gender stage model that the relative detection risk for women compared to men is only 30%. Women tend to talk most strongly about ethics, morals, and social responsibility (Dodge, 2007, 2009) and are thus less subject to crime suspicion.

Figure 2 illustrates the main convenience propositions for women in financial crime as suggested by the above referenced literature. While social concern might represent strain, the desire for acceptance and potential admiration from those taken care of reminds more strongly of greed. Accepting nurturing role obligations might be characterized as a sacrifice, yet the potential closeness and love from those favored by the offender is a benefit of great value to many offenders. In the opportunity dimension, women are simply not suspected of deviance and thus avoid the attention in a situation of organizational deterioration and decay.

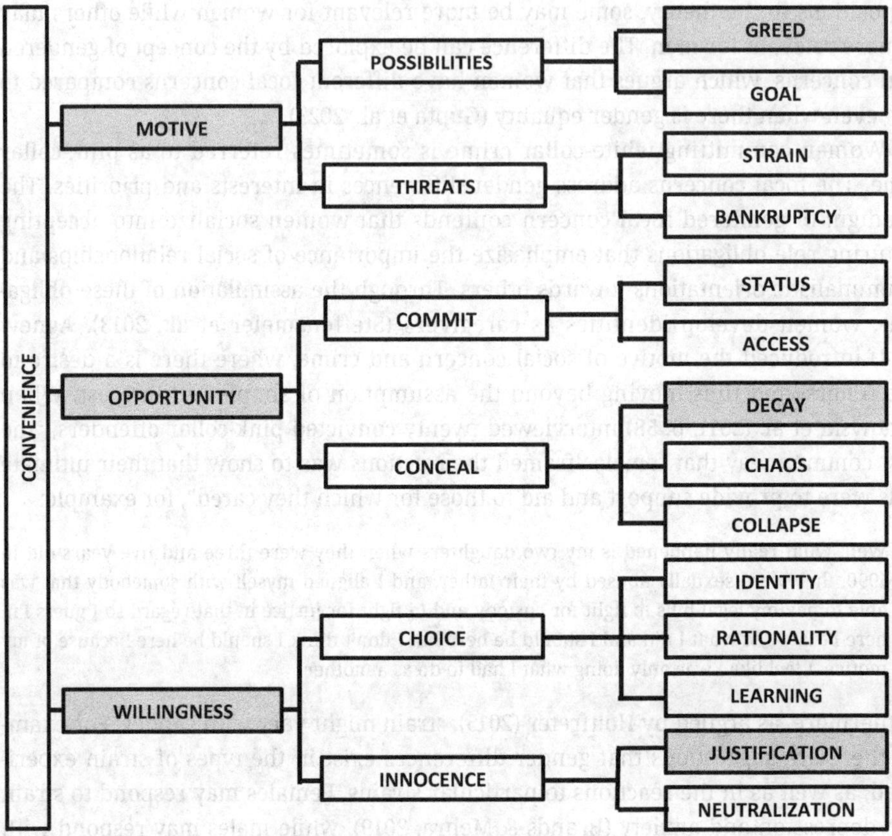

Figure 2: Convenience propositions for women in financial crime.

The willingness based on justification can be explained by the equity and equality perspective. This perspective explains how an individual can feel entitled to illegal redistribution of wealth if the current distribution is perceived as unfair (Burrai et al., 2015). When equity is not perceived in financial compensation for the same job or for work-family balance (Padavic et al., 2020), then there is a willingness to take remedial action to make the situation more equitable.

It is important to emphasize here that the analysis above illustrated in Figure 2 addresses convenience propositions for women in pink-collar crime. To what extent it is different for male offenders in terms of magnitude of crime or crime categories were not addressed. Maybe men dominate in the same convenience propositions, or maybe they do not. Previous research might indicate that the motives among men are mainly threats. For example, the strain of divorce can lead to financial crime to compensate the economic loss of giving away to the former spouse. Also, the danger of bankruptcy is found in many anecdotal studies to be the main reason for financial crime among male offenders.

In the opportunity structure, offender status and legitimate access might be the dominating opportunity propositions for men. In the willingness dimension, rationality might be the main convenience propositions. This is because the assumed detection probability is perceived as extremely low, thereby making advantages of crime exceed disadvantages of crime (Gottschalk, 2022; Gupta et al., 2023). Therefore, just as a thought experiment, female motive is greed, while male motives are strain and bankruptcy. Female opportunity is decay, while male opportunity is status and access. Female willingness is justification, while male willingness is rationality.

Of course, numerous research studies have provided evidence that women commit far less economic crime in their trusted positions compared to men in trusted positions. In fact, Gupta et al. (2023) found that the female fraction of detected white-collar crime is stable at around ten percent independent of the extent of gender equality. While countries like India, Iran, Malaysia, Norway, Romania, and the United States do indeed have different levels of gender equality or inequality, the fraction of female offenders stayed in their research at about the same level of one out of ten convicted white-collar criminals.

For a while, researchers expected that with higher representation of women in executive positions having passed the glass ceiling, the fraction of female offenders would grow accordingly. It did not. There was no support for the emancipation hypothesis suggesting proportional rise in offending. Rather, support for the focal concern hypothesis became evidenced (Dodge, 2019; Gupta et al., 2023; Ruhland & Selzer, 2020). The substantial and significant gender disparity thus continues to exist.

In terms of crime categories, women traditionally commit more embezzlement, while men are more involved in corruption. One reason for the latter seems to be that women are perceived as less bribable. Anecdotal evidence of this phenomenon is the author's experiment in many classrooms and public speeches asking the audience to tell who they would bribe in the situation of obtaining an illegal permit to build vacation home on the shoreline. The assumption is that there is a woman and a man in the municipality with the same powers to grant permission. Typically, close to one hundred percent of the audience prefers attempting to bribe the man rather than the woman.

4 Convenience Propositions from Media Coverage

The wife was alleged of being a follower in crime. Her husband had already been convicted of embezzling client funds on bank accounts in the law firm. She was now charged with money laundering of the embezzled money when doing the accounting in the law firm. The trial against the woman as a follower was scheduled in Oslo district court for three weeks starting on April 10, 2024 (Gran, 2023; Losnegård, 2023;

Ravn, 2023). Money laundering refers to concealing the proceeds of a criminal offence and in that making the proceeds appear as legally acquired funds.

Four years earlier, in 2020, shortly before the trial against her husband took place in Oslo district court (Oslo tingrett, 2021), journalist Spurkland (2021) interviewed the married couple Marianne and Halstein Sjølie in their home in the town of Moss outside the Norwegian capital Oslo. The interview took place in the kitchen. During the interview, she presented herself as a victim of the husband's crime while claiming that she would nevertheless continue to stand by his side (Spurkland, 2021, p. 208):

> Marianne stands by his side. She has done that throughout the entire process from disclosure to now. She did it although she was just as surprised as anyone else when the embezzlements were revealed, and although her life as well was turned upside down. "There were people who wondered whether I wanted to leave you", she says to her husband. "That thought did not cross my mind. But there were many other thoughts in the first weeks and months. There were moments when I thought I would never dare to go out into the light of day again.

During the interview, the married couple said that Marianne had suffered from cancer and recently been released from hospital in healthy condition. When she returned home, she noticed a depressed husband (Spurkland, 2021, p. 220):

> I thought he was tired or that he feared the cancer would return. But that it should be something like what it turned out to be? That was completely unthinkable.

The couple's perceived victimization included police raid of their house (Spurkland, 2021: 221):

> "Much of that time is a bit foggy", says Marianne. "I was panicking. I knew someone would come and raid my house, but I had no idea when it would be. I didn't dare answer the phone, couldn't bear to open the door. I basically only felt safe when the evening came, and the day could bring nothing more, or when it was Friday and a whole week was over."

To identify convenience propositions for Marianne Sjølie as the follower and woman, the following Figure 3 attempts to represent interpretation of the above statements when assuming at this stage that she is guilty of money laundering of embezzlement proceeds from her husband. The suggested convenience propositions are also grounded in self-concept-based theory, leader-follower dyadic, and work meaningfulness as discussed by Kipfelsberger et al. (2022) and Kipfelsberger & Gottschalk (2025).

Kipfelsberger et al. (2022) studied the transfer of work meaningfulness from leaders to followers. The meaningfulness transferred from Halstein to Marianne Sjølie was the acquisition of real estate that was a goal for both as indicated in Figure 3. They bought hotels together abusing embezzled money from law firm clients. The goal was to create and expand a real estate enterprise (Spurkland, 2021, p. 216):

> After a few years, we had a real estate company and a real estate complex in Moss, and a total of six hotels around in Norway.

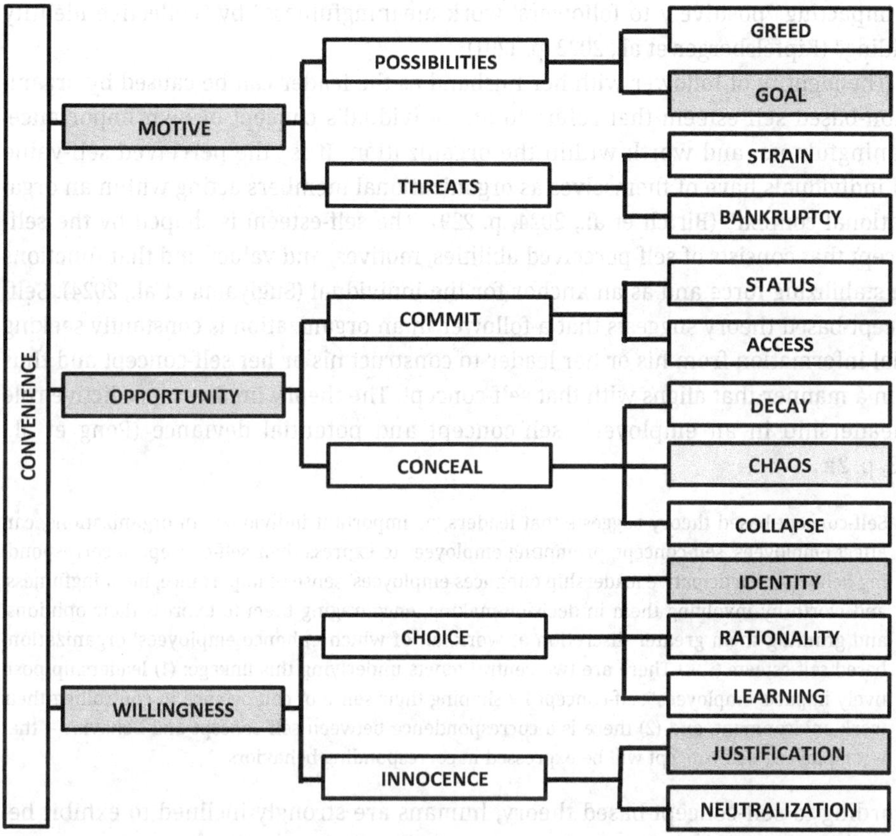

Figure 3: Convenience propositions for wife in the media.

Marianne Sjølie was Halstein Sjølie's second wife. He had divorced his first wife. When Halstein Sjølie was convicted to five-and-a-half years in prison, he had told the court that he transferred money to various hotel projects that he was managing. He said that several transfers were made both to and from each of the companies, and that the sums stated in the indictment were correct. He admitted guilt. Therefore, his trial lasted only for a few hours on one single day (Kipfelsberger & Gottschalk, 2025; Oslo tingrett, 2021).

Through collective identity building, the wife as an accountant and the husband as the lawyer might have seen the law firm as a community to which they felt committed. A follower may quickly identify with the leader due to the leader's professional status, where status refers to refers to an individual's social rank and is "a property that rests in the eyes of others" (Kakkar et al., 2020, p. 532). While "self-concept-based theory suggests that leaders behave in accordance with their inner convictions, values, and identities so as to fulfill their intrinsic needs for self-expression and self-consistency", followers perceive leaders' needs transferred to them as a factor impacting "positively to followers' work meaningfulness" by "collective identity building" (Kipfelsberger et al., 2022, p. 1291).

The identity of follower with her husband as the leader can be caused by organization-based self-esteem that refers to an individual's concept of own importance, meaningfulness, and worth within the organization. It is "the perceived self-value that individuals have of themselves as organizational members acting within an organizational context" (Birtch et al., 2024, p. 229). The self-esteem is shaped by the self-concept that consists of self-perceived abilities, motives, and values and that functions as a stabilizing force and as an anchor for the individual (Sugiyama et al., 2024). Self-concept-based theory suggests that a follower in an organization is constantly seeking social information from his or her leader to construct his or her self-concept and thus act in a manner that aligns with that self-concept. The theory implies a predictive role of leadership in an employee's self-concept and potential deviance (Peng et al., 2023, p. 2):

> Self-concept-based theory suggests that leaders, as important individuals in organizations, can affect employees' self-concept, prompting employees to express their self-concept in corresponding behavior. Participative leadership enhances employees' sense of importance, meaningfulness, and worth by involving them in decision-making, encouraging them to express their opinions, and granting them greater discretion at work, all of which enhance employees' organization-based self-esteem.(. . .) There are two central tenets underlying this linkage: (1) leadership positively impacts employees' self-concept by shaping their sense of competence in controlling their work environment, and (2) there is a correspondence between self-concept and behavior – that is, employees' self-concept will be expressed in corresponding behaviors.

According to self-concept-based theory, humans are strongly inclined to exhibit behaviors consistent with their self-concept, which is in line with self-consistency theory (Birtch et al., 2024). That is, individuals will engage in more negative behaviors when they have a negative self-concept (Peng et al., 2023). The hotel empire was a collective goal for the couple, "indeed something bigger than self" that represents meaningfulness, since "contributing to something beyond the self is a key source of meaningfulness" (Kipfelsberger et al., 2022, p. 1290). Perceptions of meaningfulness travel through the self, which implies that the same work activity may be perceived as meaningful by one person, but not by another person. Meaningfulness is also contingent on an external context that both shapes and legitimizes the subjective perspective (Kipfelsberger & Gottschalk, 2025). It was thus meaningful to the wife joining the husband's efforts to establish a hotel empire. The meaningfulness can represent a justification as indicated in Figure 3. In a justification, the actor admits responsibility for the act in question but denies its pejorative and negative content (Schoen et al., 2021, p. 730):

> People use justification mechanisms to protect their sense of self. People who sincerely believe that they are a specific kind of person but routinely demonstrate behaviors that indicate other-

wise may avoid cognitive dissonance and maintain their sense of self by using justification mechanisms that allow them to "explain away" their behavior.

There is no convenience proposition for opportunity clearly visualized in Figure 3. However, the company structure set up for the law firm was so simple that there was no legal obligation of external auditing. Therefore, oversight and guardianship were absent. The lack of such external control is labeled as the convenience proposition of chaos in the figure and could have been visualized more clearly in stronger grey color. The interesting perspective of Kipfelsberger et al. (2022) on the transfer of work meaningfulness from leaders to followers suggests that work meaningfulness can enhance followers' goal achievement. However, when misconduct and crime is the implicit meaning, the deviant behavior might become the result, according to the indictment as discussed below (Kipfelsberger & Gottschalk, 2025). The Norwegian national authority Økokrim issued the following press release on October 13, 2023, with the heading "Woman charged with concealing her husband's embezzlement of client funds":

> A woman in her 50s has been charged at the Oslo district court for concealing her husband's gross embezzlement of client funds, when she worked as a legal assistant in his company. The husband was sentenced to prison in 2021. In the period from April 2017 to September 2019, the defendant shall have managed the accounts for the business of her husband. The woman is charged with money laundering by having concealed part of her husband's embezzlement of client funds, which he did through his law firm. In 2021, the husband was sentenced to 5.5 years in prison for gross embezzlement of client funds and gross fraud. The case went as a confession case in the Oslo district court. Among other issues, the lawyer allegedly transferred the money unlawfully to his own operating account by providing fictitious invoices and falsified client account statements. The incorrect bookkeeping was done to cover up the ongoing embezzlements of the clients. The woman worked as a legal assistant and was the one who registered in the accounts in her husband's company. Now the woman is charged with, among other things, gross money laundering by concealing just under NOK 65 million [USD 6.5 million] of the embezzlement from client funds. The law firm's clients shall have been sent incorrect financial reviews and falsified bank statements. Økokrim believes that the woman must have sent these to give the impression that the clients' money was in the clients' accounts at all times. The case is serious because it concerns a significant amount and has been carried out over several years. There is also a violation of the special trust that comes with the practice of law, where the defendant worked as a legal assistant for her husband, says first state prosecutor Geir Kavlie at Økokrim.

The media reported about the press release from Økokrim. For example, Ravn (2023: 12) reported under the heading "The lawyer admitted all guilt – now the wife is also charged":

> Lawyer Halstein Sjølie admitted embezzlement of 100 million from his own clients. Økokrim is now bringing charges against his wife and legal assistant Marianne Sjølie. In September 2021, long-standing lawyer Halstein Sjølie (54) admitted embezzlement and fraud of a total of NOK 133 million [USD 13.3 million] in the Oslo district court. Sjølie was sentenced to five years and six months in prison and had to pay around NOK 50 million in compensation to 15 victims. Then Økokrim began to investigate data seizures in the case in more detail. Now his wife Marianne

> Sjølie (57) is charged with gross money laundering of around NOK 65 million, and alternatively complicity in her husband's embezzlement, according to a brand-new indictment. She has also committed bank fraud of NOK 400,000 [USD 40,000] according to the indictment.

The trial against Marianne Sjølie was scheduled for three weeks starting in Oslo district court on April 10, 2024. The local newspaper Moss Avis reported ahead of the trial (Gran, 2023):

> Three weeks have been set aside for the case, which is scheduled for next year April 10. In contrast to her husband Halstein Sjølie, who answered for himself in a confession case in the Oslo district court, the case will this time proceed as an ordinary main hearing. The indictment from Økokrim states that Marianne Sjølie allegedly laundered NOK 65 million of client funds that her husband, and former Moss lawyer Halstein Sjølie, embezzled. Two years ago, he was sentenced to five and a half years in prison for gross embezzlement and fraud totaling NOK 133 million. In this context, Økokrim believes that from April 2017 to September 2019, Marianne Sjølie managed the accounts for her husband in such a way that it helped hide Sjølie's embezzlement. According to the indictment, Sjølie operated with fictitious invoices and falsified client account statements, and transferred money to own accounts.

5 Convenience Propositions from Criminal Indictment

To identify convenience propositions for Marianne Sjølie according to the indictment, the following Figure 4 attempts to represent interpretation of the above statements when assuming at this stage that she is guilty of money laundering of embezzlement proceeds from her husband.

The indictment and the media reports cited above point mainly at the opportunity structure. She was the accountant and had thus access to resources to falsify and to conceal misleading financial transactions as indicated by access and decay in the figure. Generally, access to resources refers to access to enablers of actions such as accounting manipulation. A resource is an enabler applied and used to satisfy human and organizational needs. A resource has utility and limited availability. Access to resources may equate access to power. The resource-based perspective postulates that differences in individuals' opportunities find explanation in the extent of resource access and the ability to combine and exploit those resources (Wheelock et al., 2011). Access to resources in the organizational dimension of convenience theory makes it more relevant and attractive to explore possibilities and avoid threats by financial crime (Chan & Gibbs, 2022). Specifically, the following resources were accessed by the charged Marianne Sjølie (Kipfelsberger & Gottschalk, 2025):

– Bookkeeping is the systematic recording and organization of financial transactions of a business. The objective of bookkeeping is to create a clear and orga-

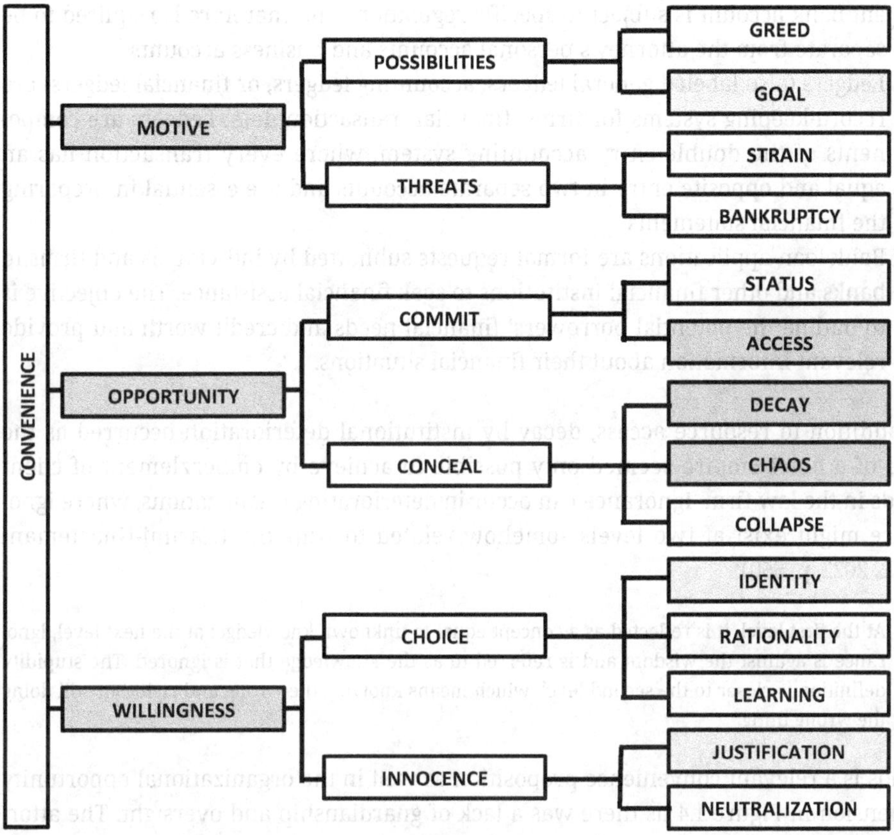

Figure 4: Convenience propositions for wife in the indictment.

nized financial trail that helps businesses track their financial health, meet legal requirements and make informed business decisions.

– Financial statements are formal records of the financial activities and position of a business. They provide a summary of a firm's performance over a certain period of time, usually according to the calendar year. It typically consists of a balance sheet, income statement, and cash flow statement. The income statement shows revenues and expenses, the balance sheets express assets, liabilities, and equity, and the cash flow statement discloses cash inflows and outflows.
– Bank statements are documents issued by a bank to an account holder that provides a summary of the financial transactions over a specified period. They include details about deposits, withdrawals, checks written, and electronic funds transfers.
– Client accounts refer to accounts in a bank held by a professional entity such as a law firm on behalf of its clients. They are typically used by professionals such as lawyers to manage funds related to their clients' transactions and activities. A cli-

ent bank account is subject to specific regulations and therefore is required to be separate from the attorney's personal accounts and business accounts.
- Ledgers (also labeled general ledgers, accounting ledgers, or financial ledgers) are record-keeping systems for firms' financial transaction data. Ledgers are components of the double-entry accounting system, where every transaction has an equal and opposite entry in two separate accounts and are essential in preparing the financial statements.
- Bank loan applications are formal requests submitted by individuals and firms to banks and other financial institutions to seek financial assistance. The objective is to outline the potential borrowers' financial needs and credit worth and provide relevant information about their financial situations.

In addition to resource access, decay by institutional deterioration occurred as the goal of a hotel empire seemed only possible to achieve by embezzlement of client funds in the law firm. Ignorance can occur in deteriorating organizations, where ignorance might exist at two levels somehow related to stupidity (Karimi-Ghartemani et al., 2022, p. 550):

> At the first level, it is reflected as a concept equal to unknown knowledge; at the next level, ignorance is against the wisdom and is referred to as the knowledge that is ignored. The stupidity definition is closer to the second level, which means knowing the wrong and right but still doing the wrong thing.

Chaos is a relevant convenience proposition as well in the organizational opportunity dimension in Figure 1.4 as there was a lack of guardianship and oversight. The attorney business of the Sjølie law firm was organized as a sole proprietorship. Sole proprietorship is characterized by the structure of ownership, decision-making, liability, taxation, and flexibility. The business is owned and operated by one individual, known as the sole proprietor, in this case Halstein Sjølie. The sole proprietor is the only one who has control over decision-making and operations. The proprietor is personally responsible for the business debt and other obligations. There is no legal distinction between business assets and personal assets. Taxation, profits, and losses are reported on the owner's personal tax return, and the business itself is not taxed separately. There is no requirement of having an auditor review accounts in a sole proprietorship.

The indictment does not talk about her motive or willingness (Kipfelsberger & Gottschalk, 2025). Therefore, Figure 4 only indicates in light grey the motive of goal achievement and the willingness based on identity and justification as discussed above based on her appearance in a book and in the media. To summarize so far, this chapter presents exploratory theoretical research by addressing the research question:

> What convenience propositions dominate depending on perspectives regarding women in white-collar crime?

In the follower perspective, the dominating motive seems to be personal strain. In the gender perspective, the dominating motive seems to be personal greed. In the self-presentation perspective, the dominating motive seems to be goal, while in the indictment perspective the dominating motive also seems to be goal. With a combination of such motives, it seems that a woman as a follower pursues the same goal as the leader based on both greed and strain.

In the follower perspective, the dominating opportunity seems to be committing by access to resources and concealing by chaos from absent guardianship. In the gender perspective, the dominating opportunity seems to be concealing by decay from institutional deterioration. In the self-representation perspective, chaos from absent guardianship from sole proprietorship seems to be the relevant convenience proposition. In the indictment perspective, all these three convenience propositions seem relevant: access, decay, and chaos. Thus, in combination, it seems that a woman as a follower has legitimate access to resources – such as an accounting system – to commit wrongdoing, while the wrongdoing remains convenient to conceal when there is institutional deterioration and lack of oversight, control, and guardianship.

In the follower perspective, the willingness for deviant behavior might derive from learning as well as justification and neutralization. In the gender perspective, only justification seems relevant. In the self-representation perspective, justification seems again to be the only relevant convenience proposition. In the indictment perspective, both identity and justification seem to be relevant convenience propositions. In combination then, it seems that a woman as a follower has a willingness for deviant behavior mainly when she can justify her actions, possibly supplied by identification with learning from the leader that might help neutralize potential guilt feelings.

While it is assumed that women tend to commit less financial crime even when they break through the glass ceiling and have similar occupational opportunities as men, it is also assumed that the detection rate for women is lower than for men. Therefore, it is important to discuss potential convenience themes for women when committing pink-collar crime. The exploratory theoretical research presented in this chapter so far suggests that women as followers tend to pursue the same goals as the leaders while having access to resources to commit and the possibility to conceal when female deviance is ignored by guardians. Justification may result from the role of follower.

6 Convenience Propositions from Trial in Court

The trial against Marianne Sjølie started in Oslo district court on Wednesday, April 10, 2024, where a business newspaper reported that she as a lawyer assistant denied criminal liability for money laundering of NOK 65 million (USD 6 million) on the first day in court (Bjørndal, 2024a, p. 11):

> According to Økokrim, among other things, the woman shall have bought Adobe, an editing program for a PC, in order to produce fake account statements. Police prosecutor Maja Salhus Røed and first state prosecutor Geir Kavlie from Økokrim believe they can prove that legal assistant Marianne Sjølie has, among other things, used Adobe Pro to hide the fact that her husband embezzled more than NOK 130 million. Now she stands accused of gross money laundering of NOK 65 million (. . .) Marianne Sjølie is charged with money laundering of NOK 65 million, violation of the Bookkeeping Act and fraud of NOK 400,000 in connection with a private loan application. 15 court days have been set aside to process the case. Marianne Sjølie will explain herself on Thursday and Friday this week. At the start of the trial, Marianne Sjølie pleaded not guilty to any of the three items in the indictment. "No," she answered in a firm and clear voice the three times district court judge Nini Ring asked the question.

When Marianne Sjølie explained herself in the courtroom on Thursday, April 11, 2024, it seemed that her personal strain dominated her motive. While she could afford most what she needed, there was a strain of having six children to feed. Therefore, Figure 5 marks strain as the motive.

> Økokrim believe Marianne Sjølie's motive must have been to hide her spouse's embezzlement (Bjørndal, 2024b, p. 10).

Her opportunity was access to resources in terms of the accounting system. The client accounting was so complex that chaos might characterize the situation. Her willingness was based on the choice of doing what her husband asked her to do.

> "I believe you do not understand how much I trusted Halstein," she said in court (Bjørndal, 2024b, p. 10).

She had a joint identity with her husband. Her perception of innocence seemed to be application of the neutralization technique of higher loyalty.

> "He had always a good explanation," she said in court (Bjørndal, 2024b, p. 10).

The offender denies the act was motivated by self-interest, claiming that it was instead done out of obedience to some moral obligation. The offender appeals to higher loyalties. Those who feel they are in a dilemma employ this technique to indicate that the dilemma must be resolved at the cost of violating a law or policy. In the context of an organization, an employee may appeal to organizational values or hierarchies (Sims & Barreto, 2022).

Marianne Sjølie was back in the witness box on Tuesday, April 16, 2024. Both prosecutors asked her detailed questions about changes in numbers in the internal accounting as well as on bank statements sent to law firm clients. She repeatedly responded that "I don't remember", "I don't know", and "You have to ask Halstein", thus referring to her husband Halstein Sjølie. This kind of responses from the defendant went on for several hours. The joint identity as illustrated in Figure 5, while sharing the vision of her husband by being the follower, seemed to indicate that she perceived herself as no independent individual who could answer questions from the prosecution that should be answered by her leader and husband. The identity might also be explained by the marriage, where she took care of the household at home, while he took care of the administration in the office.

At the time of writing this part of the case study, the outcome of the trial was not known. While of importance to understand the relevance of convenience propositions, the final verdict was not expected until 2026 or 2027 as typically the losing party will appeal the verdict. Whether the prosecution or the defense loses in the district court, one of them will send the case to a court of appeal. If then appealed further to the Norwegian Supreme Court, then the final verdict will be known several years from now.

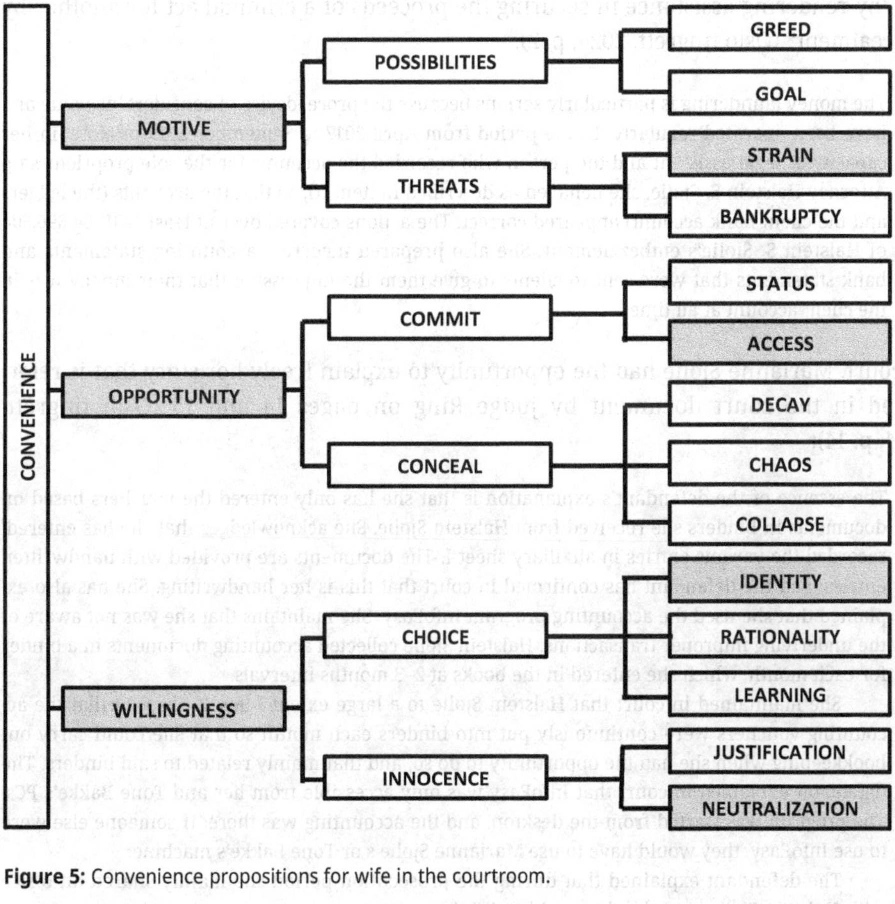

Figure 5: Convenience propositions for wife in the courtroom.

7 Convenience Propositions from Verdict Document

Given that the verdict became available, the following is an interpretation of the message in the court verdict regarding Marianne Sjølie (Oslo tingrett, 2024). The professional judge at Oslo district court was Nini Ring, while Bjørn Gunnar Fjellheim and Bjørn Krok were two lay judges in court. The prosecution was headed by first state attorney Geir Kavlie supported by police attorney Maja Salhus Røed. The defendant Marianne Sjølie had defense lawyers Tormod Tingstad and Thomas Skjelbred. The verdict document is 61 pages long.

The verdict document starts with the indictment by the prosecution. Marianne Sjølie was charged with violating Norwegian penal codes § 324, 325, 337, 338, 371, and 372 "by rendering assistance in securing the proceeds of a criminal act for another by concealment" (Oslo tingrett, 2024, p. 2):

> The money laundering is particularly serious because the proceeds are of considerable value and have been operated regularly. In the period from April 2017 to September 2019 in Moss, in her capacity as legal assistant and the person who recorded the accounts for the sole proprietorship Attorney Halstein S. Sjølie, she behaved as described in item III, so that the accounts (the ledgers and the client bank account) appeared correct. The actions covered over at least NOK 64,696,504 of Halstein S. Sjølie's embezzlement. She also prepared incorrect accounting statements and bank statements that were sent to clients to give them the impression that their money was in the client account at all times.

In court, Marianne Sjølie had the opportunity to explain freely her story that is referenced in the court document by judge Ring on pages 14 and 15 (Oslo tingrett, 2024, p. 14):

> The essence of the defendant's explanation is that she has only entered the vouchers based on documents in binders she received from Halstein Sjølie. She acknowledges that she has entered/recorded the various entries in auxiliary sheet I. The documents are provided with handwritten entries, and the defendant has confirmed in court that this is her handwriting. She has also explained that she used the accounting program InfoEasy. She maintains that she was not aware of the underlying improper transactions. Halstein Sjølie collected accounting documents in a binder for each month, which she entered in the books at 2–3 months intervals.
>
> She maintained in court that Halstein Sjølie to a large extent himself ensured that the accounting vouchers were continuously put into binders each month so that she could carry out bookkeeping when she had the opportunity to do so, and that mainly related to said binders. The defendant explained in court that InfoEasy was only accessible from her and Tone Bakke's PCs. The program was started from the desktop, and the accounting was there. If someone else were to use InfoEasy, they would have to use Marianne Sjølie's or Tone Bakke's machine.
>
> The defendant explained that during the prosecution period she mainly shared an office with Halstein Sjølie, and that he used her PC if he was going to use the accounting program InfoEasy, which she claims he did. He sent various documents to her PC, continued working there, and then sent the documents back to himself. This is the same explanation Halstein Sjølie has given in court. Marianne Sjølie has also maintained that she was not in the office much, and that there were many problems with the children that she had to deal with. She was also seriously ill

at several times during the indictment period. The defendant maintained that she trusted Halstein Sjølie in every way, had no suspicions, and that the revelation in September 2019 came as a surprise and a great shock to her.

The explanation is supported by Halstein Sjølie's explanation, who claims that he has made all the forgeries, and that it was done from Marianne Sjølie's PC when there was a lot of mess in his office space. He logged into her PC, made changes and forgeries, and then sent it back to his own PC. He finds it incomprehensible that no traces of forgeries have been found on his PC, and maintains that this cannot be the case. He claims that the defendant knew nothing about his embezzlement. The court disregards these explanations, and shall say why in the following.

As mentioned, in her explanation, Marianne Sjølie maintained that she mainly dealt with attachments in binders, but the evidence shows that she was more involved in the bookkeeping than she expressed in court, which the court will return to in more detail. The evidence further reveals that extensive actions have been taken to cover up the defendant's ongoing embezzlement. These were made on Marianne Sjølie's PC, and from her user. No forgeries have been found on Halstein Sjølie's PC. Had Halstein Sjølie done this in accordance with the defendant's and Halstein Sjølie's explanations, it is likely that traces of this would have been found. Both Halstein Sjølie and Marianne Sjølie have maintained that her PC was used by both of them, and that he mainly used it to manipulate documents. The court perceives their reasons as somewhat different. Marianne has indicated that it is because the InfoEasy program is only available there, while he has also indicated that it was "messy" at his office.

In the court's opinion, Marianne Sjølie's explanation, seen in the light of other evidence, seems contravened, adapted and also not credible.

The last statement in this quote is really strong. It simply says that the judges did not believe what the defendant was telling in court. It seems that the court considered her a colluder rather than a conformer, where a conformer is prone to obedience to the leader while a colluder actively contributes to the leader's mission. This distinction was made by Thoroughgood et al. (2012: 902) who suggested that

> there is a distinction between destructive follower behaviors performed in response to authority and those initiated by the followers

as some followers are conformers while other followers are colluders:

> While conformers are prone to obedience, and thus do not engage in destructive behavior alone, colluders actively contribute to the leader's mission.

Thoroughgood et al. (2012) suggested three conformer sub-types: lost souls, authoritarians, and bystanders. They also suggested two colluder sub-types: acolytes and opportunists. Lost souls are conformers with negative self-evaluations and ill-defined self-concepts. Authoritarians are conformers who accept leaders' legitimate right to exert power over them. Bystanders are conformers who are passive and motivated primarily by fear. Acolytes are colluders because they share congruent values and goals with their leaders. Opportunists are colluders viewing their cooperation and alliance with their leaders as a vehicle for personal gain that makes them willing to follow to acquire financial, political, professional or other benefits.

If Marianne Sjølie is to be classified as a colluder, it seems that the label of opportunist is the most appropriate as she enjoyed higher status by being married to a seemingly successful lawyer, entrepreneur, and hotel owner. "Status is a property that rests in the eyes of others and is conferred to individuals who are deemed to have a higher rank or social standing in a pecking order based on a mutually valued set of social attributes" (Kakkar et al., 2020: 532).

In the following, the court verdict will be analyzed with the intent to identify what motive, opportunity, and willingness the court emphasized in their judgment. The court verdict was released on June 14, 2024, and concluded with Marianne Sjølie being guilty without reasonable doubt and sentenced to three years in prison for serious money laundering with related violation of accounting rules. Six and a half weeks after the court trial ended, was the devasting verdict published, concluding that Marianne Sjølie was guilty without reasonable or sensible doubt, sentencing her to three years in jail. The unanimous verdict came somewhat as a surprise, as the question of guilt did not seem as straight forward during trial as the judges of Oslo district court seemed to believe. Oslo district court's conclusion was that Marianne's statement and questions were constructed and not credible (Oslo tingrett, 2024: 15).

This was not the spectator experience by Muri (2024) at the closing of the completed trial left her with even more uncertainties than when she first entered. Despite Marianne's selective memory and her having unquestionably a role in the crime, whether she was guilty without reasonable and sensible doubt was not as clear to Muri (2024) as a student writing her master thesis about the case. After listening to witnesses' testimonies, she got the impression that Marianne was not good at accounting and finance in general due to the lack of interest and knowledge and therefore was dependent on help from others to complete the accounts in the law firm.

This left Muri (2024) with doubt of whether she was able to successfully hide and conceal the crime. It also was doubtful of whether Marianne was to blame as it seemed she just did what she was told to do by her husband, who was a seemingly successful and knowledgeable lawyer who reassured her and made her trust his orders, and therefore, could have made her believe that it would work out legally in the end and no one would get hurt, which was also something the court judges mentioned in the final pages of the verdict but did not seem to be significant for them when concluding. Another factor as to why it was not as evident as the verdict makes it out be to, according to Muri (2024), was how they seemed to disagree on the IT technical questions, and how it seemed doubtful which point in time could be linked to which activity on the computer. This doubt came to light when the IT expert had to return to the court for the second time and testify once more to clarify certain terms and findings.

In terms of Marianne Sjølie's motive, despite accumulating several real estate properties and significant values, the judges emphasized Marianne and Halstein Sjølie's strained liquidity. The real estate properties were financed by short-term seller credits and involved substantial loans. It was also mentioned that the couple obtained several small loans, which illustrated the "constant lack of liquidity" (Oslo tingrett, 2024, p. 6). In addition to this, Marianne and Halstein obtained two emergency loans from Marianne's brother-in-law in 2017 and 2018. The court also mentioned the fact that Marianne had her own self-interest in the money laundering, because the embezzlement of client funds "benefitted her directly" (Oslo tingrett, 2024, p. 52) Furthermore, the court mentioned that Marianne Sjølie was dependent on Halstein Sjølie, and that it would have been difficult for her to "not clean up" after him (Oslo tingrett, 2024, p. 53). This illustrated, according to Muri (2024), another type of pressure that Marianne was subject to, that is her husband. Overall, the court seemed to believe that Marianne faced several challenges which was threatening to her, and this was her convenience into the alleged concealing of crime, identified as strain in Figure 6.

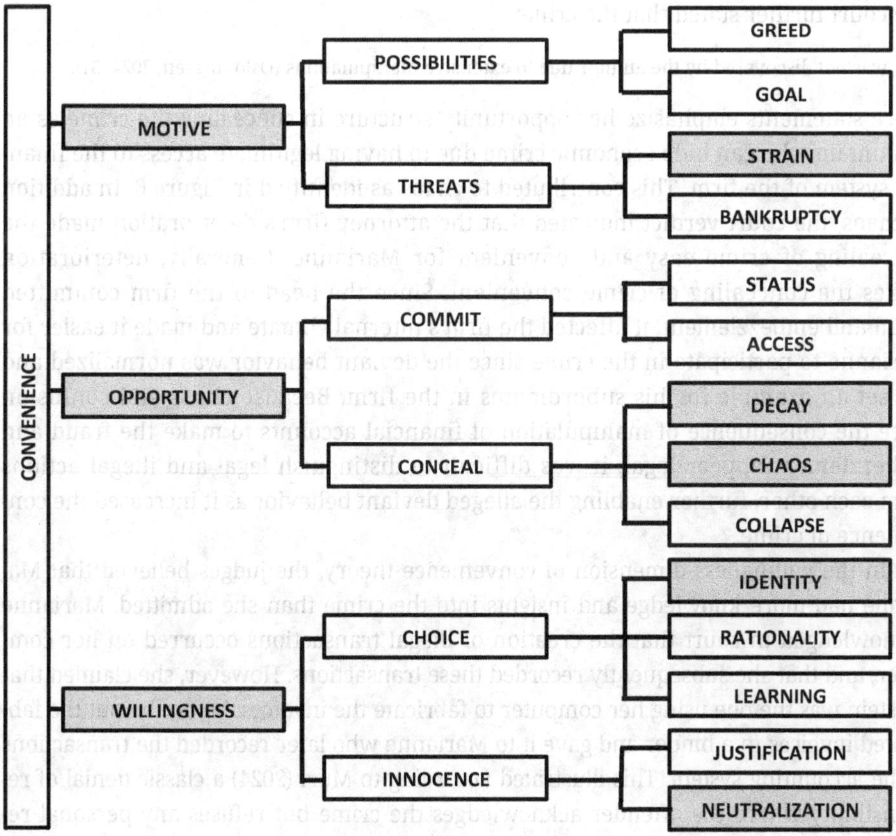

Figure 6: Convenience propositions for wife in the verdict document.

In the opportunity dimension of convenience theory, the key point to Marianne's alleged involvement with the crime was her role in the attorney firm, especially regarding her responsibility as the accountant and attorney assistant for Halstein Sjølie. The court emphasized in the verdict the fact that her colleagues and several auditors from BDO stated that Marianne was the one who continuously updated the accounts and was responsible for balance sheet, status reports, and interest calculations, as well as ongoing control of entrusted funds, e.g., client funds (Oslo tingrett, 2024, p. 16). Her role as the accountant and Halstein's closest coworker made it convenient to conceal his embezzlement of client funds and bank fraud because the crime was difficult to uncover due to the lack of oversight over client accounts, and because the financial statements were in such a mess that it made the auditor's job of detecting crime almost impossible. The court states that

> it is clear that Marianne Sjølie, by virtue of her position and role, had a real opportunity to influence the firm's accounts (Oslo tingrett, 2024, p. 51).

The court further stated that the crime

> was not discovered by the auditor due to extensive manipulations (Oslo tingrett, 2024: 51).

These statements emphasize her opportunity structure in concealing the crime as an accountant who can hide economic crime due to having legitimate access to the financial system of the firm. This contributed to chaos as identified in Figure 6. In addition to chaos, the court verdict indicated that the attorney firm's deterioration made the concealing of crime easy and convenient for Marianne. Generally, deterioration makes the concealing of crime convenient. Since the head of the firm committed fraud and embezzlement, it affected the firm's internal climate and made it easier for Marianne to participate in the crime since the deviant behavior was normalized and did set an example for his subordinates in the firm. Because chaos and confusion were the consequence of manipulation of financial accounts to make the fraud and embezzlement appear legal, it was difficult to distinguish legal and illegal actions from each other, further enabling the alleged deviant behavior as it increased the convenience of crime.

In the willingness dimension of convenience theory, the judges believed that Marianne had more knowledge and insights into the crime than she admitted. Marianne acknowledged in court that the creation of illegal transactions occurred on her computer, and that she subsequently recorded these transactions. However, she claimed that Halstein was the one using her computer to fabricate the invoices, before he put the fabricated invoices in a binder and gave it to Marianne who later recorded the transactions in the accounting system. This illustrated according to Muri (2024) a classic denial of responsibility where the offender acknowledges the crime but refuses any personal responsibility in committing it, that is then to neutralize potential feelings of guilt.

This is identified as a neutralization technique where Marianne denies responsibility for crime. Denial of responsibility occurs when the criminals admit to crime but claim it was due to reasons beyond their control. The court also seemed to believe Marianne's identity and social status was closely attached to the successful attorney husband from Moss, quite in contrast to the fast food-job in Lofoten she previously held before meeting Halstein. These two contradicting identities seemed to be a reason as to why the court was of the opinion that she had been manipulated by Halstein and had a "dependent relationship" to him (Oslo tingrett, 2024, p. 53). If she did not go along into the crime, but exposed her husband, or even blew the whistle on him, there would be an identity collision in her identity as a wife to a successful lawyer, which made her relying on Halstein and his professional success, that further contributed to explaining her willingness to partake in the crime. The court also mentioned that the "initiator" for committing the crime was Halstein and due to their dependent relationship, it would have been difficult for Marianne to refuse to hide his crime (Oslo tingrett, 2024, p. 53).

This issue seems closely related to a leader-follower dynamic, where the follower is subordinate to the leader and dependent on him or her (Kremer et al., 2024). The court indicated that Marianne was more of a colluder-follower. As mentioned previously in the literature review, colluders are the active kind of followers who want to contribute to the leaders' goals, while conformers are prone to obedience and do not engage in crime alone (Thoroughgood et al., 2012). While previous steps showed Marianne as more of a conformer who passively took part in the crime out of obedience to her strong, leading husband, the court assumed that Marianne had more of a self-interest in participating and contributing in the crime due to both having the same financial interest and therefore she was more of an active follower.

This also gives support to the findings that followers can be more leading of nature and work in alliances with the leader as they see a reward for themselves. A follower who is opportunist will be easy to convince if they see a clear benefit for themselves. Thoroughgood et al. (2012, p. 909) provided an example of Andrew Fasto, Enron's CFO, being an opportunist-colluder who manipulated financial records to hide losses and make the company look more successful to satisfy his drive for ambition and greed. This example is similar to Marianne Sjølie who did hide her husband's fraud and embezzlement in the attorney firm's accounts to prevent outsiders from detecting it. From the court verdict it seems to be that the judges believe Marianne had a desire for more as she was a co-owner of the hotels and other real estate projects, and supporting her leader in the crime would help them both in achieving their personal goals and made her more willing to comply with her husband and follow along into the criminal activities.

8 Conclusion

In the present case the initial vision came from the leader; however, it could also be that the follower or followers come up with visionary ideas in which the leader buys in.

Based on a single case, the generalizability of the present analysis and interpretation is obviously limited. The case study with its research propositions serves as anecdotal evidence of a human phenomenon of barriers to changing direction and correcting mistakes when in a professional and personal relationship. While the present research reveals some potential dynamics between a leader and a follower in a criminal setting (and in our perception: the most important ones), it cannot claim that these dynamics are all-embracing. Rather they should be considered as a starting point to further unfold in future research the dynamics between partners in crime.

It is important to mention here that in every democratic society with criminal justice, a charged and indicted defendant should have the benefit of the doubt. Until a final verdict is passed regarding guilt, the person is to be considered innocent. Guilt has to be proven beyond any reasonable and sensible doubt before the court can pass a sentence. If there is reasonable and sensible doubt, then the defendant is to be acquitted. At the time of writing this article, the accused wife was in the criminal justice system, but she had not yet received any verdict from the district court and not yet experienced any appeal of that verdict. A final verdict – especially if the case ends up in Norwegian Supreme Court – might not emerge until 2027 or 2028. At the time of finishing this chapter, the district court published the sentence: Marianne Sjølie was convicted to 3 years in prison (Aasen, 2024; Bjørndal & Mikalsen, 2024).

The in-depth case study presented in this chapter regarding partners in crime served the purpose of linking a number of theoretical perspectives to shed light on a leader-follower phenomenon in misconduct and crime. In a small business such a small law firm, exemplified by the case of a law firm with only the husband working as a lawyer and the wife working as an accountant, oversight and guardianship is of importance to prevent economic misconduct and crime. While the two persons in the firm share the same vision and work accordingly, someone else needs to review the business from outside. Typically, this is the role of an external auditor. In addition, given the client-attorney privilege for law firm business, there is a need to counter this form of secrecy with some form of transparency.

References

Aasen, E. S. (2024). Marianne Sjølie dømt til fengsel for grov hvitvasking: -Hun er svært skuffet (Marianne Sjølie convicted of serious money laundering: -She is very disappointed), daily local newspaper *Moss Avis*, www.moss-avis.no, published June 14.

Agnew, R. (2014). Social concern and crime: Moving beyond the assumption of simple self-interest. *Criminology*, *52*(1), 1–32.

Asting, C., & Gottschalk, P. (2023). Attorney fraud in the law firm: A case study of crime convenience theory and crime signal detection theory. *Deviant Behavior*, *44*(4), 591–602.

Baird, J. E., & Zelin, R. C. (2009). An examination of the impact of obedience pressure on perceptions of fraudulent acts and the likelihood of committing occupational fraud. *Journal of Forensic Studies in Accounting and Business*, *1*(1), 1–14.

Birtch, T. A., Cai, Z., & Chiang, F. F. T. (2024). Effects of formal mentoring support on newcomer-protégé affective organizational commitment: A self-concept-based perspective. *Human Resource Management*, *63*(2), 225–242.

Bjørndal, B. (2024a). Advokatassistent nekter straffskyld for hvitvasking av 65 millioner kroner (Lawyer assistant denies criminal liability for money laundering of NOK 65 million), daily Norwegian business newspaper *Dagens Næringsliv*, Thursday, April 11, page 11.

Bjørndal, B. (2024b). –Jeg har mistet alt. Arbeidsplassen min, kolleger og huset (-I have lost everything. My workplace, colleagues and the house), daily Norwegian business newspaper Dagens Næringsliv, *Saturday*, April 13, pages 10–11.

Bjørndal, B., & Mikalsen, B.E. (2024). Advokatassistent dømt for hvitvasking (Attorney assitant convicted of money laundering), daily Norwegian business newspaper *Dagens Næringsliv*, www.dn.no, published June 14.

Braaten, C. N., & Vaughn, M.S. (2021). Convenience theory of cryptocurrency crime: A content analysis of U.S. federal court decisions. *Deviant Behavior*, *42*(8), 958–978.

Brands, R. A., & Mehra, A. (2019). Gender, brokerage, and performance: A construal approach. *Academy of Management Journal*, *62*(1), 196–219.

Burrai, E., Xavier, F., & Cochraine, J. (2015). Destination stakeholders' perceptions of volunteer tourism: An equity theory approach. *International Journal of Tourism Research*, *17*, 451–459.

Chan, F., & Gibbs, C. (2022). When guardians become offenders: Understanding guardian capability through the lens of corporate crime. *Criminology*, 60, 321–341.

Cressey, D. (1972). *Criminal organization: Its elementary forms*. New York, NY: Harper and Row.

Dion, M. (2020). Bribery, extortion and "morally ambiguous" leadership in organizations, *Journal of Financial Crime*, *27*(4), 1027–1046.

Dodge, M. (2007). Women who commit white-collar crimes. In H.N. Pontell and G. Geis (editors), *International handbook of white-collar and corporate crime* (pp. 379–405). New York, NY: Springer Science.

Dodge, M. (2009). *Women and white-collar crime*. Saddle River, NJ: Prentice Hall.

Dodge, M. (2019). Women and white-collar crime, in: *Oxford Encyclopedia of Criminology and Criminal Justice*, doi.org/10.1093/acrefore/9780190264079.013.493.

Ferraro, F., Pfeffer, J., & Sutton, R.I. (2005). Economics language and assumptions: How theories can become self-fulfilling. *Academy of Management Review*, *30*(1), 8–24.

Gao, P., & Zhang, G. (2019). Accounting manipulation, peer pressure, and internal control. *The Accounting Review*, *94*(1), 127–151.

Gottschalk, P. (2017). Convenience in white-collar crime: Introducing a core concept. *Deviant Behavior*, *38*(5), 605–619.

Gottschalk, P. (2022). Gender and crime: Convenience for pink-collar offenders. *Deviant Behavior*, *43*(2), 213–227.

Gottschalk, P. (2023). Trusted chief executives in convenient white-collar crime. *Crime & Delinquency*, 1–29, published online doi 10.1177/00111287221104737.

Gran, J. (2023). Rettssaken mot Marianne Sjølie skal gå i Oslo (The trial against Marianne Sjølie will be held in Oslo), local daily Norwegian newspaper *Moss Avis*, www.moss-avis.no, published November 17.

Gupta, C. M., Gottschalk, P., & Kamaei, M. (2023). Role of gender in white-collar crime: An examination of the emancipation and focal concern hypothesis. *Journal of Financial Crime*, *31*(4), 849–863.

Holtfreter, K. (2015). General theory, gender-specific theory, and white-collar crime. *Journal of Financial Crime*, *22*(4), 422–431.

Kakkar, H., Sivanathan, N., & Globel, M.S. (2020). Fall from grace: The role of dominance and prestige in punishment of high-status actors. *Academy of Management Journal*, *63*(2), 530–553.

Karimi-Ghartemani, S., Khani, N., & Isfahani, A.N. (2022). Designing a conceptual model for organizational stupidity using a combination of grounded theory and interpretive structural modeling. *Iranian Journal of Management Studies*, *15*(3), 549–568.

Kipfelsberger, P., & Gottschalk, P. (2025). The transfer of meaningfulness from leaders to followers as partners in crime: The case of a married lawyer and his accountant wife in embezzlement and money laundering. *Deviant Behavior*, published first online.

Kipfelsberger, P., Raes, A., Herhausen, D., Kark, R., & Bruch, H. (2022). Start with why: The transfer of work meaningfulness from leaders to followers and the role of dyadic tenure. *Journal of Organizational Behavio*r, 43(8), 1287–1309.

Klenowski, P. M., Copes, H., & Mullins, C. W. (2011). Gender, identity, and accounts: How white-collar offenders do gender when making sense of their crime. *Justice Quarterly*, *28*(1), 46–69.

Kremer, H., Villamor, I., & Ormiston, M. (2024). The ripple effect: When leader self-group distancing responses affect subordinate career trajectories. *Journal of Business Ethi*cs, 195, 813–829.

Losnegård, A. S. (2023). Kona til Halstein Sjølie er tiltalt for å ha skjult i underkant av 65 millioner kroner av underlaget fra klientmidler (The wife of Halstein Sjølie is charged with concealing just under NOK 65 million of the embezzlement from client funds), *AdvokatWatch*, www.advokatwatch.no, published October 13.

Mawritz, M. B., Greenbaum, R. L., Butts, M. M., & Graham, K.A. (2017). I just can't control myself: A self-regulation perspective on the abuse of deviant employees. *Academy of Management Journal*, 60(4), 1482–1503.

Muri, S. F. (2024). *The accomplice in crime: Exploring the spouse's alleged involvement in white-collar crime and deviant behavior*. Master thesis, BI Norwegian Business School, Oslo, Norway, 88 pages.

Murphy, P. R., & Free, C. (2015). Broadening the fraud triangle: Instrumental climate and fraud. *Behavioral Research in Accounting*, *28*(1), 41–56.

Oslo tingrett (2021). Court case number 21-126664ENE-TOSL/03, trial September 22, verdict October 1, *Oslo tingrett (Oslo District Court)*, judge Toini Oulie-Hauge, 26 pages, Oslo, Norway.

Oslo tingrett (2024). Court case number 23-163067MED-TOSL/02, trial April 2024, verdict June 14, *Oslo tingrett (Oslo District Court)*, jugde Nini Ring, 61 pages, Oslo, Norway.

Padavic, I., Ely, R. J., & Reid, E. M. (2020). Explaining the persistence of gender inequality: The work-family narrative as a social defense against the 24/7 work culture. *Administrative Science Quarterl*y, 65(1), 61–111.

Peng, J., Hou, N., Zou, Y., & Long, R. (2023). Participative leadership and employees' cyberloafing: A self-concept-based theory perspective. *Information & Manageme*nt, 60(8), 103878.

Rashidian, C., & Archie, K. (2025). A multi-theoretical approach to understanding the Tom Girardi embezzlement scheme: Integrating convenience theory, game theory, and social network theory. *Proceedings of the 58th Hawaii International Conference on Systems Sciences*, 6607–6616.

Ravn, L. K. (2023). Advokaten innrømmet all skyld – nå er også kona tiltalt (The lawyer admitted all guilt – now the wife is also charged), daily Norwegian business newspaper *Dagens Næringsliv*, Saturday, October 14, page 12.

Ruhland, E. L., & Selzer, M. (2020). Gender differences in white-collar offending and supervision. *Criminal Justice Studi*es, 33(1), 13–30.

Saad, N. A., Othman, S. Z., & Noor, W. S. W. M. (2022a). Exploring the characteristics of white-collar criminals: A cross-case analysis. *Asian Journal of Research in Business and Management*, *4*(3), 423–431.

Saad, N. A., Othman, S. Z., & Noor, W. S. W. M. (2022b). Does individual personality contribute to the occurences of white-collar crime? A qualitative study. *Journal of Social Sciences and Humanities*, *1*(6), 53–57.

Schoen, J. L., DeSimone, J. A., Meyer, R. D., Schnure, K. A., & LeBreton, J. M. (2021). Identifying, defining, and measuring justification mechanisms: The implicit biases underlying individual differences. *Journal of Management*, *47*(3), 716–744.

Sims, R. L., & Barreto, T. S. (2022). In defense of leader misconduct: The use of neutralization techniques by ingroup members. *The Journal of Social Psychology*, *162*(5), 621–639.

Spurkland, M. (2021). *Ut av krisen: Beretninger om sammenbrudd og tilsynelatende håpløshet, men også om mot og den ukjente styrken som bor i oss alle (Out of the Crisis: Reports of Collapse and Apparent Hopelessness, but also about the Courage and the Unknown Strength that Lives in All of Us)*, Cappelen Damm publishing, Oslo, Norway.

Srivastava, S. B., & Goldberg, A. (2017). Language as a window into culture. *California Management* Review, 60(1), 56–69.

Steffensmeier, D., Schwartz, J., & Roche, M. (2013). Gender and twenty-first-century corporate crime: Female involvement and the gender gap in Enron-era corporate fraud. *American Sociological Re*view, 78(3), 448–476.

Sugiyama, K., Ladge, J. J., & Dokko, G. (2024). Stable anchors and dynamic evolution: A paradox theory of career identity maintenance and change. *Academy of Management Review*, *49*(1), 135–154.

Szalma, J. L., & Hancock, P. A. (2013) A signal improvement to signal detection analysis: fuzzy SDT on the ROCs. *Journal of Experimental Psychology: Human Perception and Performance*, *39*(6), 1741–1762.

Thoroughgood, C. N., Padilla, A., Hunter, S. T., & Tate, B. W. (2012). The susceptible circle: A taxonomy of followers associated with destructive leadership. *The Leadership Quarterly*, *23*, 897–917.

Wheelock, D., Semukhina, O., & Demidov, N.N. (2011). Perceived group threat and punitive attitudes in Russia and the United States. *British Journal of Criminol*ogy, 51, 937–959.

Anita Zehrer and Martin Pfaffinger

The Adaptive Capacity of Tourism Family Firms – An Owners' Perspective on Risk Resilience

Abstract: Despite the growing interest in resilience in family businesses, the current literature overlooks the contribution of owners to the exercise of resilience, i.e. there is only limited systematic evidence on how family business owners manage and cope with crises. This study investigates how family business owners perceive, strengthen and maintain their resilience when facing entrepreneurial challenges and risks. Using semi-structured interviews, we show that sustainable investments, employee commitment, quick adjustments during crises and diversification of offerings are key strategies to strengthen resilience. Additionally, close bonding and continuous training of employees enhance their loyalty and contribute positively to the stability of the business. Finally, the findings provide practical recommendations for family businesses.

Keywords: Resilience, Adaptive capacity, Family business owners

1 Introduction

Tourism is a vital economic sector for many countries. It significantly contributes to national wealth (Glaesser, 2005). However, its complex and interconnected structure makes it highly susceptible to crises and disasters (Aliperti et al., 2019). The effects of such crises on tourism are multifaceted and extensive (Backer & Ritchie, 2017). Preparing for these disruptions is challenging, but it must be done. External crises bring unexpected changes that businesses struggle to control (Faulkner, 2001).

A business' ability to recover from crises hinges on its resilience. Resilient businesses are better equipped to respond to unforeseen situations through enhanced operational flexibility (Prayag, 2018). The growing complexity and dynamics of modern tourism – shaped by structural changes, political and economic crises, and climate change – require a stronger focus on crisis management within the industry. Consequently, negative events, crises and disasters present new strategic and operational challenges for tourism (Glaesser, 2005; Siller & Zehrer, 2016; Zehrer & Mössenlechner, 2010).

Family businesses are the backbone of the economy, particularly in German-speaking regions, where they make up about 80% of all companies (Felden et al., 2019). In Austria alone, 157,000 family businesses employ nearly 1.8 million people and generate around 393.5 billion euros in revenue. This encompasses both small enterprises and globally successful corporations. The tourism industry is 70% family-owned. (KMU Forschung Austria, online)

https://doi.org/10.1515/9783110790344-008

Family businesses face unique challenges in crises due to the influence of the entrepreneur's family, which can impact the crisis process both positively and negatively (Gómez-Mejía et al., 2007; Großmann & Schlippe, 2015; Rüsen, 2009). High levels of family ownership often result in a lack of adherence to formal crisis' procedures (Faghfouri et al., 2015). These businesses prioritise long-term survival over short-term profits, valuing the preservation of the family legacy (Kraus et al., 2020; Lins, Volpin & Wagner, 2013). Emotional ties to the business also shape family members' crisis responses, setting family firms apart from other types of businesses (Arrondo-García, et al. 2016; Anderson & Reeb, 2003). Family businesses are more resilient than other forms, and this quality is essential for success in today's uncertain environment (Chrisman et al., 2011; Beech et al., 2020; Luthe & Wyss, 2014). Long-established family firms, in particular, demonstrate impressive longevity (Bertrand & Schoar, 2006). However, despite the prominence of family-owned SMEs in tourism, there is a clear need for more research on their crisis management and the role of the owner respectively (Kraus et al., 2020; Toubes et al., 2020).

2 Literature Review

A systematic literature review is undertaken for family firms, crises and resilience including the different types of resilience as well as the theory of adaptive cycle to understand owner behaviour in a crisis situation.

2.1 Family Firms

The EU defines a family business as one in which the majority of decision-making rights are held by the owning family (including founders, buyers, heirs, etc.), with at least one family member actively involved in management (EU, online). Davis (1983) characterizes family businesses as shaped by the interplay between family and business systems. Baumgartner (2009) specifies a family business as one managed by a family member, founder, or outsider, with the family holding over 50% of equity. Similarly, Pirmanschegg (2016) views family businesses as economic organizations where an involved family influences business operations and seeks to transfer this influence to future generations. Generally, family businesses are defined by significant family control over ownership and management (Arosa, Iturralde & Maseda, 2010; De Massis et al., 2016; Sciascia & Mazzola, 2008). However, definitions vary widely and lack consistency (Ampenberger, 2010; Chua et al., 2012; Corbetta & Salvato, 2004). Family businesses are marked by close, intensive management and a strong focus on customer relations (Ampenberger, 2010). Family members typically hold key leadership and management roles (Anderson & Reeb, 2003), values like reliability and familiarity, reinforced through personal interactions with stakeholders, shape their corporate culture (Gehrig & Lux, 2020). The main objective of family businesses is ensuring sustainable succession to the next generation (Siller et al., 2016).

2.2 Crises

A crisis involves unexpected changes that companies frequently have limited control over (Faulkner, 2001). In today's complex world, vulnerabilities to crises increase as natural and human-induced crises become less distinct (Capra, 1996). The tourism industry is particularly susceptible, underscoring the need for thorough preparation (Aliperti et al., 2019; Pforr & Hosie, 2008). Since 9/11, organizations have encountered an escalating variety of crises, threats, and dangers (Glaesser, 2005; Pforr & Hosie, 2008; Tarlow, 2014), such as COVID-19 (Kraus et al., 2020). These can strike unexpectedly, highlighting the critical role of crisis management in tourism (Dwyer & Čavlek, 2019; Lerbinger, 2012).

The term "crisis" originates from the Greek "krisis," meaning distinction or decision (Glaesser, 2005). It is interpreted differently across fields, from finance and management to employee relations (Hale et al., 2005; Elliott et al., 2005), without a universally accepted definition. Generally, a crisis is an unexpected event that disrupts normal operations and demands leadership intervention (Faulkner, 2001; Ghaderi et al., 2012; Pforr & Hosie, 2008). Effective responses can reduce damage and help restore stability, though severe crises may endanger a company's survival (Ghaderi et al., 2012). While "crisis" and "catastrophe" are often used interchangeably (Faulkner, 2001; Kim & Lee, 1998), they differ: catastrophes typically arise from external forces like extreme weather, whereas organizational crises stem from internal tensions, which are sometimes manageable and avoidable (Faulkner, 2001; Ghaderi et al., 2012).

2.3 Crises in Family Firms

Family-run businesses often forgo formal crisis procedures, prioritizing family interests and assets even during crises (Faghfouri et al., 2015). Focused on long-term survival, family members are typically willing to sacrifice short-term profits to preserve the family legacy (Kraus et al., 2020; Lins, et al. 2013; Minichilli, et al., 2016). Their strong emotional attachment to the business shapes their responses to crises (Berrone et al., 2012; Arrondo-García, et al. 2016). This emotional connection and commitment to long-term goals set family businesses apart from non-family firms (Anderson & Reeb, 2003; Lumpkin, Brigham & Moss, 2010; Zahra, Hayton & Salvato, 2004). However, conflicts and disharmony within family-run businesses can adversely impact operations (Corbetta &Salvato, 2012). The blending of personal and professional life often generates tension (Ortín García et al., 2018), making the workplace atmosphere vulnerable and potentially affecting employees (Chrisman et al., 2012). Issues such as inheritance disputes, parental divorce, and the involvement of siblings' partners can further strain the business (Sanchez-Ruiz et al., 2018). In the hospitality and tourism sector, particularly during peak seasons, the intense demands push family members to their mental and physical limits (Zehrer & Siller, 2007). Additionally, resistance to external changes can create rigidity, as traditional practices may narrow perspectives on adapting to market shifts (Felden et al., 2019). Internal conflicts often arise from the complex interplay between family and business roles (Habbershon & Williams, 1999; Kellermanns & Eddleston, 2004).

2.4 Resilience

Resilience is widely studied across disciplines such as psychology, social sciences, and engineering (Folke & Gunderson, 2010; Klein, et al. 2003; Lee, et al., 2013; Martin-Breen & Anderies, 2011; Eiser et al., 2012) and applied in various contexts (Keenan, 2020; Schwaiger & Zehrer, 2020). Derived from the Latin word "resilire," meaning "to spring back" (Xiao & Cao, 2017), resilience also refers to preventing businesses from repeating past weaknesses (Esnard, 2013). The concept originated in ecology and engineering, where it describes a system's ability to recover from disturbances while maintaining its core functions and structure (Beech et al., 2020; Berbés-Blázquez & Scott, 2017; Hall et al., 2017; Schwaiger & Zehrer, 2020; Smith et al., 2008; Tsao & Ni, 2016). Across various fields—ecology (Walker & Cooper, 2011), engineering (Hollnagel et al., 2012), psychology (Powley, 2009), and organizational management (Gilbert et al., 2012) – resilience is interpreted and developed differently. Its interdisciplinary application has led to multiple dimensions of resilience, all aimed at ensuring a system's survival and adaptability in the face of disturbances.

Resilience differs from flexibility, agility, and robustness (Duchek, 2020). While flexibility and agility are vital for managing everyday challenges, resilience is key to addressing unexpected and severe crises (Lengnick-Hall et al., 2011). It also involves the ability to adapt, enabling businesses to emerge stronger from crises (Madni & Jackson, 2009). In contrast, robustness refers to a system's capacity to maintain functionality despite disturbances (Kitano, 2004). Unlike traditional crisis management, resilience posits that systems can adapt, respond, and evolve in the face of both extraordinary events and gradual changes (Prayag, 2018). This perspective provides an alternative, often more effective approach to understanding how systems cope with various adversities (Prayag, 2018).

Resilience is a multifaceted concept, typically categorized into three types. *Personal resilience* refers to an individual's ability to adapt to challenges and emerge stronger. Entrepreneurs, in particular, require high personal resilience to navigate the constant challenges that affect their business survival (Portuguez Castro & Gómez Zermeño, 2021). Resilient entrepreneurs demonstrate a high tolerance for uncertainty, adapt swiftly to change, leverage difficult situations to their advantage, and learn from their mistakes (Ayala & Manzano, 2014). This adaptability is crucial for long-term business success. Smith et al. (2008) define personal resilience as the ability to recover, resist illness, and adapt to stress or adversity. Garcia-Dia et al. (2013) describe it as the capacity to recover, adapt, and even thrive following misfortune. Kalisch et al. (2015) emphasize that resilience is observable when an individual does not develop lasting mental health issues despite adverse conditions. Taormina (2015) views it as a multifaceted construct that encompasses determination, endurance, and the ability to adapt and recover from adversity.

Organizational resilience refers to an organization's ability to manage unexpected events, recover from crises, and ensure long-term success (Duchek, 2020). In times of increasing volatility and uncertainty, this resilience becomes especially critical. Companies must have the right resources—such as financial reserves, assets, and strong relationships—to support their resilience (Duchek et al., 2020). Diversity is essential, as varied perspectives and skills enhance adaptability and innovation (Hong & Page, 2004). Somers (2009) emphasizes that organizational resilience is not just about survival; it also involves identifying risks and taking proactive measures to ensure growth despite adversity. Lengnick-Hall et al. (2011) define it as an organization's ability to absorb disruptions, develop context-specific responses, and engage in transformative actions to turn disruptions into opportunities. Ortiz-de-Mandojana and Bansal (2016) describe resilience as an organization's incremental ability to anticipate and adjust to environmental changes. Xiao and Cao (2017) characterize it as the ability to restore to its original state and even acquire new skills in the face of disruptions.

Interorganizational Resilience, also known as network or industry resilience, refers to the collective ability of communities or industries to respond to complex ecological, political, and socioeconomic changes (Faulkner et al., 2018). Foster (2006) defines regional resilience as a region's capacity to anticipate, prepare for, respond to, and recover from disturbances. Hill et al. (2008) emphasize the importance of a region's ability to recover from economic shocks that could disrupt its growth trajectory. Briguglio (2016) describes economic resilience as the extent to which an economy can withstand or manage the negative effects of external shocks. Brinkmann et al. (2017) define industry resilience as an economy's ability to prepare for crises, mitigate immediate impacts, and adapt to changing conditions. Resilience in this context is shaped by interactions within a complex system, governing the mechanisms through which resilience occurs (Matin & Taylor, 2015). A rapid industry response to changes and shocks is vital for a country's economic development, highlighting the importance of innovation and adaptability (Aldianto et al., 2021).

3 Empirical Study

3.1 Methodology

The sample comprises thirteen owners of 3-star and 4-star family-run hotel businesses in Salzburg, Austria. All businesses are founded in Salzburg, operate within the hotel industry, and qualify as family businesses. Most interviews were conducted on-site, with some held digitally or via phone. All interviews were recorded and transcribed. Transcripts followed the simplified transcription system of Dresing and Pehl (2020), rendering them verbatim rather than paraphrased. Participants provided consent for data processing through a consent form. The interviews were analyzed using transcription-based qualitative content analysis following Mayring (2022). The sample is presented in Table 1.

Table 1: Sample overview (own illustration).

Respondent	Star rating	No. of rooms	generation
1	4*	23	Gen Y
2	3*	15	Gen X
3	4*	32	Gen X
4	3*	16	Gen Y
5	4*	20	Gen X
6	4*	23	Gen Y
7	3*	15	Gen Y
8	3*	38	Gen Y
9	4*	85	Gen X
10	3*	22	Gen Y
11	3*	14	Gen Y
12	4*	95	Gen X
13	4*	26	Gen Y

3.2 Main Results

An inductive approach was used for category development, where categories were derived directly from the data and classified based on a coding guide. Each code in the guide included a definition, an anchor example, and a coding rule to ensure clarity in the process. The text material was coded by assigning statements to the relevant codes. After coding 4 out of the 13 interviews (approximately 25%), the codes were reviewed for relevance and their interrelationships. Minor adjustments were made to ensure content consistency. In total, 15 codes were derived, as outlined below.

Hotel operators employ various *strategies to mitigate risks*, with a central focus on sustainable investments in technology and infrastructure. One operator stated,

> We have invested in sustainable concepts in advance, namely photovoltaic, biomass heating, our own water supply, and similar initiatives. (Hotel 9/16)

These investments have proven effective in reducing operating costs and minimizing environmental impact. Another owner emphasized the importance of sustainable operations:

> We have invested in renewable energy and water treatment to become more independent and environmentally friendly in the long term. (12/56)

Another key aspect of risk management is fostering strong bonds with employees and ensuring continuous training. One respondent shared:

> We kept all employees registered because we wanted to maintain cohesion within the company. This helped us be stronger externally and better manage the crisis. (5/133)

Another noted,

> It's important to be well-prepared financially. We have built up reserves to react flexibly in times of crisis. (7/211)

These measures not only enhance employee loyalty but also contribute positively to the business' stability.

In response to unexpected crises like the COVID-19 pandemic, *quick adjustments and measures* were necessary to ensure business continuity. One owner explained:

> During the pandemic, we put all employees on short-time work, but none were laid off. (13/37)

This swift response helped maintain stability during the crisis, highlighting the importance of flexibility and rapid action in minimizing the pandemic's impact. Another operator, underlining the critical role of clear communication during a crisis, emphasized:

> We focused on communication and transparency to maintain the trust of our guests. (11/145)

Another respondent shared:

> We made our website more dynamic and increased our presence on social media to keep our guests continuously informed. (9/65)

These efforts enabled a flexible response to ever-changing conditions and maintained contact with customers. The increased use of digital channels was essential to transparently communicate updated information and safety measures, thus reinforcing guests' trust.

Another operator said:

> We also increasingly relied on digital services, such as online check-in and digital guest directories, to minimize contact and increase safety. (4/52)

Preventive measures aimed at strengthening the long-term resilience of family-run hotel businesses are highly valued. Many businesses have prioritized building financial reserves to ensure flexibility in times of crisis. One operator stated,

> Building reserves and provisions is extremely important, not only in the hotel industry. (2/176)

These financial reserves have been essential in ensuring the stability of the business and providing a solid foundation for managing future challenges. In addition to financial preparation, diversification of services plays a critical role in enhancing resilience. As one operator explained:

> We have diversified our offerings to cater to different target groups and spread our risk. (5/132)

This strategy has been effective in supporting the long-term stability of the business. By expanding the range of services and targeting new customer segments, businesses can reduce their reliance on specific markets, thus strengthening their overall resilience. Another operator noted:

> By diversifying, we can better meet the needs of our guests and are less dependent on individual markets. (8/72)

A *significant competitive advantage* for many family-run tourism businesses lies in their unique resources and characteristics that differentiate them from competitors. One key factor is the value of long-term employees. As one operator mentioned:

> Our long-term employees are a great advantage. They know the business and the guests very well. (12/41)

These long-standing employees contribute significantly to the stability and continuity of the company, bringing their deep experience and understanding of both the business and its clientele. The close relationship between employees and guests helps to build trust, enhancing customer satisfaction, and contributing to the long-term resilience of the business. Another advantage for some family-run hotels is their unique location. One operator highlighted:

> The location is certainly a significant point because it is very central in Austria and in the suburban area of Salzburg, but still in a green area. (9/172)

Another operator added:

> Our location in the middle of the old town is unbeatable. Our guests appreciate the proximity to the sights. (11/96)

While such locations provide a distinct appeal to guests, they also present challenges. For example, structural changes like installing photovoltaic systems may not be feasible due to monument protection laws. Despite these restrictions, businesses leverage their unique historical settings as a marketing advantage, attracting guests who are seeking an authentic stay in a culturally rich and historically significant environment.

Employees play a central role in the risk management strategies and resilience of family-run tourism businesses. One operator emphasized:

> We have many long-term employees who know the company well and are highly committed. (6/82)

This long-term commitment and familiarity with the business foster a sense of loyalty and stability, making employees key contributors to the company's resilience. Another operator, highlighting the personalized service that strengthens customer relationships and enhances business stability, added:

> Because we are still a personal house with nice people, where someone is standing behind the reception desk. (4/130)

To support and maintain this resilience, businesses implement various measures aimed at fostering employee loyalty and satisfaction. These include offering incentives such as employee housing and flexible working hours, which contribute to higher employee retention and satisfaction. Additionally, continuous training is a key strategy to build resilience. One operator explained:

> We place great importance on training our employees so they are always up to date. (7/251)

These training programs not only cover technical aspects of the job but also include crucial skills like crisis management and stress management. This preparation helps employees cope with challenges more effectively and strengthens the overall ability of the business to navigate potential crises.

Family values and the company culture are integral to the resilience of family-run tourism businesses, particularly in times of crisis. One operator, underlining how the close-knit nature of the family business fosters stability, emphasized:

> The family environment is important to us. We have long-term employees who have been with us for years. (12/137)

Another operator, suggesting that the sense of tradition and shared values contributes to both employee loyalty and the company's enduring success, noted:

> I think they appreciate the tradition and the family values that still prevail with us. (5/149)

These values of trust, loyalty, and mutual support form the foundation of the business and significantly impact its operations and resilience. This strong internal culture creates an environment where employees feel a sense of belonging and commitment, which translates into better performance and stability during challenging times. These values also resonate with guests. As one operator put it:

> Our guests appreciate the family atmosphere and the personal attention we offer them. (1/62)

This personalized service, rooted in family values, helps distinguish family-run businesses from larger, more impersonal hotel chains, fostering strong customer satisfaction and loyalty. The combination of a family-oriented work environment and a culture of care and trust enhances the business's ability to overcome crises and maintain long-term success.

The *importance of cooperation and networks* in risk management was a consistent theme across the interviews, highlighting their role in strengthening resilience for family-run tourism businesses. One operator, emphasizing the collaborative approach to managing risks, shared:

> We rely on cooperation with other businesses and networks to strengthen our resilience. (9/124)

Another, illustrating how key service providers and collaborators are crucial for operational flexibility, noted:

> Networking is very important. Generally, we entrepreneurs are totally dependent on plumbers, electricians, to be spontaneous, and I have been doing this for many years. (16/130)

These collaborations provide opportunities for businesses to exchange resources, knowledge, and best practices, which is especially valuable during crises. Moreover, networks support joint marketing strategies and package deals that can increase visibility and attractiveness, helping businesses attract a broader customer base. One operator explained:

> Through cooperation, we can present a stronger front and learn from each other's experiences. (4/75)

This sharing of insights and resources not only offers immediate support but also creates a platform for innovation, allowing businesses to grow and adapt together in the face of challenges. The interconnectedness fostered through networks is vital for building resilience and ensuring long-term success.

The *integration of ecological and social factors* into risk management strategies was a significant theme in the interviews, with many family-run tourism businesses recognizing the dual benefits of sustainability—both as an ethical responsibility and an economic advantage. One operator, highlighting the financial and environmental benefits of sustainable investments, stated:

> We have invested in sustainable technologies to reduce our energy costs and environmental impact. (8/139)

Another manager, showcasing a commitment to environmental stewardship and its potential to mitigate long-term risks, mentioned:

> We have analyzed our CO2 footprint and participate in reforestation and renaturation projects. (1/217)

These sustainability efforts contribute to the long-term resilience of businesses by lowering operating costs, reducing dependence on external energy sources, and aligning with growing consumer preferences for eco-friendly practices. One operator, underlining how sustainability can improve customer satisfaction and loyalty, added:

> Our guests greatly appreciate when we implement environmentally friendly practices. (3/52)

In addition to enhancing brand image, sustainable practices demonstrate a long-term commitment to the future, which positively influences both guests and employees. Overall, these initiatives not only support the resilience of the business but also foster a positive reputation and stronger relationships with customers and the community.

Experiences from past crises, particularly the COVID-19 pandemic, have played a pivotal role in helping family-run tourism businesses develop more robust strategies for future planning. Many operators noted that the lessons learned from the pandemic have been invaluable for refining their approaches to crisis management. One operator, reflecting a proactive stance on adapting to future challenges, explained:

> We have learned from the pandemic and are adjusting our strategies to be better prepared for future crises. (12/32)

Another, emphasizing the learning curve and the importance of experience in crisis preparedness, shared:

> So you definitely know how to do something. It's always the first time. You don't know how to do something and can remember it in the event of a new crisis. (1/208)

These lessons have led businesses to adjust their strategies by improving internal processes, diversifying their offerings, and enhancing financial security to withstand future shocks. One operator, reinforcing the importance of agility in mitigating the effects of crises, highlighted that

> flexibility and quick responsiveness are crucial. (14/193)

Financial strategies and management are critical to ensuring the stability and resilience of family-run hotel businesses, particularly in times of crisis. A common strategy highlighted by operators is the importance of building financial reserves. One operator, illustrating how having savings can provide a safety net, allowing businesses to remain stable even in the face of sudden revenue losses or unforeseen expenses, emphasized:

> We have built up financial reserves to remain operational in times of crisis. (2/181)

This proactive approach to financial security enables businesses to cope with financial storms without compromising their operations. In addition to reserves, cautious investment strategies are also emphasized. As one operator mentioned:

> We invest cautiously and only in projects that make sense in the long term to avoid influencing our financial stability. (6/49)

This careful approach ensures that the company does not overextend itself in ways that could jeopardize its long-term viability. By focusing on investments that align with long-term goals and sustainability, these businesses aim to maintain financial stability, supporting their resilience and ensuring they can navigate both expected and unexpected challenges effectively.

Investments in technology to enhance efficiency and adaptability are essential for building risk resilience. Many businesses rely on modern technologies to optimize operations and respond flexibly to market changes. For example, one company uses a revenue management program to generate forecasts and explore "what-if" scenarios, providing valuable support for decision-making (1/121). This technology allows businesses to adjust prices dynamically based on market demand, maximizing occupancy. Another noted:

> The digitization of our processes has improved efficiency and helps us better meet guest needs. (16/284)

Technological innovations thus boost both operational efficiency and competitiveness.

Customer retention and effective communication are vital for business resilience. Strong communication with guests and maintaining relationships with regular customers foster business stability. As one operator noted:

> We rely heavily on social media to stay in touch with our guests. (6/121)

Another shared:

> I sent out a newsletter after the first lockdown at Easter to keep in touch and inform our guests. (3/175)

These platforms allow businesses to communicate directly with guests, share updates, and respond to feedback. Regular communication, such as newsletters and special offers, reinforces customer loyalty (15/231). An operator explained:

> We listen to our guests' feedback and continuously adapt our offerings to their needs. (12/143)

This ongoing engagement and responsiveness build trust and satisfaction, enhancing long-term stability and resilience.

Intergenerational risk management emerged as a crucial theme in the interviews, with collaboration across generations significantly enhancing risk resilience. One manager observed:

> The collaboration between generations helps us consider different perspectives and make better decisions. (9/148)

Another noted:

> Usually my grandma, my mom, and I are at the table, everyone has a different age, and that is helpful. (16/539)

This intergenerational approach blends traditional and modern risk management practices, creating a more robust and adaptable strategy. In family businesses, the involvement of both younger and older generations combines the experience and stability of the older with the innovation and technological insight of the younger. This synergy enables the creation of well-rounded risk management strategies that address both immediate and long-term challenges.

Meeting and exceeding customer expectations is crucial for a business's long-term resilience. Many operators highlighted the importance of incorporating guest feedback to continuously refine their offerings. As one operator stated:

> We listen to our guests' feedback and continuously adapt our offerings to their needs. (3/356)

Another, emphasizing adaptability to customer priorities, noted:

> The quality doesn't need to be four stars in the old city center; it could be three stars in the periphery. (2/65)

This customer-focused approach builds guest loyalty, which is especially valuable in times of crisis. High service standards and tailored offerings distinguish a business from competitors. One operator shared:

> We ensure our service meets the highest standards and that our guests are satisfied. (5/52)

Such commitment to excellence fosters a loyal customer base that supports the business even in challenging times.

A *willingness to innovate and adapt* is essential for the resilience of family-run tourism businesses. As one operator noted:

> We are always open to new ideas and adapt our strategies to stay competitive. (10/347)

However, another operator highlighted challenges, stating:

> For example, if we need a photovoltaic system, I can forget it due to the monument office and old town preservation board. (4/31)

This openness to change, alongside a commitment to improvement, allows businesses to respond flexibly to challenges. Investment in new technologies and processes also plays a critical role. One operator reported:

> We have invested in modern systems to increase our efficiency and better meet the needs of our guests. (1/164)

These investments not only enhance operations but also improve service quality, boosting guest satisfaction and loyalty.

3.3 Interpretation of Findings

The qualitative content analysis of interviews with 13 hotel owners in Salzburg provides comprehensive insights into the strategies and measures for risk resilience in family-run tourism businesses. This analysis highlights various dimensions of risk management practices and their importance for the long-term stability and adaptability of these businesses.

Regarding ***personal resilience***, the *willingness to innovate and the ability to adap*t to changing conditions are key factors for the resilience of entrepreneurs of family-run tourism businesses. Openness to change and the continuous search for improvement opportunities help businesses respond flexibly to new challenges. Willingness to invest in new technologies and processes is also an important aspect. By continuously adapting to new market conditions and technological developments, entrepreneurs show personal resilience, which can secure their competitiveness of the business in the long term. *Intergenerational risk management* also plays an important role. Collaboration between generations within a company contributes to risk resilience by integrating different perspectives and experiences. Older generations bring experience and proven practices, while younger generations bring new ideas and technological innovation. This synergy of personal resilience across generations promotes the development of comprehensive risk management strategies that can address both short-term and long-term challenges. By involving different generations, businesses can respond more flexibly and innovatively to changes. After succession, succeeding entrepreneurs are often more willing to invest, while they become more cautious later.

Regarding ***organizational resilience***, *sustainable investments and financial reserves* are central elements of risk resilience. Hotel operators emphasize the importance of photovoltaic systems, biomass heating, and their own water supply to reduce operating costs and environmental impact. Such investments contribute to long-term stability and make the businesses more independent of external resources. Financial reserves provide financial security and enable businesses to react flexibly in times of crisis. The cautious investment strategy of only investing in projects that make long-term sense further supports financial stability. These measures ensure both short-term liquidity and long-term financial health by focusing on sustainability and resource independence. The ability to *quickly adapt to unexpected crises*, such as the COVID-19 pandemic, has proven essential. Measures such as short-time work and the use of digital communication channels have allowed businesses to maintain operations and minimize the impact of the crisis. This quick response and adaptation helped manage the crisis effectively. Preventive measures, such as diversifying the offer and building financial reserves, strengthen the long-term resilience of the businesses. By diversifying their services, such as offering farm holidays or seminars, businesses can reduce dependencies on single market segments and increase flexibility. These measures help make the businesses more resilient to future crises. By expanding their services and catering to various customer needs, they create additional income streams and reduce the risk of revenue loss. The *specific resources of the businesses*, particularly long-term employees and unique locations, are critical competitive advantages. Long-term employees know the business and the guests well, contributing to stability and continuity. Employees play a central role in the risk management of the businesses. Long-term employees who know the company well and are highly committed significantly contribute to resilience. Businesses promote this loyalty through continuous training and incentives such as employee housing. Strong employee retention is essential to ensure the stability of the business. By providing training opportunities and additional benefits like housing, companies can increase employee satisfaction and engagement. *Family values and company culture* are also of great importance. Trust, respect, and loyalty create a strong foundation that provides stability in times of crisis. These values shape the company culture and promote long-term loyalty among both employees and guests. A strong family environment and a pronounced company culture help employees and guests identify with the business and commit long-term. *Good communication with guests and strong customer retention* are crucial for business resilience. Social media and digital platforms enable businesses to communicate quickly and directly with their guests. These measures strengthen customer loyalty and promote long-term guest loyalty. Continuously adapting the offer to meet the needs of guests creates trust and satisfaction, contributing to the long-term stability and resilience of the business. This customer orientation is a key factor in successfully navigating crises. Through regular communication and tailored offers, businesses can build strong relationships with their guests and secure their loyalty. Additionally, by using digital media, they can increase their reach and attract new guests.

As regards ***interorganizational resilience*** across the industry, a specific difference between businesses in the old town and those in the surrounding areas lies in *structural possibilities*. While old town hotels cannot install photovoltaic systems or heat pumps due to monument protection, hotels in the surrounding areas do not have these restrictions and can invest accordingly. Nonetheless, old town hotels leverage their central location as an advantage, despite these structural limitations. The historical location of many businesses in the old town offers a unique appeal to guests. An interesting point from the interviews was that three-star hotels had better booking situations in the high season compared to four-star hotels. This indicates that guests are willing to save on accommodation to spend more on sightseeing and activities. This insight can help businesses better plan their pricing strategy and market positioning. The *importance of cooperation and networks* for risk management was clearly evident in the interviews. Collaboration with other tourism businesses and industry associations offers valuable opportunities to strengthen resilience. This cooperation enables the exchange of resources, knowledge, and best practices, which is particularly important in times of crisis. By participating in industry associations and local networks, businesses can benefit from the experiences and knowledge of others and support each other. Additionally, networks promote the development of joint marketing strategies and package deals, which can increase both visibility and attractiveness. This collaboration not only provides support but also a platform for innovation and growth. Cooperation allow businesses to increase their market presence and respond to challenges together, further strengthening their resilience.

4 Summary and Conclusions

The present study on risk resilience in family-run tourism businesses offers valuable insights, but several limitations must be considered. First, a primary limitation is the relatively small sample size of 13 hotel owners, which may not be representative of the entire population of family-run tourism businesses in Salzburg or other regions. Second, the results are based on qualitative interviews, which can be subjective and influenced by the personal opinions and memories of the respondents. Third, the study was conducted at a specific point in time, meaning the results represent a snapshot and may not account for future changes in economic conditions or new crises. Important topics such as specific financial metrics or the precise role of suppliers and partners may not have been sufficiently addressed. Fourth, the generalizability of the findings is limited because the study focuses on family-run tourism businesses, whose structures and challenges may differ from other types of businesses. Fifth, the responses of the interview partners may have been influenced by a desire to provide socially desirable answers.

Despite these limitations, the study offers important insights that should be considered when interpreting the results and applying them to other contexts. As regards *personal resilience*, we found our interview partners show the ability to adapt to challenges that affect their business survival. They also demonstrate a high tolerance for uncertainty, adapt swiftly to change, leverage difficult situations to their advantage, and learn from their mistakes. As regards *organizational resilience*, sustainable investments are crucial for the long-term stability of businesses. Investing in cost-efficient and environmentally friendly technologies, reduces operating costs and increases independence from external energy sources. Financial stability is achieved by systematically building reserves, allowing businesses to respond flexibly during crises. This requires careful financial planning, setting aside profits during good times, and diversifying investment portfolios to spread risk and enhance financial security. Flexible crisis management is essential. Businesses should develop and regularly update emergency plans and provide crisis management training for employees. Effective use of digital communication channels enables transparent and prompt communication with guests, maintaining trust and customer relationships during crises. Diversifying offerings, such as farm holidays and seminars, generates additional income streams and reduces dependence on single market segments. Employee retention and development are vital. Providing continuous training and incentives, fostering a positive work environment, and recognizing employee contributions enhance loyalty and morale. Encouraging innovation and adaptability is key. Businesses should invest in modern technologies, adopt new business models, and enhance customer communication through social media and digital platforms. As regards *interorganizational resilience*, cooperation and networks offer valuable support, allowing businesses to share knowledge, develop joint marketing strategies, and innovate collectively. These strategies ensure resilience and competitiveness in a dynamic market environment.

The findings of this work have significant implications for both theoretical research and practical implementation in family businesses, particularly in the tourism sector. Theoretical underpinnings in literature are complemented and expanded upon by the empirical findings of this thesis. The study shows that family businesses can enhance their resilience through targeted measures, which is an important addition to existing theoretical models. The results suggest that integrating sustainability aspects, promoting employee commitment, and leveraging networks are crucial factors for the long-term stability and success of family businesses. This expands the understanding of how family businesses can improve their resilience to crises and provides new avenues for future theoretical research.

For practical applications, this thesis offers several concrete recommendations that family businesses in the tourism sector can implement to strengthen their resilience. Family businesses should invest in sustainable technologies and infrastructures to reduce operating costs and environmental impact. This not only contributes to financial stability but also enhances brand image and customer loyalty. The close bond and continuous training of employees are crucial for the stability of the business. Measures to increase employee satisfaction, such as flexible working hours and further training opportunities, should be prioritized. Family businesses must be able to respond quickly to unexpected crises, which requires flexible business models and strong internal communication. Utilizing digital channels can be supportive in this regard. Diversifying the range of services can help reduce dependencies on specific market segments and make the business more resilient to market changes. This includes expanding the service portfolio and targeting new customer groups. Collaboration with other businesses and industry associations offers valuable opportunities to strengthen resilience. Networks enable the exchange of resources, knowledge, and best practices, which is particularly beneficial in times of crisis.

In summary, these practical insights provide concrete approaches for family-run tourism businesses to strengthen their resilience and secure long-term stability and competitiveness. Future research could address these limitations and provide a more comprehensive picture of risk resilience in various industries and regions. In summary, this research provides a snapshot of the current situation. Due to the rapid changes in today's world, many factors can quickly evolve, creating new challenges for managers. It is important to consider that many factors are significant when analyzing the results, highlighting the boundaries of the present work. The subjectivity of the author, in particular, influences the selection of literature and interview partners for the empirical study. To obtain more reliable findings, larger, more representative surveys and a combination with quantitative research are necessary.

References

Ampenberger, M. (2010). Unternehmenspolitik in börsennotierten Familienunternehmen. Wiesbaden: Gabler.

Anderson, R. C. & Reeb, D. M. (2003). Founding-Family Ownership and Firm Performance: Evidence from the S&P 500. *The Journal of Finance, 58*(3), 1301–1328.

Aldianto, L., Anggadwita, G., Permatasari, A., Raafaldini, I. & Williamson, I. (2021). Toward a Business Resilience Framework for Startups. Sustainability. 13. 3132.

Aliperti, G., Sandholz, S., Hagenlocher, M., Rizzi, F., Frey, M., & Garschagen, M. (2019). Tourism, crisis, disaster: An interdisciplinary approach. *Annals of Tourism Research, 79*, 102808.

Arosa, B., Iturralde, T. & Maseda, A. (2010). Ownership structure and firm performance in non-listed firms. *Journal of Family Business Strategy, 1*(2), 88–96.

Arrondo-García, R., Fernández-Méndez, C., & Menéndez-Requejo, S. (2016). The growth and performance of family businesses during the global financial crisis: The role of the generation in control. *Journal of Family Business Strategy, 7*(4), 227–237.

Ayala, J. C., & Manzano, G. (2014). The resilience of the entrepreneur. Influence on the success of the business. A longitudinal analysis. Journal of Economic Psychology, *42*, 126–135.

Baumgartner, B. (2009). *Familienunternehmen und Zukunftsgestaltung. Schlüsselfaktoren zur erfolgreichen Unternehmensnachfolge*. Wiesbaden: Springer.

Backer, E, & Ritchie, B.W. (2017). VFR travel: A viable market for tourism crisis and disaster recovery? *International Journal of Tourism Research, 19*(4), 400–411.

Beech, N., Devins, D., Gold, J., & Beech, S. (2020). In the family way: An exploration of family business resilience. *International Journal of Organizational Analysis, 28*(1), 160–182.

Bertrand, M., & Schoar, A. (2006). The role of family in family firms. *Journal of Economic Perspectives, 20*(2), 73–96.

Berrone, P., Cruz, C., & Gomez-Mejia, L. R. (2012). Socioemotional wealth in family firms: Theoretical dimensions, assessment approaches, and agenda for future research. *Family Business Review, 25*(3), 258–279.

Berbés-Blázquez, M., & Scott, D. (2017). The development of resilience thinking. Tourism and Resilience, CABI Wallingford.

Brigham, K. H. & Moss, T. W. (2010). Long-term orientation: Implications for the entrepreneurial orientation and performance of family businesses. *Entrepreneurship & Regional Development, 22*(3/4), 241–264.

Briguglio, L. P. (2016). Exposure to external shocks and economic resilience of countries: evidence from global indicators. *Journal of Economic Studies*, *43*(6), 1057–1078.

Brinkmann, H., Harendt, C., Heinemann, F., & Nover, J. (2017). Ökonomische Resilienz — Schlüsselbegriff für ein neues wirtschaftspolitisches Leitbild? *Wirtschaftsdienst*, *97*(9), 644–650.

Capra, F. (1996). The Web of Life: A New Scientific Understanding of Living Systems. Hamburg: Anchor Publishing.

Chua, J.H., Chrisman, J.J., Steier, J.P., & Rau, S.B. (2012). Sources of heterogeneity in family firms: An introduction. *Entrepreneurship Theory and Practice*, *36*(6), 1103–1113.

Chrisman, J. J., Chua, J. H., Pearson, A. W. & Barnett, T. (2012). Family involvement, family influence and family centered non-economic goals in small firms. *Entrepreneurship Theory and Practice*, *36*(2), 267–293.

Chrisman, J. J., Chua, J. H., & Steier, L. P. (2011). Resilience of family firms: An introduction. *Entrepreneurship Theory and Practice*. *35*(6), 1107–1119.

Corbetta, G., & Salvato, C.A. (2012). *Strategies for longevity in family firms: A European perspective*. London, UK: Palgrave MacMillan.

Corbetta, G., & Salvato, C. A. (2004). The board of directors in family firms: One size fits all? *Family Business Review*, *17*(2), 119–134.

Davis, J. A. & Tagiuri, R. (1989). The influence of life stage on father-son work relationships in family companies. *Family Business Review*, *2*(1), 47–74.

Davis, P. (1983). Realizing the Potential of the Family Business. Organizational Dynamics 12(1), 47–56

De Massis, A., Frattini, F., Kotlar, J., Petruzzelli, A.M., & Wright, M. (2016). Innovation through tradition: lessons from innovative family businesses and directions for future research. *Academy of Management Perspectives*, *30*(1), 93–116.

Dresing, T. & Pehl, T. (2020). Transkription. In Handbuch Qualitative Forschung in der Psychologie (p. 835–854). Springer, Wiesbaden.

Duchek, S., Raetze, S., & Scheuch, I. (2020). The role of diversity in organizational resilience: a theoretical framework. *Business Research*, *13*(2), 387–423.

Dwyer, L. & Čavlek, N. (2019). Economic globalisation and tourism. In D. Timothy (Ed.), Handbook of globalisation and tourism (pp. 12 –26). Edward Elgar Publishing.

Elliott, D., Harris, K., & Baron, S. (2005). Crisis management and services marketing. Journal of Services Marketing, *19*(5), 336–345.

Eiser, J.R., Bostrom, A., Burton, I., Johnston, D.M., McClure, J., Paton, D., van der Pligt, J., & White, M.P. (2012). Risk interpretation and action: A conceptual framework for responses to natural hazards. *International Journal of Disaster Risk Reduction*, *1*(1), 5–16.

Esnard, A.-M. (2013). Taking action in uncertain environments – connecting resilience to hazards. In: Kapucu, N., Hawkins, C.V., & Rivera, F.I. (eds). *Disaster resiliency – interdisciplinary perspectives* (pp.121–125). New York, NY: Routledge.

Faghfouri, P., Kraiczy, N. D., Hack, A., & Kellermanns, F. W. (2015). Ready for a crisis? How supervisory boards affect the formalized crisis procedures of small and medium-sized family firms in Germany. *Review of Managerial Science*, *9*(2), 317–338.

Faulkner, B. (2001) Towards a framework for tourism disaster management. *Tourism Management*, *22*, 135–147.

Faulkner, L., Brown, K., & Quinn, T. (2018). Analyzing community resilience as an emergent property of dynamic social-ecological systems. Ecology and Society, *23*(1), 1–10.

Felden, B., Hack, A., & Hoon, C. (2019). *Management von Familienunternehmen: Besonderheiten – Handlungsfelder – Instrumente*. Wiesbaden: Springer.

Folke, C., & Gunderson, L. (2010). Resilience and global sustainability. *Ecology and Society*, *15*(4), 43.

Foster, K.A. (2006). A Case Study Approach to Understanding Regional Resilience. Working Paper, University of California.

Garcia-Dia, M.J., DiNapoli, J.M., Garcia-Ona, L., Jakubowski, R., O'Flaherty, D. (2013). Concept Analysis: Resilience, Archives of Psychiatric Nursing, *27*(6), 264–270.

Gehring, M. & Lux, W. (2020). Strategisches Controlling für Familienunternehmen. *Controlling & Management Review*, *64*(1), 30–38.

Ghaderi, Z., Mat Som, A. P., & Henderson, J. C. (2012). Tourism crises and island destinations: Experiences in Penang, Malaysia. Tourism Management Perspectives, *2*(3), 79–84.

Gilbert, C., Eyring, M., & Foster, R. N. (2012). Two routes to resilience. *Harvard Business Review*, *90*(12), 65–73.

Glaeßer, D. (2005). *Handbuch Krisenmanagement im Tourismus: Erfolgreiches Entscheiden in schwierigen Situationen*. Berlin: Erich Schmidt GmbH & Co.

Gómez-Mejía, L. R., Haynes, K. T., Núñez-Nickel, M., Jacobson, K. J. L., & Moyano- Fuentes, J. (2007). Socioemotional wealth and business risks in family- controlled firms: Evidence from Spanish olive oil mills. *Administrative Science Quarterly*, *52*(1), 106–137.

Großmann, S., & Schlippe, A. von. (2015). Family businesses: fertile environments for conflict. *Journal of Family Business Management*, *5*(2), 294–314.

Habbershon, T. G., & Williams, M. L. (1999). A Resource-Based Framework for Assessing the Strategic Advantages of Family Firms. Family Business Review, *12*, 1–25.

Hale, J. E., Dulek, R. E., & Hale, D. P. (2005). Crisis response communication challenges: Building theory from qualitative data. Journal of Business Communication, *42*(2), 112–134.

Hall, C. M., Prayag, G., & Amore, A. (2017). Tourism and resilience: Individual, organisational and destination perspectives. In Tourism and Resilience: Individual, Organisational and Destination Perspectives. https://doi.org/10.21832/HALL6300

Hill, E., Wial, H. & Wolman, H. (2008). Exploring Regional Economic Resilience. UC Berkeley, IURD Working Paper Series.

Hong, L., & Page, S. E. (2004). Groups of diverse problem solvers can outperform groups of high-ability problem solvers. *Proceedings of the National Academy of Sciences of the United States of America*, *101*(46), 16385–16389.

Kalisch, R., Müller, M. B., & Tüscher, O. (2015). A conceptual framework for the neurobiological study of resilience. BEHAVIORAL AND BRAIN SCIENCES, *38*, 1–79.

Keenan, J.M. (2020). COVID, Resilience, and the built environment. *Environment Systems & Decisions*, *40*, 216–221.

Kellermanns, F.W. and Eddleston, K.A. (2004) Feuding Families: When Conflict Does a Family Firm Good. Entrepreneurship Theory and Practice, *28*, 209–228.

Kim, P. S., & Lee, J. E. (1998). Emergency management in Korea and its future directions. Journal of Contingencies and Crisis Management, *6*(4), 189–201

Kitano, H. (2004). Biological robustness. Nature Reviews Genetics, *5*(11), 1–7.

Klein, R. J. T., Nicholls, R. J., & Thomalla, F. (2003). Resilience to natural hazards: How useful is this concept? *Environmental Hazards*, *5*(1), 35–45.

Kraus, S., Clauss, T., Breier, M., Gast, J., Zardini, A., & Tiberius, V. (2020). The economics of COVID-19: Initial empirical evidence on how family firms in five European countries cope with the corona crisis. *International Journal of Entrepreneurial Behaviour and Research*, *26*(5), 1067–1092.

Lee, A.V., Vargo, J., & Seville, E. (2013): Developing a tool to measure and compare organizations' resilience. *Natural Hazards Review*, *4*(1), 29–41.

Lengnick-Hall, C. A., Beck, T. E., & Lengnick-Hall, M. L. (2011). Developing a capacity for organizational resilience through strategic human resource management. *Human Resource Management Review*, *21*(3), 243–255.

Lerbinger, O. (2012). The Crisis Manager: Facing Disasters, Conflicts, and Failures. Routledge.

Lew, A. A. (2013). Scale, change and resilience in community tourism planning. *Tourism Geographies*, *16*(1), 14–22.

Lins, K., Volpin, P., & Wagner, H. (2013). Does family control matter? International evidence from the 2008–2009 Financial Crisis. *The Review of Financial Studies*, *26*(10), 2583–2619.

Luthe, T., & Wyss, R. (2014). Assessing and planning resilience in tourism. *Tourism Management*, *44*, 161–163.

Martin-Breen, P., & Anderies, J.M. (2011). Resilience: A literature review. *The Bellagio Initiative*, November.

Matin, N., & Taylor, R. (2015). Emergence of human resilience in coastal ecosystems under environmental change. *Ecology and Society*, *20*(2), 43.

Mayring, P. (2022): Qualitative Inhaltsanalyse. Weinheim/Basel: Beltz Verlag.

Madni, A. M., & Jackson, S. (2009). Towards a conceptual framework for resilience engineering. *IEEE Systems Journal*, *3*(2), 1–12.

Minichilli, A., Brogi, M., & Calabrò, A. (2016). Weathering the storm: Family ownership, governance, and performance through the financial and economic crisis. *Corporate Governance: An International Review*, *24*(6), 552–568.

R.-Toubes, D., Araújo-Vila, N., & Fraiz-Brea, J. A. (2020). Be water my friend: Building a liquid destination through collaborative networks. *Tourism Management Perspectives*, *33*, 100619.

Ortiz-de-Mandojana, N., & Bansal, P. (2016). The long-term benefits of organizational resilience through sustainable business practices. Strategic Management Journal, *37*(8), 1615–1631.

Ortín García, J., Martín, Castejón, Pedro Juan & Pérez Pérez, C. (2018). The culture of conflict in family business. *European Journal of Family Business*, *4*(2), 25–35.

Pforr, C., & Hosie, P. (2008). Crisis management in tourism – preparing for recovery. *Journal of Travel & Tourism Marketing*, *23*, 249–264.

Portuguez Castro, M., & Gómez Zermeño, M. G. (2021). Being an entrepreneur post-COVID-19 – resilience in times of crisis: a systematic literature review. *Journal of Entrepreneurship in Emerging Economies*, *13*(4), 721–746.

Powley, E. H. (2009). Reclaiming resilience and safety: Resilience activation in the critical period of crisis. Human Relations, *62*(9), 1289–1326

Prayag, G. (2018). Symbiotic relationship or not? Understanding resilience and 83 crisis management in tourism. *Tourism Management Perspectives*, *25*, 133.

Pirmanschegg, P. (2016). *Die Nachfolge in Familienunternehmen: Aus Konflikten lernen*. Wiesbaden: Springer.

Rüsen, T. (2009). *Krisen und Krisenmanagement in Familienunternehmen: 84 Schwachstellen erkennen Lösungen erarbeiten Existenzbedrohungen meistern*. Wiesbaden: Springer.

Sanchez-Ruiz, P., Maldonado-Bautista, I.A., & Rutherford, M. (2018). Business stressors, family-business identity, and divorce in family business: A vulnerability-stress-adaptation (VSA) model. *Journal of Family Business Strategy*, *9*(3), 167–179.

Sciascia, S, & Mazzo, P. (2008). Family Involvement in Ownership and Management: Exploring Nonlinear Effects on Performance. *Family Business Review*, *21*(4), 331–345.

Somers, S. (2009). Measuring resilience potential: An adaptive strategy for organizational crisis planning. *Journal of Contingencies and Crisis Management*, *17*(1), 12–23.

Schwaiger, K., & Zehrer, A. (2020). Familienunternehmen: Resilienz in Krisenzeiten. *TourismusWissenQuarterly*, *21*, 210–215.

Siller, H., & Zehrer, A. (2016). *Entrepreneurship & Tourismus. Unternehmerisches Denken und Erfolgskonzepte aus der Praxis*. Wien: Linde Verlag.

Smith, B. W., Dalen, J., Wiggins, K., Tooley, E., Christopher, P., & Bernard, J. (2008). The brief resilience scale: Assessing the ability to bounce back. International Journal of Behavioral Medicine, *15*(3), 194–200.

Tarlow, P. (2014). Reflective epilogue: Concerns in tourism safety. *International Journal of Religious Tourism and Pilgrimage*, *2*(1), 68–70.

Taormina, R. J. (2015). Adult personal resilience: A new theory, new measure, and practical implications. Psychological Thought, *8*(1), 35–46.

Tsao, C. Y., & Ni, C. C. (2016). Vulnerability, resilience, and the adaptive cycle in a crisis-prone tourism community. Tourism Geographies, *18*(1), 80–105.

Walker, J., & Cooper, M. (2011). Genealogies of resilience: From systems ecology to the political economy of crisis adaptation. *Security Dialogue*, *42*(2), 143–160.

Woods, D. D., & Hollnagel, E. (2012). Prologue: Resilience engineering concepts. In E. Hollnagel, D. D. Woods & N. Leveson (Eds.), *Resilience engineering: Concepts and precepts* (pp. 1–8). Boca Raton, RL: CRC Press.

Xiao, L., & Cao, H. (2017). Organizational resilience: The theoretical model and research implication. *ITM Web of Conferences*, 12, 1–4.

Zahra, S., Hayton, J., & Salvato, C. (2004). Entrepreneurship in Family vs. Non-Family Firms: A Resource-Based Analysis of the Effect of Organizational Culture. Entrepreneurship: Theory and Practice, *28*(4), 363–381.

Zehrer, A., & Mössenlechner, C. (2010). Leadership-Kompetenzen in Krisensituationen. In H. Pechlaner, M. Raich, Schön Silvia, & K. Matzler (Eds.), *Change Leadership: Den Wandel antizipieren und aktiv gestalten* (S. 181–209). Wiesbaden: Springer.

Zehrer, A., & Siller, H. (2007). Destination goods as travel motives – the case of the Tirol. Tourism Review, *62*(3/4), 39–46.

Michael Kuttner

Corporate Social Responsibility during the COVID-19 Pandemic: Learnings from Austrian Family Businesses

Abstract: This qualitative study explores the impact of the COVID-19 pandemic on corporate social responsibility (CSR) in ten Austrian family businesses. Results show that CSR and non-financial goals, particularly stakeholder relationships, remained priorities during the COVID-19 pandemic. The integration of financial and non-financial objectives underscores CSR as a long-term investment. While CSR strategies largely remained stable, operational adjustments included a heightened focus on employees, enhanced CSR communication, and the implementation of tools like materiality analyses to better align with stakeholder needs. Key stakeholders (e.g., employees, customers) emerged as critical for building resilience. Furthermore, the results illustrate the high relevance of socioemotional wealth (SEW), which is developed and maintained through CSR and can strengthen resilience. Practical implications suggest family businesses focus on non-financial goals and CSR during crises to enhance resilience. Prioritizing employee well-being, fostering stakeholder trust, and integrating economic considerations into CSR strategies are essential. Future research should examine other industries, organizational forms, and international contexts to deepen understanding of CSR's role in resilience.

Keywords: Corporate Social Responsibility (CSR), COVID-19 Pandemic, Family Business, Resilience, Qualitative Study

1 Introduction

The COVID-19 pandemic is an external crisis that challenges companies of all categories and sizes worldwide (Eggers, 2020; Kraus et al., 2020; Calabrò et al., 2021; Amore et al., 2022; Shan & Tang, 2023). External crises are unexpected situations characterized by devastating adversity (Hällgren et al., 2018). Furthermore, external crises are becoming increasingly unpredictable (Doern et al., 2019) and are only comparable to a limited extent due to their unique specifics (Issah et al., 2023). The COVID-19 pandemic also affects family businesses (Kraus et al., 2020; Calabrò et al., 2021), for which crises often represent dangerous events, as they jeopardize the continued existence of the company (Faghfouri et al., 2015; Kraus et al., 2020; Shan & Tang, 2023).

Family businesses are highly relevant worldwide (Gedajlovic et al., 2012; Sharma et al., 2012; Botero et al., 2015; Rumanko et al., 2021), which also applies to Austria. In Austria, between 51% and 88% of all companies are family businesses (depending on

https://doi.org/10.1515/9783110790344-009

the definition), to which 65% of all Austrian employees can be attributed (WKO, 2023). There is no consensus on the definition of family businesses in literature and practice (Steiger et al., 2015). A frequently used definition comes from *Chua et al.* (1999, p. 25), who describe family business as

> a business governed and/or managed with the intention to shape and pursue the vision of the business held by a dominant coalition controlled by members of the same family or a small number of families in a manner that is potentially sustainable across generations of the family or families.

Within family businesses, non-financial objectives are considered of great relevance, which are discussed in the academic literature under the term *"socioemotional wealth (SEW)"* (Gómez-Mejía et al., 2007; Berrone et al., 2012; Kalm & Gómez-Mejía, 2016).[1] SEW involves the non-financial aspects of the business that satisfy the affective needs of the corporate family, the ability to exert family influence, and the maintenance of the family dynasty (Gómez-Mejía et al., 2007; Kalm & Gómez-Mejía, 2016). SEW also influences companies' ecological, economic, and social responsibility (collectively referred to as corporate social responsibility (CSR)) and is a way for family businesses to maintain or expand their SEW (Izzo & Ciaburri, 2018; Diéguez-Soto et al., 2024). Thus, SEW causes CSR to be organized differently in family businesses than in non-family businesses (Dick et al., 2021; Kuttner et al., 2021; Rudyanto, 2023). For example, image and reputation are highly relevant for family businesses (Dyer & Whetten, 2006; Block & Wagner, 2014), relationships with stakeholders (especially employees) are of great importance (Marques et al., 2014; Kuttner et al., 2021), and CSR measures are predominantly of a long-term nature (Berrone et al., 2012; Kuttner & Fürthner, 2024).

The CSR discussion in relation to crises is also often associated with resilience (e.g., Le Breton-Miller & Miller, 2022; Kuttner & Fürthner, 2024). Following *Duchek* (2020), resilience entails the proactive anticipation of threats, effective coping with adverse events, and the dynamic adaptation to evolving conditions. For example, *Le Breton-Miller & Miller* (2022) highlight that resilience within family businesses is due to the long-term orientation and the desire for continuity and that, for example, reputation, human capital, and networks of relationships help family businesses to survive external crises. However, the authors also mention the negative side and its effects (e.g., corruption).

The case study by *Kuttner & Fürthner* (2024) also illustrates that trusting and long-term stakeholder relationships can contribute to strengthening resilience within a family business. Further results show that the development of resilience within family businesses through ecological, economic, and social responsibility takes time (Mörth & Kuttner, 2024). *Mzid et al.* (2019) also found that social capital in family businesses helps cushion external shocks, reallocate resources, and introduce management prac-

1 Further information on the SEW in family businesses can be found in Jiang et al. (2018), Swab et al. (2020), and Smajić et al. (2023).

tices that promote the handling of future crises. Nevertheless, there remains a gap in research on the relationship between CSR and resilience in family businesses (Kuttner & Fürthner, 2024). Therefore, the following research questions will be answered within the scope of this study:

> *How has the COVID-19 pandemic changed CSR within the investigated family businesses?*
>
> *What relevance do non-financial versus financial objectives have?*
>
> *How has the CSR strategy changed? Has the focus of CSR activities changed?*
>
> *To what extent and how do CSR activities influence resilience to external crises such as the COVID-19 pandemic within the investigated family businesses?*

This study focuses on the short-term effects of the recent COVID-19 pandemic in Austria. As a member state of the European Union and located in the center of Europe, Austria is particularly suitable for this study, as its understanding of CSR in Austria has been significantly shaped by the European Union (Strigl, 2005; Mark-Ungericht & Weiskopf, 2007), and family businesses have always been highly relevant there (WKO, 2023). The results contribute to a better understanding of CSR in family businesses, the influence of external crises on CSR, and the link between CSR and resilience. Several implications for business practice and future research can be derived from the results.

For example, the results show that CSR can support family businesses in overcoming crises and thus contribute to their resilience. Moreover, the results provide examples of how CSR can influence resilience and offer insights into family businesses for interested parties (e.g., future employees, financiers, investors). In particular, the study promotes an understanding of the high relevance of socioemotional factors, such as relationships with internal (e.g., employees) and external stakeholders (e.g., customers, suppliers), as well as image and reputation, which influence CSR on the one hand and contribute significantly to the resilience of family businesses on the other. However, it also becomes apparent that research on the link between CSR and resilience is still in its infancy and that further research is needed. Future studies could, for example, focus on contextual factors such as sectors and company size or confirm or refute the results using quantitative studies.

2 Methodology

The article uses a qualitative research design, in line with previous articles (e.g., Laguir et al., 2016; Kuttner et al., 2021; Kuttner & Fürthner, 2024), which is particularly suitable for answering questions about how and why, as well as for gaining an in-depth understanding of complex situations (Eriksson & Kovalainen, 2015). The results stem from ten Austrian family businesses selected based on personal contacts and online research. Problem-centered interviews were conducted with the managing director or CSR manager, depending on the responsibility for and expertise in CSR in the family business. If a CSR manager was available, they were chosen, as they have CSR expertise and are responsible for CSR strategy, the associated implementation, and the outcomes (Kanashiro & Rivera, 2019). To increase the generalizability of the results, family businesses of different sectors and sizes were included in the study.

The COVID-19 pandemic first emerged in China at the end of 2019. In Austria, the first COVID-19 case was reported in February 2020, and the situation worsened by March 2020, when the first lockdown in Austria (e.g., closure of restaurants and shops except for essential services, restrictions on public life) happened. By May 2020, these measures had been eased again. However, the second COVID-19 wave in Austria began in September 2020, and another lockdown was imposed from November to December 2020. The third lockdown started after Christmas 2020 until the beginning of February 2021. It is also worth mentioning that the vaccination campaign in Austria started at the end of 2020 (Bauer & Egger, 2023). The interviews, which form the basis of this study, were conducted after the peak of the COVID-19 pandemic in Austria, between February and August 2021.[2]

Table 1 illustrates the descriptive data of the case family businesses and the interviewees. The case family businesses belong to different industries (e.g., trade, trade & crafts, information), whereby the manufacturing industry (e.g., metal processing industry, food industry) predominates. The smallest family business has five employees (FB 6), while the largest has around 2,200 (FB 1). The oldest family businesses were founded in 1905 (FB 5) and 1912 (FB 8). Only one family business was established after the turn of the millennium (FB 6). The CSR manager[3] was interviewed in six cases, and the managing director was interviewed in four (five women and five men). The interviews were conducted mostly online, recorded with the consent of the interviewees, and transcribed promptly.

To analyze the data, it is referred to *Thomas*'s (2006) *"general inductive approach."* This data evaluation method offers an easy-to-use systematic approach for analyzing qualitative data to generate meaningful and reliable results. Repeated reading leads to a systematic and successive reduction of the data material to a general level of abstraction to achieve comparable results. Example statements were translated from German into English without changing the basic meaning. In the next chapter, the findings will be presented in line with the research questions and the inductively derived meta categories.

2 The COVID-19 pandemic was not over in Austria at that time. For instance, a fourth lockdown happened from November 2021 to January 2022. Bauer & Egger (2023) published a detailed overview of the measures and lockdowns in Austria.

3 Positions such as sustainability manager, internal communication manager, director of sustainability, and corporate sustainability manager were summarized under the term "CSR manager."

Table 1: Descriptive data of the case family businesses and interviewees.

Case	Sector	Number of employees	Founding year	Interviewee	Gender
FB 1	Trade	~ 2,200	1932	CSR Manager	Female
FB 2	Trade & Crafts	~ 550	1978	CSR Manager	Female
FB 3	Industry	~ 750	1919	CSR Manager	Male
FB 4	Industry	~ 450	1976	CSR Manager	Female
FB 5	Trade & Crafts	~ 400	1905	Managing Director	Male
FB 6	Information	~ 5	2005	Managing Director	Female
FB 7	Industry	~ 100	1945	Managing Director	Male
FB 8	Information	~ 50	1912	Managing Director	Male
FB 9	Industry	~ 950	1976	CSR Manager	Male
FB 10	Industry	~ 500	1988	CSR Manager	Female

3 Findings

3.1 Changes to CSR due to the COVID-19 Pandemic

Despite the COVID-19 pandemic, the non-financial goals within the investigated family businesses remained highly relevant. *CSR Manager 1's* statement can be used as an example:

> It is not only about increasing sales and maximizing profits but also about maintaining a liveable future for following generations (. . .).

The CSR focus of *FB 2* lies primarily on the customer and communication, so that it is recognizable to what extent the family business assumes ecological, economic, and social responsibility. In *FBs 2 and 7*, the high relevance of stakeholder relations and the resulting networks is particularly emphasized in the context of non-financial goals. Similar results emerge from *FBs 4 and 5*, where the relevance of employees is explicitly highlighted, as *Managing Director 6* illustrates by example:

> When you walk through the company and see that the employees are smiling and feel comfortable, that is valuable.

In *FB 6*, the high relevance of non-financial goals and the associated values (e.g., appreciation, fairness) is explicitly mentioned. At the same time, however, it must be stated that these values have existed since the company was founded and are not linked to the COVID-19 pandemic (Managing Director 6). However, the connection with financial goals is frequently mentioned (e.g., FBs 2, 6, 7). Still, the cost factor also plays an important role in achieving non-financial goals, as *CSR Manager 2* notes:

> Of course, costs are associated with goals in terms of what [the CSR measures] are intended to achieve.

Managing Director 6 emphasizes the high relevance of financial goals for future CSR investments and explains:

> (. . .) we need a profit, it doesn't have to be large, but we need it to invest.

Managing Director 7 also emphasizes the necessity of the economic efficiency of CSR measures but also points out the underlying long-term nature of family businesses. CSR measures in *FB 7* sometimes only pay off after several years, which is only possible in an owner-managed family business without an external managing director

> who has to account to anyone else.

Furthermore, the results show a heterogeneous picture regarding the CSR strategy of the case family businesses. Within seven family businesses, the CSR strategy has not changed because of the COVID-19 pandemic (FBs 1, 2, 4, 5, 8, 9, 10), as *CSR Manager 2* confirmed:

> I would say that not much has really changed in terms of the strategic direction. We have simply been confirmed in our direction.

A continuous improvement process is in place in *FB 5,* where the strategy is adapted annually. In this context, *Managing Director 5* explicitly mentions that, due to the COVID-19 pandemic,

> the path has changed, but not the goal.

In *FB 1,* there would have been some initial effects, and only

> projects that are necessary

should have been carried out. However, no changes were made when it became clear that the COVID-19 pandemic was not an existential threat for the mentioned family business (CSR Manager 1). In *FB 10,* CSR was only institutionalized shortly before the COVID-19 pandemic. In this context, it is not possible to assess the strategic changes. Still, *CSR Manager 10* believes that the COVID-19 pandemic has made CSR more relevant for society and that it is also increasingly accepted within the company. However, it should be noted that CSR is an essential part of business activity in all family businesses studied (CSR Manager 10).

The CSR strategy has changed within the *FBs 3, 6, and 7* due to the COVID-19 pandemic and can be seen as a driver for CSR. For example, an even stronger strategic focus was placed on CSR goals (e.g., increasing the share of regional suppliers) (CSR Manager 3). In *FB 6,* a greater focus on CSR was evident due to COVID-19, as illustrated by the statement of *Managing Director 6*:

> We want to contribute to making Austria more sustainable, simply contribute, (. . .) so that all people are doing well.

In *FB 7*, the CSR strategy was adapted due to the COVID-19 pandemic. From the perspective of *Managing Director 7*, pushing for cuts would be the wrong approach. Instead, the CSR and communication strategies must adapt to market changes so that customers recognize this focus and consciously choose the product (Managing Director 7).

Within the analyzed family businesses, there was no reduction in CSR commitment—only *FB 8* reported no changes regarding CSR from an operational perspective, as confirmed by the following statement from *Managing Director 8*:

> I cannot confirm that we have reduced anything.

It should be noted that *FB 8* is already a pioneer and role model in terms of CSR and that its CSR engagement is already at a high level (Managing Director 8). The remaining nine companies reported various operational changes related to CSR. For example, *CSR Manager 1* mentions that specific topics (e.g., sustainability week) could not be implemented due to COVID-19 restrictions. However, other issues without legal restrictions due to COVID-19, such as energy efficiency processes, were implemented as planned (CSR Manager 1). Within *FB* 2, CSR communication with internal employees was strengthened. Due to increased CSR awareness (e.g., preference for regional, biological products), it was necessary to keep customers well informed about CSR measures, which is why employees needed this information more (CSR Manager 2).

Another family business introduced a materiality matrix for CSR activities during COVID-19 to involve stakeholders in an even more targeted way. This materiality matrix clarified that the highest relevance and impact in *FB 3* could be achieved through ecological product innovation, which was implemented accordingly as part of the operational CSR measures (CSR Manager 3). In *FB 10*, climate protection measures were increasingly implemented during COVID-19. However, the main reason was societal pressure (e.g., Fridays for Future) and not COVID-19 (CSR Manager 10). Within *FB 4*, CSR measures were also intensified during COVID-19. However, *CSR Manager 8* attributed this primarily to a change process in the corporate structure and organizational culture, driven by the company's growth:

> We have added 150 new employees since 2019.

Managing Director 7 also points to an increase in CSR measures, justifying this with an economic component:

> We don't really sell [products], but we sell attention.

CSR measures in *FB 7* currently serve to acquire customers and sell products to compensate for the decline in sales (Managing Director 7). Within *FBs 6 and 9*, the increased employee focus as part of the social CSR measures is particularly addressed.

Managing Director 6 explicitly emphasizes the high relevance of treating each other with care. In *FB 9*, certain regulatory requirements had to be implemented in production so that operations could be maintained during COVID-19. Accordingly, social CSR measures regarding employee health and occupational safety were intensified (CSR Manager 9).

3.2 Influence of CSR on Resilience

The results regarding the influence of CSR on resilience to external crises are very homogeneous. In general, all interviewees confirm that CSR can positively influence resilience. The statement by *CSR Manager 3* can be used as an example:

> Sustainable thinking and acting certainly strengthens the company itself, especially in crises.

Managing Director 6 provides another argument, linking CSR with forward-looking action and confirming that CSR

> naturally mitigates crises because I am forward-looking and think about what is coming and can act accordingly. This is resilience.

Moreover, stakeholder relationships are essential for resilience and can be strengthened through CSR measures (FBs 1, 2, 3, 4, 5, 7, 9, 10). *CSR Manager 9* explains the strengthening of stakeholder relationships through CSR measures, particularly in terms of team spirit and solidarity:

> (. . .) moving things forward together, whether it's in corporate giving, reducing CO2 emissions or going rubbish collecting together brings people together, and this team spirit is certainly important in a crisis.

Managing Director 7 also points out the resilience-building effect of CSR measures, as confirmed by the following statement:

> Yes, it builds resilience because the trust of customers, society, the population is simply there.

Within stakeholder relationships, employees in particular are considered to be highly relevant (FBs 1, 2, 4, 7, 8), as *CSR Manager 8* exemplifies:

> CSR gives a certain sense of purpose (. . .) the more sense I can give (. . .) they will probably go that extra mile too.

In this context, *CSR Manager 2* particularly mentions the high relevance of employee retention for resilience:

> (. . .) the company does good things [CSR], and I am valued in the company and looked after by the company. That naturally strengthens employee retention.

Suppliers are also explicitly mentioned as a relevant stakeholder group building up resilience in terms of CSR (FBs 5, 10). *CSR Manager 10* explicitly refers to the security of the supply of raw materials and the necessity of greater diversification of suppliers, which can be achieved through CSR measures and responsible relationship management. *Managing Director 5* argues that reducing supplier dependencies goes hand in hand with responsible behavior:

> Reducing dependencies on Asia is sustainable and at the same time strengthens resilience. It's simply better to work with European partners.

4 Discussion and Summary

Based on a qualitative study, the extent to which the COVID-19 pandemic has changed CSR within ten Austrian family businesses is analyzed. With regard to non-financial goals, the study confirms the high priority of non-financial goals for family businesses even in times of crisis, such as the COVID-19 pandemic. CSR remains a high priority for family businesses during the COVID-19 pandemic. Furthermore, in the context of non-financial goals, maintaining and developing stakeholder relationships is particularly important, focusing on employees and their well-being. However, the integration of financial and non-financial goals is often referred to. The case family businesses emphasize the need to balance the costs of CSR activities and the resulting benefits. However, CSR is also seen as a long-term investment, the outcomes of which are sometimes only visible years later.

The results also show that the strategic direction of CSR has not changed. Most family businesses did not show any significant changes in their CSR strategy due to COVID-19. In some cases, the COVID-19 pandemic acted as a driver for a stronger CSR focus. With regard to the operational level, changes were identified in the vast majority of family businesses. Some CSR measures had to be discontinued due to legal requirements during the lockdown, and others were increasingly prioritized. One example of this is the implementation of energy efficiency and climate measures. During COVID-19, there was also an increased focus on employees in the context of CSR measures. For example, social CSR measures addressing employee health and occupational safety were prioritized. In the area of employee health, in particular, it is questionable to what extent the social idea outweighs the economic benefit or whether legal regulations prescribe the supposedly social measures. Furthermore, the results confirm an increase in CSR communication and the implementation of new instruments, such as materiality analysis, to enhance stakeholder focus and integration.

Moreover, the extent to which CSR influences resilience to external crises was examined. The findings indicate a homogenous picture and acknowledge the positive influence of CSR on resilience. The family businesses analyzed show that CSR is widely recognized as enhancing resilience to the COVID-19 pandemic through forward-thinking strategies, stakeholder relationships, trust, and preparedness for the future. Targeted CSR measures strengthen stakeholder relationships, for instance, by fostering team spirit, solidarity, and trust. With regard to stakeholder relations, it is clear that employees, suppliers, and customers, in particular, are seen as key stakeholders. Thus, CSR strengthens employee retention and motivation and thus increases organizational adaptability as a key factor for resilience. The focus on social CSR measures addressing employees was also observed in Austrian family businesses outside of crises (Kuttner et al., 2021). Moreover, responsible supplier management due to CSR, including diversification and reducing dependencies, can also increase resilience.

Furthermore, the results explicitly highlight the importance of the SEW in the connex of CSR, which is already confirmed by former studies (Gómez-Mejía et al., 2007; Kuttner et al., 2021). The study emphasizes stakeholder relationships, image, and reputation, which are strengthened by CSR measures, indirectly leading to the maintenance and enhancement of SEW and influencing resilience. Several potential fruitful implications for business practice can be derived from the results. The results show that family businesses should also focus on non-financial goals in times of crisis. Maintaining such priorities during crises ensures organizational integrity and contributes to long-term resilience. Secondly, the study's results highlight the high relevance of stakeholder relationships.

Key stakeholders (e.g., employees, suppliers, customers) play a decisive role in resilience. During crises, CSR measures should prioritize employees to foster motivation, loyalty, and trust. Furthermore, CSR initiatives can promote team spirit and solidarity and build a cohesive and committed workforce. Another important aspect is balancing financial and non-financial objectives. While CSR does come at a cost, it should be viewed as a strategic long-term investment. Benefits such as enhanced reputation, stakeholder loyalty, and operational efficiency often outweigh the initial outlay. Family businesses can ensure financial viability and successfully implement environmental and social initiatives by integrating economic considerations into CSR strategies.

The adaptability and flexibility of CSR measures are also crucial. Furthermore, CSR communication is also highly relevant. Targeted, transparent, and consistent communication ensures that internal and external stakeholders are informed about CSR initiatives. Tools such as materiality analysis can help identify stakeholder priorities and enable targeted and effective CSR activities. Finally, CSR should be used as a mechanism to strengthen resilience. By specifically promoting stakeholder relationships, diversifying supplier networks, and reducing dependencies, family businesses can better withstand external crises. Resilience driven by CSR ensures business continuity and strengthens stakeholder trust in uncertain times.

The study illustrates that research on CSR and resilience in family businesses is only at the beginning. Future research could examine other contextual factors (e.g., company size, industry). A comparison of results with family businesses in other countries could also provide new insights. In addition to the need for further qualitative studies to obtain more findings on the linkage between CSR and resilience, future quantitative studies could refute, confirm or expand the existing results. In addition to the study of family businesses, a comparison with other organizational forms (e.g., non-family businesses, non-profit organizations) could also provide new insights.

However, the present study also has limitations. For example, the results only apply in the context of the study and cannot be generalized. Furthermore, a certain subjectivity is associated with the results. On the one hand, the interview partners may have tried to present the company in a better light, and on the other hand, the subjectivity of the author who evaluated the results must be mentioned. Other authors might have come to different conclusions.

References

Amore, M. D., Pelucco, V., & Quarato, F. (2022). Family ownership during the Covid-19 pandemic. *Journal of Banking & Finance*, *135*, 106385.

Bauer, C., & Egger, R. (2023). *Chronologie der COVID-19 Pandemie in Österreich*. Springer VS, Wiesbaden.

Botero, I. C., Cruz, C., Massis, A. D., & Nordqvist, M. (2015). Family business research in the European context. *European Journal of International Management*, *9*(2), 139–159.

Berrone, P., Cruz, C., & Gómez-Mejía, L. R. (2012). Socioemotional wealth in family firms: Theoretical dimensions, assessment approaches, and agenda for future research. *Family Business Review*, *25*(3), 258–279.

Block, J., & Wagner, M. (2014). Ownership versus management effects on corporate social responsibility concerns in large family and founder firms. *Journal of Family Business Strategy*, *5*(4), 339–346.

Calabrò, A., Frank, H., Minichilli, A., & Suess-Reyes, J. (2021). Business families in times of crises: The backbone of family firm resilience and continuity. *Journal of Family Business Strategy*, *12*(2), 100442.

Chua, J. H., Chrisman, J. J., & Sharma, P. (1999). Defining the family business by behavior. *Entrepreneurship Theory and Practice*, *23*(4), 19–39.

Dick, M., Wagner, E., & Pernsteiner, H. (2021). Founder-controlled family firms, overconfidence, and corporate social responsibility engagement: Evidence from survey data. *Family Business Review*, *34*(1), 71–92.

Diéguez-Soto, J., Campos-Valenzuela, M., Callejón-Gil, Á. M., & Aldeanueva-Fernández, I. (2024). Family firm heterogeneity on CSR approach: A socio-emotional (SEW) perspective. *BRQ Business Research Quarterly*, *27*(4), 443–466.

Doern, R., Williams, N., & Vorley, T. (2019). Special issue on entrepreneurship and crises: business as usual? An introduction and review of the literature. *Entrepreneurship & Regional Development*, *31*(5–6), 400–412.

Duchek, S. (2020). Organizational resilience: a capability-based conceptualization. *Business Research*, *13*(1), 215–246.

Dyer Jr, W. G., & Whetten, D. A. (2006). Family firms and social responsibility: Preliminary evidence from the S&P 500. *Entrepreneurship Theory and Practice*, *30*(6), 785–802.

Eggers, F. (2020). Masters of disasters? Challenges and opportunities for SMEs in times of crisis. *Journal of Business Research*, *116*, 199–208.

Eriksson, P. & Kovalainen, A. (2015). *Qualitative methods in business research: A practical guide to social research*. London: Sage.

Faghfouri, P., Kraiczy, N. D., Hack, A., & Kellermanns, F. W. (2015). Ready for a crisis? How supervisory boards affect the formalized crisis procedures of small and medium-sized family firms in Germany. *Review of Managerial Science*, *9*, 317–338.

Gedajlovic, E., Carney, M., Chrisman, J. J., & Kellermanns, F. W. (2012). The adolescence of family firm research: Taking stock and planning for the future. *Journal of Management*, *38*(4), 1010–1037.

Gómez-Mejía, L. R., Haynes, K. T., Núñez-Nickel, M., Jacobson, K. J., & Moyano-Fuentes, J. (2007). Socioemotional wealth and business risks in family-controlled firms: Evidence from Spanish olive oil mills. *Administrative Science Quarterly*, *52*(1), 106–137.

Hällgren, M., Rouleau, L., & De Rond, M. (2018). A matter of life or death: How extreme context research matters for management and organization studies. *Academy of Management Annals*, *12*(1), 111–153.

Issah, W. B., Anwar, M., Clauss, T., & Kraus, S. (2023). Managerial capabilities and strategic renewal in family firms in crisis situations: The moderating role of the founding generation. *Journal of Business Research*, *156*, 113486.

Izzo, M. F., & Ciaburri, M. (2018). Why do they do that? Motives and dimensions of family firms' CSR engagement. *Social Responsibility Journal*, *14*(3), 633–650.

Jiang, D. S., Kellermanns, F. W., Munyon, T. P., & Morris, M. L. (2018). More than meets the eye: A review and future directions for the social psychology of socioemotional wealth. *Family Business Review*, *31*(1), 125–157.

Kalm, M., & Gómez-Mejía, L. R. (2016). Socioemotional wealth preservation in family firms. *Revista de Administração*, *51*, 409–411.

Kanashiro, P., & Rivera, J. (2019). Do chief sustainability officers make companies greener? The moderating role of regulatory pressures. *Journal of Business Ethics*, *155*, 687–701.

Kuttner, M., Feldbauer-Durstmüller, B., & Mitter, C. (2021). Corporate social responsibility in Austrian family firms: Socioemotional wealth and stewardship insights from a qualitative approach. *Journal of Family Business Management*, *11*(2), 238–253.

Kuttner, M., & Fürthner, B. (2024). Corporate social responsibility and COVID-19: A case study of a family-owned printery. *Journal of the International Council for Small Business*, *5*(1), 9–16.

Kraus, S., Clauss, T., Breier, M., Gast, J., Zardini, A., & Tiberius, V. (2020). The economics of COVID-19: initial empirical evidence on how family firms in five European countries cope with the corona crisis. *International Journal of Entrepreneurial Behavior & Research*, *26*(5), 1067–1092.

Laguir, I., Laguir, L., & Elbaz, J. (2016). Are family small-and medium-sized enterprises more socially responsible than nonfamily small-and medium-sized enterprises?. *Corporate Social Responsibility and Environmental Management*, *23*(6), 386–398.

Le Breton-Miller, I., & Miller, D. (2022). Family businesses under COVID-19: Inspiring models–Sometimes. *Journal of Family Business Strategy*, *13*(2), 100452.

Mark-Ungericht, B., & Weiskopf, R. (2007). Filling the empty shell. The public debate on CSR in Austria as a paradigmatic example of a political discourse. *Journal of Business Ethics*, *70*, 285–297.

Marques, P., Presas, P., & Simon, A. (2014). The heterogeneity of family firms in CSR engagement: The role of values. *Family Business Review*, *27*(3), 206–227.

Mörth, T. R., & Kuttner, M. (2024). Developing resilience through sustainability: Qualitative insights from family businesses. *Journal of the International Council for Small Business*, 1–10, https://doi.org/10.1080/26437015.2024.2417015.

Mzid, I., Khachlouf, N., & Soparnot, R. (2019). How does family capital influence the resilience of family firms? *Journal of International Entrepreneurship*, *17*(2), 249–277.

Rudyanto, A. (2023). Socioemotional wealth of family firms during the COVID-19 pandemic: the role of slack resources. *Journal of Family Business Management*, *13*(4), 1320–1342.

Rumanko, B., Lušňáková, Z., Moravanská, M., & Šajbidorová, M. (2021). Succession as a risk process in the survival of a family business – Case of Slovakia. *Journal of Risk and Financial Management*, *14*(10), 458.

Shan, C., & Tang, D. Y. (2023). The value of employee satisfaction in disastrous times: Evidence from COVID-19. *Review of Finance*, *27*(3), 1027–1076.

Sharma, P., Chrisman, J. J., & Gersick, K. E. (2012). 25 years of family business review: reflections on the past and perspectives for the future. *Family Business Review*, *25*(1), 5–15.

Smajić, H., Palalić, R., & Ahmad, N. (2023). Future perspective of socioemotional wealth (SEW) in family businesses. *Journal of Family Business Management*, *13*(4), 923–954.

Steiger, T., Duller, C., & Hiebl, M. R. (2015). No consensus in sight: an analysis of ten years of family business definitions in empirical research studies. *Journal of Enterprising Culture*, *23*(01), 25–62.

Strigl, A. (2005), Concerted action towards sustainable development, in: Habisch, A., Jonker, J., Wegner, M. and Schmidpeter, R. (Eds.), Corporate Social Responsibility across Europe (pp. 125–139). Springer: Berlin.

Swab, R. G., Sherlock, C., Markin, E., & Dibrell, C. (2020). "SEW" what do we know and where do we go? A review of socioemotional wealth and a way forward. *Family Business Review*, *33*(4), 424–445.

Thomas, D. R. (2006). A general inductive approach for analyzing qualitative evaluation data. *American Journal of Evaluation*, *27*(2), 237–246.

WKO (2023). *WKO-Analyse: Familienunternehmen in Österreich*, https://www.wko.at/oe/news/wko-analyse-familienunternehmen-oesterreich, Access: June 10, 2024.

Stefan Märk and Mario Situm

Resilience beyond Metrics: How Hidden Resources in Small Family Firms Challenge the Resource-Based View

Abstract: Family businesses play a key role in economic development and are often analyzed through the Resource-Based View (RBV). However, in small firms, the RBV shows inconsistent explanatory power. This study investigates "hidden resources" such as unpaid family labor and informal commitments, which are typically excluded from financial reporting and RBV metrics. Based on a qualitative case study of a small Austrian family business, findings reveal that nearly 40% of labor is unpaid, artificially inflating profitability indicators. Once accounted for, key financial ratios drop significantly. These hidden contributions also reflect a form of informal resilience – enabling flexible responses to challenges through mobilization of hidden family-based capacities. The study argues that such resilience constitutes a dynamic capability and should be integrated into RBV frameworks. It calls for broader operationalizations of resources and mixed-method approaches to better capture the strategic role of informal, intangible inputs in small family firms.

Keywords: Case study, Family business, Hidden resources, Resource-based view

1 Introduction

Family businesses are the most common ownership model worldwide and have a tremendous impact on the global economy. They contribute significantly to national GDPs – for example, 64% in the U.S. – and generate trillions in revenue globally. Many leading corporations, such as Walmart and Volkswagen, are family-owned, underlining their central role in driving economic growth (Birdthistle & Hales, 2023). They secure employment, promote regional stability, and are often characterized by long-term orientation. Their strategic direction and sustainable success are therefore not only crucial for the families themselves but also for entire economies.

To explain business success, the Resource-Based View (RBV) has become a dominant paradigm in management research. The RBV posits that differences in firm performance can largely be explained by differences in the availability and use of resources (Barney & Arikan, 2001; Foss et al., 1995; Grant, 1996). Firms that possess valuable, rare, inimitable, and organizationally embedded resources can achieve sustainable competitive advantages. Resource efficiency is thus considered a key driver of entrepreneurial success.

https://doi.org/10.1515/9783110790344-010

The RBV has also been widely applied to family businesses. Studies show that specific characteristics such as strong emotional attachment, trust, tacit knowledge, or intergenerational commitment can be interpreted as valuable and hard-to-imitate resources (Habbershon & Williams, 1999; Cabrera-Suárez et al., 2001). Empirical research partly confirms that such resources contribute to above-average performance (Cook et al., 2011; Costa et al., 2013).

However, strategic management research has long neglected the influence of the family itself – such as its impact on decision-making, resource allocation, or strategic orientation (Arregle et al., 2021). Especially in areas like internationalization or succession, the so-called "family factor" is often not systematically accounted for. Moreover, other studies have shown that smaller companies can also be successful without pronounced resource advantages (Døving & Gooderham, 2008; Sandvig & Coakley, 1998). These divergent research findings raise fundamental questions: Why are some firms able to perform above average with limited resources? Why does the RBV appear explanatory in some contexts but not in others?

Rather than viewing these inconsistencies as theoretical flaws, Lado et al. (2006) argue that such tensions reflect inherent paradoxes within the RBV – for example, between resource transparency and inimitability, or between firm-specificity and generalizability. These paradoxes challenge linear cause-effect logic but can serve as catalysts for theoretical refinement. In this spirit, the present study does not seek to resolve the RBV's contradictions, but to engage with them constructively. The case analysis presented here illustrates one such paradox: the coexistence of high financial performance and the absence of formally measurable resource advantages. It is precisely this tension that reveals the need to expand traditional RBV assumptions – particularly in the context of small family businesses.

A promising explanation for this divergence lies in the concept of organizational resilience. Resilience describes the capacity of an organization to absorb shocks, adapt, and emerge stronger from crises (Duchek, 2019). Particularly in family businesses, resilience is closely tied to the social fabric of the organization: trust-based relationships, long-term orientation, and a deep sense of responsibility are not only culturally embedded but act as resilience-enhancing resources (Beech et al., 2020; Schwaiger et al., 2021). These characteristics can buffer against volatility and enable rapid, flexible responses when external conditions change – qualities that are increasingly relevant in uncertain environments.

However, such resources often remain informal or hidden: unpaid work by family members, emotional commitment, or tacit knowledge transfer between generations are difficult to quantify and thus frequently excluded from traditional RBV-based empirical analyses. As a result, they remain under-theorized despite their strategic relevance. This study argues that these "hidden resources", which are central to resilience, may be key to understanding why some family firms succeed even without obvious resource advantages.

Moreover, resilience research offers conceptual tools to extend the RBV. Duchek (2019) frames resilience as a meta-capability, encompassing three stages: anticipation, coping, and adaptation. These dynamic processes enable firms not just to survive, but to transform in response to adversity. Such capabilities can be interpreted as resource orchestration mechanisms that mobilize and reconfigure existing resources in ways not captured by static RBV models.

In family firms, this process is often embedded in the concept of "familiness," which Beech et al. (2020) describe as a mediating system of relational and emotional capital. Familiness strengthens the socio-ecological system of the business and family and supports resilience through shared values, meaning-making, and long-term identity construction. The implication is clear: resilience and RBV are not mutually exclusive but can be synergistically linked – especially when applied to the unique context of family businesses. Shepherd & Williams (2023) support this perspective by identifying different organizational response paths to resilience. Their findings highlight that resilience is not solely a result of resource endowment but also of how firms perceive adversity, interpret uncertainty, and make strategic decisions under pressure. This implies a need to integrate cognitive and behavioral dimensions into the RBV framework.

Therefore, the central thesis of this paper is expanded as follows: The divergence in the empirical applicability of the RBV to family firms may be attributed not only to the lack of recognition and operationalization of informal, family-specific resources, but also to the neglect of resilience as a dynamic capability that shapes how resources are used in times of adversity. This has methodological implications: If key variables used to measure RBV assumptions are invalid or distorted, empirical analyses can only offer limited insights into the theory's validity. Especially for micro and small enterprises, new approaches are needed to transform these "hidden" and dynamic resilience-related resources into measurable constructs.

In line with Kellermanns et al. (2016), who emphasize the divergence between researchers' theoretical constructs and entrepreneurs' resource perceptions, this study aims to bridge this gap through an empirically grounded case analysis of informal, yet strategically significant, family firm resources. The contribution of this study lies in the combination of theoretical reflection and empirical case analysis. It demonstrates how the exclusion of family-specific and resilience-related resources can lead to misinterpretations of success factors and offers perspectives on how this issue might be addressed in future research. The structure of this paper is as follows: after this introduction, a literature review discusses the theoretical foundations of the RBV and organizational resilience and its application to family firms. This is followed by a detailed explanation of the case study methodology, before presenting the core empirical findings and reflecting on them in the discussion section. The paper concludes with final remarks, implications for research and practice, and an outlook on future research needs.

2 Literature Review

2.1 Resource-Based View

The Resource-Based View (RBV) has emerged as a widely applied theoretical framework within strategic management research. According to Newbert (2008) and Priem & Butler (2001), the RBV serves as a valuable lens for analyzing firm-specific sources of competitive advantage and explaining performance heterogeneity. As Mathews (2002) emphasizes, differences in firm performance can be attributed to the heterogeneity of resources – where firms competing in the same environment may possess and utilize resources differently, leading to varying degrees of efficiency and profitability (Barney & Arikan, 2001; Costa et al., 2013). These differences are not a function of market power but of internal capabilities and resource configurations (Foss et al., 1995; Lenox et al., 2011; Peteraf, 1996).

Empirical research has confirmed the RBV in numerous contexts. Studies show that company-specific resources such as know-how, brand image, or technological capabilities can lead to significant performance advantages (Foss et al., 1995; Lenox et al., 2011). Grant (1996) emphasizes that sustainable competitive advantages are built through the development of core competencies over time. In the context of family businesses, the RBV appears particularly suitable as an explanatory model. Research by Cook et al. (2011) and Costa et al. (2013) shows that the performance of SMEs can be well explained using RBV logic. Family firms often exhibit high levels of stability, long-term orientation, and strong social networks – factors that can be interpreted as valuable and hard-to-imitate resources (Habbershon & Williams, 1999). The concept of "familiness" – the unique bundle of resources arising from the interaction between the family and the business – is central here (Cabrera-Suárez et al., 2001).

However, the RBV's applicability is increasingly being questioned. Arend & Lévesque (2010) and Lockett et al. (2009) argue that the RBV is too narrowly focused when used as a stand-alone perspective. Especially in the case of family firms, challenges like succession, emotional dynamics, power structures, and implicit expectations often cannot be captured by objectively measurable resources alone. Chrisman et al. (2005, 2009) point out that the impact of resources in family firms depends on the nature and intensity of family involvement.

In addition, other studies demonstrate that smaller companies can succeed without pronounced resource advantages (Døving & Gooderham, 2008; Sandvig & Coakley, 1998). These findings call into question the universality of RBV assumptions, particularly the notion that superior firm performance is always rooted in resource differentials. Instead, contextual factors such as agility, proximity to customers, or informal governance structures may explain performance in ways that extend beyond RBV's original scope. A particularly underexplored issue is the existence of so-called hidden resources. In line with these concerns, Kellermanns et al. (2016) reveal a fundamental disconnect between how scholars conceptualize resources within the RBV and how entrepreneurs perceive and use them in practice. While academic applications tend to focus on abstract VRIN criteria, entrepreneurs often emphasize contextual, relational, and immediately actionable resources, such as personal networks, trust, or family-based labor contributions. This divergence highlights a conceptual blind spot in many RBV-based studies: by privileging measurable, formalized assets, they risk overlooking the informal, often invisible resource dynamics that are central to entrepreneurial behavior – particularly in small family firms. The findings of this study reinforce this gap and underscore the need to reconcile theoretical abstraction with practical resource realities.

Many small family firms rely heavily on informal or unpaid contributions – such as work provided by family members without formal contracts. These resources are typically absent from financial statements and are often excluded from empirical analyses, leading to distorted assessments of performance. Despite these limitations, the RBV remains a foundational theory for understanding competitive advantage. It argues that competitive superiority arises not from market positioning but from the internal ability to develop and leverage valuable, rare, inimitable, and organizationally embedded resources (VRIO). Companies that successfully build such resource profiles – especially through core competencies (Armstrong & Shimizu, 2007; Becker & Meise, 2008, p. 117) – can sustain long-term performance advantages and superior returns (Deb, 2009, p. 4; Grant, 1996).

Larger firms are generally better positioned to develop such resources due to their greater capacity for innovation and organizational complexity (Jovanovic & MacDonald, 1994). Empirical studies confirm that size and age are proxies for resource accumulation and are positively correlated with survival and performance (Altman, 1968; Chava & Jarrow, 2004; Esteve-Pérez & Mañez-Castillejo, 2008). Consequently, firm size is often used as an indicator of strategic resource capacity, a measure of past performance and risk (Ben-Zion & Shalit, 1975). For strategy development, this implies a need to align strategic choices with the existing and developable resource base. According to Grant (1999), Pfeffer & Salancik (1978, p. 2) and Rasche (2008, p. 54), managers must:

1. Identify internal resources and capabilities,
2. Analyze competitor strengths and weaknesses,
3. Determine how resources can be deployed more effectively than competitors.

From an economic standpoint, ensuring access to critical resources – particularly those necessary for core competencies – is essential. Barney (2001) and Brahma & Chakraborty (2011) argue that resource markets must exhibit inelasticity; otherwise, increased demand will raise factor prices and erode potential returns. In conclusion, while the RBV is conceptually robust and empirically supported in many respects, it must be applied with caution in the context of small family firms. Informal structures and hidden resources challenge the assumptions of resource visibility and measurability. Therefore, this study contributes to the academic discourse by critically evaluating the applicability of the RBV in family firm contexts and proposing directions for future pluralistic and methodologically refined research.

2.2 Organizational Resilience

In recent years, the concept of organizational resilience has become a focal point in strategic management research, particularly within the context of family businesses. Resilience, in this regard, is not merely a reactive capacity to overcome crises, but a proactive, dynamic ability to adapt, reorganize, and even transform in response to internal and external disruptions (Leppäaho & Ritala, 2022; Hadjielias et al., 2022). From a theoretical perspective, the Resource-Based View (RBV) offers a solid foundation to analyze resilience, as it emphasizes the strategic value of resources that are valuable, rare, inimitable, and non-substitutable (Barney, 2001; Kraaijenbrink et al., 2010; Lin & Wu, 2014).

However, resilience cannot be derived from resources alone, but from their specific deployment in firm-specific performance processes, especially through the development of dynamic capabilities that enable firms to reconfigure resources in response to change (Deakins & Scott, 2024, p. 163; Newbert, 2008). In family firms, resilience emerges from a complex interplay between strategic routines, cultural continuity, and adaptive leadership. As Czakon et al. (2023) argue, strategic resilience in family businesses is not improvisational but rather rooted in long-standing decision-making repertoires accumulated over generations. These capabilities are often informal and embedded in familial social capital – making them hidden resources that are crucial but difficult to measure through traditional RBV lenses.

Moreover, organizational evolution, driven by intergenerational learning and shared values, forms the backbone of resilient family firms (Chirico et al., 2012; Zainal, 2022). This evolutionary adaptation allows family firms to develop adaptive routines rather than rely on reactive strategic shifts, which aligns with Porter's (1991) notion of a "dynamic theory of strategy." Thus, the RBV's focus on static resource conditions must be expanded toward a more dynamic and processual perspective in order to capture resilience as a long-term strategic asset.

Nevertheless, the RBV in its traditional form exhibits conceptual limitations when applied to resilience in family firms. First, the theory assumes the existence of objective, measurable resources, which conflicts with the often informal, implicit, and non-quantifiable nature of familial resources such as unpaid labor, trust-based coordination, or tacit intergenerational knowledge (Habbershon & Williams, 1999; Chrisman et al., 2005). Second, resilience is inherently context-dependent and time-sensitive. It is not enough to possess a resource – resilience requires the ability to reconfigure and repurpose it under changing conditions. As such, dynamic capabilities (Lin & Wu, 2014; Teece, 2007) serve as a crucial complement to the RBV, enabling the evolutionary transformation of a firm's resource base over time.

Third, the "familiness" construct (Habbershon & Williams, 1999) represents a unique configuration of tangible and intangible resources that underpin both competitive advantage and resilience. However, as Arregle et al. (2021) note, the role of the family factor has been underexplored, particularly in research areas such as internationalization, innovation, and crisis management. This omission limits the explanatory power of RBV-based studies when applied to family firms. To address these limitations, scholars have begun to argue for a pluralistic theoretical integration, combining RBV with institutional theory, agency theory, or socioemotional wealth (SEW) perspectives (Chrisman et al., 2009; Prencipe et al., 2014; Zahra, 2021). Such integrations allow for a more nuanced understanding of how resilience is cultivated and sustained within the overlapping spheres of family and business.

In conclusion, while the RBV offers critical insights into the foundation of competitive advantage, its current application to family firm resilience requires refinement. Specifically, resilience in family businesses must be understood as an evolving capability shaped by hidden, non-traditional resources and long-term strategic routines. This calls for new conceptual models and measurement approaches that integrate both tangible and intangible, formal and informal, resources into a coherent framework of analysis.

3 Methodology

3.1 Research Design and Methodological Approach

To answer the research question, a qualitative single case study was conducted. The choice of this methodology is justified both theoretically and empirically. Case studies are considered particularly suitable for examining complex and context-dependent phenomena in their natural setting (Gibbert et al., 2008; Ridder, 2017). They enable an in-depth understanding of real-life management situations and are especially helpful for generating new insights in research areas that are still underexplored (Rule & John, 2015; Tripathy, 2009).

According to Van Wynsberghe & Khan (2007), the case study serves as a transdisciplinary and transparadigmatic heuristic in which the research phenomenon – here: "hidden resources" in family businesses – is clearly delineated and systematically examined. Dumez (2015) emphasizes that the defining feature of case studies lies in their comparability: when conducted with methodological rigor, the findings can be transferred to other, similar cases. Berg (1968) also highlights the relevance of case studies for decision-makers, as they enable practical problem-solving and context-related recommendations for action.

In this paper, the case study was deliberately designed as a single case study in order to analyze a previously overlooked phenomenon – namely, the invisible contribution of family members within a typical but empirically underrepresented context: a small family business with fewer than 10 employees and multiple business units. The selected company does not represent an outlier or extreme case but reflects a structure commonly found in small and medium-sized family businesses both in German-speaking countries and internationally. It thus constitutes a representative case and allows conclusions to be drawn about broader entrepreneurial realities.

Following Starman (2013), the single case study is particularly appropriate when aiming to uncover the "unknown within well-known borders." This case meets that criterion: its formal structure, ownership model, and business segments are typical of many rural family businesses, yet the specific role of non-monetized resources remains largely unexplored. The in-depth analysis therefore offers a valuable contribution to the theoretical development and empirical grounding of the Resource-Based View (Scapens, 2004). By combining document-based analyses (e.g., financial statements), activity logs, and qualitative interviews – collected as part of a consulting project – a deep, holistic understanding of the case was achieved, going far beyond purely quantitative analyses.

3.2 Description and Information about the Family Business

he family business under analysis is located in Western Austria (specific federal state anonymized) and has existed for several generations. The company structure is broad and comprises several economically independent units that are nevertheless closely linked through family ownership. These include, in particular, a gastronomy unit, a farm, a small brewery, and a rental and leasing division. The legal structure spans multiple company forms, with formal ownership entirely held by the second generation.

The family consists of six actively and potentially actively involved members from the second and third generations. While the second generation (the parents) currently manages the operations entirely, some members of the third generation are engaged in the business to varying degrees – some under formal contracts, others informally without financial compensation. The future succession is currently a matter of internal discussion, but no clear rules have yet been defined regarding responsibilities, roles, or timelines. Interviews revealed both uncertainty and expectations within the family, but there has been no open communication about specific succession arrangements.

A central finding of the case study concerns the distribution of labor within the family business. According to the collected activity logs, a total of 127.48 working hours per week are contributed by family members. Notably, around 50.33 hours (approximately 40%) are unpaid and not compensated through any contractual or financial means. If these tasks were performed by external employees, the business would incur additional personnel costs estimated at around € 81,480 per year. These services therefore represent a resource of substantial economic relevance, yet they remain invisible in the company's profit and loss statement.

From a scientific perspective, this can be interpreted through the concept of opportunity costs: in a non-family business, such unpaid contributions would not be feasible, as market-based remuneration would be required. As a result, the company's economic representation in the profit and loss statement does not reflect the "true and fair view" of the actual efforts required to generate revenues. Conversely, some of the listed expenses indirectly benefit family members (e.g., through the use of company-owned housing, vehicles, or meals).

This situation leads to a specific problem: on the one hand, there are hidden performance contributions ("hidden resources"); on the other, there are unspoken expectations within the family that are neither financially rewarded nor strategically managed. The analyzed family discussions and interviews revealed that this issue has not yet been explicitly addressed – despite its importance for the future succession and the equitable distribution of roles within the third generation. The resulting discrepancy between the formal financial data and the actual contribution of labor complicates not only the economic evaluation of the business but also challenges the application of theoretical models such as the Resource-Based View (RBV), which relies on measurable resources.

4 Results

The empirical investigation of the case study provides key insights into the extent to which the Resource-Based View (RBV) serves as a suitable theoretical framework for explaining the performance of small family businesses. The focus of the analysis is a family-run micro-enterprise with several operational business units, including gastronomy, agriculture, brewing, and rental services. While these units are legally distinct entities, they are tightly connected through family ownership and operationally integrated.

A detailed analysis of financial statements over several years reveals consistently high profitability. For instance, in 2020, the EBIT margin for one company was an impressive 24.64%, while the net profit margin (Profitability II) reached 23.62%. These figures suggest a high level of managerial quality and particularly efficient resource utilization (Dambolena & Khoury, 1980; Drobetz & Wanzenried, 2006) – two core pillars of RBV theory (Barney & Arikan, 2001; Grant, 1996). Considering that this is a micro-enterprise, the outcome appears all the more remarkable, as common RBV assumptions – such as those related to economies of scale and access to resources – typically suggest that larger firms hold structural advantages (Lumpkin et al., 2010; Ben-Zion & Shalit, 1975).

This finding aligns with empirical work by Døving & Gooderham (2008) and Sandvig & Coakley (1998), who demonstrate that under certain conditions, even small firms are capable of utilizing resources highly effectively. However, the question arises as to what specific resource strategies have contributed to this above-average performance, and whether these strategies have been adequately captured in existing literature.

To gain deeper insight, a qualitative investigation was conducted within the company, including interviews with all family members and the compilation of systematic activity logs. These logs recorded both paid and unpaid labor contributions. The results show that a total of 127.48 working hours per week were provided by family members. Of this, only 77.15 hours (60.52%) were financially compensated, while 50.33 hours (39.48%) were unpaid. Particularly notable is the fact that two members of the third generation contribute daily in areas such as farming, maintenance, and guest services without formal employment or remuneration.

To quantify the impact of these "hidden resources," an opportunity cost calculation was performed. Based on industry-standard wage rates, this translates into a potential annual labor cost of approximately EUR 81,480. In a simulated income statement, this amount was included in the cost structure. The results are significant: the EBIT margin would drop from 24.64% to 12.32%, and the net profit margin would fall from 23.62% to 11.31%. This shift in profitability fundamentally alters the assessment of economic performance and significantly relativizes the previously inferred "management quality."

These findings raise fundamental questions about the applicability of the RBV to small family firms. When critical resources – such as unpaid family labor, implicit obligations, or emotional attachment – are not captured in accounting systems, they also remain invisible to theoretical frameworks. The typical operationalization of "resources" through objective variables such as employee count, personnel costs, or assets proves insufficient in this context (Chrisman et al., 2005).

This issue becomes even more problematic when such distortions lead to erroneous conclusions in empirical studies. For example, RBV-based regression analyses that assume highly efficient resource use in small family firms may in fact be based on invisible resource foundations. As a result, common proxy variables such as firm size, as well as performance indicators themselves, are systematically distorted – a classic case of endogeneity due to omitted variable bias and measurement error.

The present case study also makes clear that this is not an outlier case. The observed patterns – informal labor division, implicit expectations, lack of transparency – are common practice in many small family firms. This has also been documented in succession research and role allocation studies, as well as in broader family business literature. The result is a kind of "informal resilience": the company is able to overcome economic challenges because family resources can be mobilized quickly, flexibly, and without monetary compensation. As shown by Santoro et al. (2020), such resilience emerges from a multilevel dynamic: entrepreneurial resilience at the owner level amplifies employee-level cognitive, behavioral, and contextual resilience capacities, which together contribute to sustained firm performance. This dynamic is particularly relevant in small family firms, where the entrepreneur's mindset shapes not only strategic decisions but also the emotional and motivational climate within the business.

Moreover, the ability to activate such hidden reserves under pressure reflects not only strategic intent but also a resilience capability portfolio, as conceptualized by Manfield & Newey (2018). These include routinized responses for familiar challenges and more heuristic, adaptive responses for unfamiliar disruptions – capacities often embedded in family routines, trust-based cooperation, and informal knowledge transfer. These mechanisms, though not codified in formal management systems, enable continuity and responsiveness even under resource constraints.

However, this resilience occurs "through the backdoor" and thereby escapes conventional economic measurement tools. It is difficult to plan, not institutionally embedded, and difficult to transfer in the context of generational succession. Precisely for this reason, it is crucial to make it theoretically visible and methodologically measurable. This study contributes to that goal by highlighting the discrepancy between officially reported performance and actual resource use – thereby addressing a critical explanatory gap within the application of the RBV.

5 Summary and Conclusion

The aim of this study was to examine the suitability of the Resource-Based View (RBV) as a theoretical framework for explaining the performance of small family businesses. The core focus was a critical reflection on the phenomenon of "hidden resources" – that is, resources that are not adequately captured by traditional accounting systems or empirical research. Using a qualitative case study, it was demonstrated that unpaid labor by family members significantly influences the representation of business performance. These contributions not only play a key role in profitability, but in many cases, they are a prerequisite for the firm's ability to operate successfully at all. If this contribution is ignored, a distorted picture emerges – both in financial metrics and in theoretical interpretations.

A central contribution of this study is the interpretation of these "hidden resources" not only as economically relevant inputs but also as expressions of organizational resilience. Especially in small family businesses, it is often informal, hard-to-measure resources such as dedication, tacit knowledge, intergenerational responsibility, and emotional attachment that enable a firm to respond flexibly to external shocks and to exhibit exceptional resilience. However, this form of resilience occurs outside formal structures, is not institutionally secured, and thus escapes conventional measurement systems. Resilience thereby becomes a kind of "hidden capability" that cannot be captured by financial data or standard management systems.

This insight also offers a possible resolution to the inconsistent empirical application of the RBV to small firms: it is not necessarily that the RBV is incorrect, but that it overlooks resilience as a critical, dynamic capability. Recent research (e.g., Duchek, 2019; Beech et al., 2020; Shepherd & Williams, 2023) has emphasized that resilience – especially in the form of anticipation, coping, and adaptation – is itself a valuable and inimitable resource. In the context of family firms, resilience is often embedded in "familiness" and emerges from the interaction of the business and family systems. These capabilities remain largely unmeasured yet are instrumental in long-term survival and performance – particularly in times of crisis.

The findings of this case study partly align with the existing literature: studies by Habbershon & Williams (1999) or Cabrera-Suárez et al. (2001) highlight the unique nature of family businesses, which allows them to create distinctive resources. Chrisman et al. (2005, 2009) and Costa et al. (2013) also emphasize the significance of implicit resources and their impact on firm performance. At the same time, however, the empirical results contradict the common assumption that high profitability is automatically a reflection of efficient resource use in the RBV sense – particularly in the case of small firms. The case study shows that perceived efficiency was overestimated due to the omission of unpaid labor, a point that has been only marginally addressed in RBV literature to date (Arend & Lévesque, 2010; Lockett et al., 2009).

These findings can be further substantiated through a conceptual framework developed in connection with this study (see Figure 1). The figure illustrates the cascading effects of hidden resources across four critical stages of empirical research: from the information base, to the operationalization of variables, to statistical inference, and finally, to the interpretation of theoretical findings. As the graphic shows, the presence of unrecorded family labor or informal commitments distorts input variables such as firm size or efficiency. This distortion can propagate through regression models as endogeneity or omitted variable bias, ultimately resulting in erroneous conclusions that appear inconsistent with the RBV – although the deviation is rooted in measurement deficiencies, not in theoretical inadequacy.

By integrating the concept of resilience, this study suggests a broader view of what constitutes a strategic resource in family businesses – one that accounts not only for tangible inputs but also for dynamic, informal, and deeply embedded capabilities. This has significant implications for future research and theory development: rather than rejecting the RBV for its limited applicability to small firms, scholars may instead seek to expand it by incorporating resilience as a critical construct – particularly in the context of resource-constrained, owner-managed enterprises. The framework derived from the accompanying analysis clearly illustrates the mechanisms behind this distortion:

- Misrepresentation in informational content: Hidden resources do not appear in officially available data, leading to reduced informational quality.
- Distorted proxies and variables: Metrics such as firm size (e.g., number of employees) or efficiency indicators (e.g., profitability) are systematically over- or underestimated.

- Impact on statistical analyses: Regression models suffer from endogeneity issues (e.g., omitted variable bias), resulting in erroneous conclusions.
- Impact on results and interpretation: Studies may arrive at conclusions that seem to contradict RBV, while in fact only the informational basis is flawed.

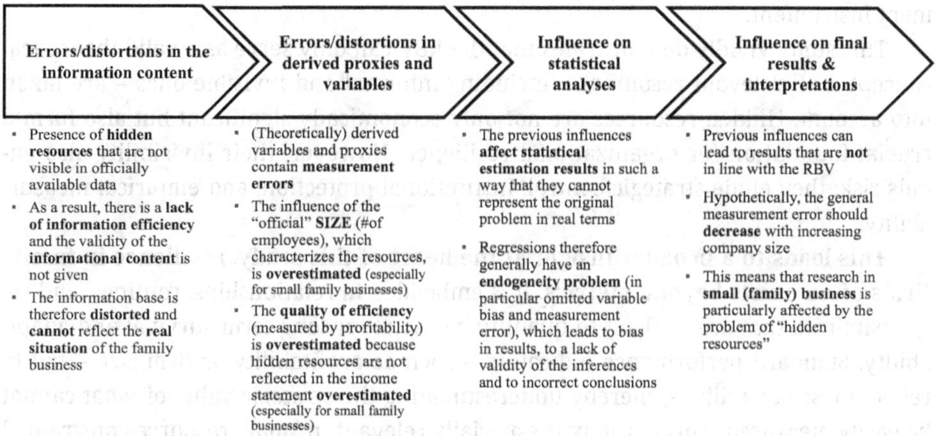

Figure 1: Systematic effects of hidden resources on empirical research processes in family business studies.

These insights make clear: the validity of many empirical studies in the field of family business research is limited if they rely solely on formal, quantitative data. Especially in the field of resilience research, it becomes apparent that many contemporary indicators – such as capital structure, profitability, or liquidity ratios- fail to adequately reflect the true adaptive and survival capacities of small firms. The resilient performance observed in this case is based on a familial structure that is neither standardized nor generalizable. At the same time, it remains unclear how sustainable this form of resilience is – particularly in the context of succession or under changing economic conditions.

Future studies should build upon the findings of this case study and investigate them further. Particularly relevant are:

- The development of mixed-methods approaches that combine qualitative and quantitative data,
- The operationalization of implicit, informal resources as measurable variables (e.g., time contributions, emotional commitment, tacit responsibilities),
- The integration of resilience concepts into existing RBV frameworks,
- The examination of the long-term implications of hidden resources in the context of succession and generational transitions.

The case study is based on a single company, which limits its generalizability. The opportunity cost calculation is an approximation and does not account for all economic and social effects. Furthermore, it remains unclear how the identified mechanisms would manifest in other industries, regions, or family constellations. Finally, resilience was observed and described, but not captured using a standardized measurement instrument.

This study vividly demonstrates that the RBV can only serve as a valid theoretical concept if all relevant resources – including informal and invisible ones – are taken into account. Hidden resources are not only economically significant but also form a crucial foundation for organizational resilience. However, their invisibility also entails risk: they elude strategic control, institutional protection, and empirical measurability.

This leads to a broader insight at the heart of this study: resilience in family firms often exists beyond metrics. It is embedded in relationships, routines, and responsibilities that are difficult to quantify, yet vital for long-term survival and adaptability. Standard performance indicators – such as profitability or firm size – fail to reflect these capabilities, thereby underestimating the strategic value of what cannot be easily measured. This paradox is especially relevant in small, resource-constrained enterprises where resilience emerges not from formal systems but from embedded social structures and informal commitments.

By highlighting this disconnect, the study not only addresses an empirical gap but also contributes to the ongoing theoretical refinement of the RBV. It aligns with recent research (e.g., Gupta et al., 2021; Kellermanns et al., 2016) calling for pluralistic models that move beyond static resource inventories and engage with the dynamic, lived realities of entrepreneurship. In this sense, "resilience beyond metrics" becomes both a conceptual challenge and a guiding perspective for future research on the strategic potential of small family firms.

References

Altman, E. I. (1968). Financial ratios, discriminant analysis and the prediction of corporate bankruptcy. *The Journal of Finance*, *23*(4), 589–609.

Arend, R. J., & Lévesque, M. (2010). Is the resource-based view a practical organizational theory? *Organization Science*, *21*(4), 913–930.

Armstrong, C. E., & Shimizu, K. A. (2007). Review of approaches to empirical research on the resource-based view of the firm. *Journal of Management*, *33*(6), 959–986.

Arregle, J.-L., Chirico, F., Kano, L., Kundei, S. K., Majocchi, A., & Schulze, W. S. (2021). Family firm internationalization: Past research and an agenda for the future. *Journal of International Business Studies*, *52*(6), 1159–1198.

Barney, J. B. (2001). Ressource-based theories of competitive advantage: A ten-year retrospective on the resource-based view. *Journal of Management*, *27*(6), 643–650.

Barney, J. B., & Arikan, A. M. (2001). The resource based view: Origins and implications. In: M. A. Hitt, R. E. Freeman & J. S. Harrison (Hrsg.), *The Blackwell handbook of strategic management* (pp. 124–188). Oxford, UK: Blackwell Publishers.

Becker, J., & Meise, V. (2008). Strategie und Ordnungsrahmen. In: J. Becker, M. Kugeler & M. Rosemann (Hrsg.), *Prozessmanagement: Ein Leitfaden zur prozessorientierten Organisationsgestaltung* (pp. 105–154). Berlin-Heidelberg: Springer.

Beech, N., Devins, D., Gold, J., & Beech, S. (2020). In the family way: An exploration of family business resilience. *International Journal of Organizational Analysis, 28*(1), 160–182.

Ben-Zion, U., & Shalit, S. S. (1975). Size, leverage, and dividend record as determinants of equity risk. *The Journal of Finance, 30*(4), 1015–1026.

Berg, C. (1968). Case studies in organizational research and education. *Acta Sociologica, 11*, 1–11.

Birdthistle, N., & Hales, R. (2023). The meaning of a family business and why they are important to economies. In: N. Birdthistle & R. Hales (Eds.),*Attaining the 2030 sustainable development goal of gender equality (Family businesses on a mission)* (pp. 13–25). Leeds: Emerald Publishing Limited.

Brahma, S. S., & Chakraborty, H. (2011). From industry to firm resources: Resource-based view of competitive advantage. *The IUP Journal of Business Strategy, 8*(2), 7–21.

Cabrera-Suárez, K., De Saá-Pérez, P., & García-Almeida, D. (2001). The succession process from a resource- and knowledge-based view of the family firm. *Family Business Review, 14*(1), 37–48.

Chava, S., & Jarrow, R. A. (2004). Bankruptcy prediction with industry effects. *Review of Finance, 8*(4), 537–569.

Chirico, F., Nordqvist, M., Colombo, G., & Mollona, E. (2012). Simulating dynamic capabilities and value creation in family firms: Is paternalism an "asset" or a "liability"? *Family Business Review, 25*(3), 318–338.

Chrisman, J. J., Chua, J. H., & Kellermanns, F. W. (2009). Priorities, resource stocks, and performance in family and non-family firms. *Entrepreneurship Theory and Practice, 33*(3), 739–760.

Chrisman, J. J., Chua, J. H., & Sharma, P. (2005). Trends and directions in the development of a strategic management theory of the family firm. *Entrepreneurship Theory and Practice, 29*(5), 555–575.

Cook, G. A.S., Pandit, N. R., & Milman, D. (2011). A resource-based analysis of bankruptcy law, SMEs and corporate recovery. *International Small Business Journal, 30*(3), 275–293.

Costa, L. A., Cool, K., & Dierickx, I. (2013). The competitive implications of the deployment of unique resource. *Strategic Management Journal, 34*(4), 445–463.

Czakon, W., Hajdas, M., & Radomska, J. (2023). Playing the wild cards: Antecedents of family firm resilience. *Journal of Family Business Strategy, 14*(1), 100484.

Dambolena, I. G., & Khoury, S. J. (1980). Ratio stability and corporate failure. *The Journal of Finance, 35*(4), 1017–1026.

Deakins, D., & Scott, J. M. (2024). Resources for entrepreneurship. In: D. Deakins & J. M. Scott (Eds.), *Entrepreneurship: A contemporary & global approach* (pp. 163–194). Thousand Oaks, CA: Sage Publications.

Deb, T. (2009). *Compensation management: Text & cases*. New Dehli: Excel books.

Døving E., Gooderham P. N. (2008). Dynamic capabilities as antecedents of the scope of related diversification: The case of small firm accountancy practices. *Strategic Management Journal, 29*(8), 841–857.

Drobetz, W., & Wanzenried, G. (2006). What determines the speed of adjustment to the target capital strucutre? *Applied Financial Economics, 16*(3), 941–958.

Duchek, S. (2019). Organizational resilience: A capability-based conceptualization. *Business Research, 13*(1), 215–246.

Dumez, H. (2015). What is a case, and what is a case study?. *Bulletin of Sociological Methodology, 127*, 43–57.

Esteve-Pérez, S., & Mañez-Castillejo, J. A. (2008). The resource-based theory of the firm and firm survival. *Small Business Economics, 30*(3), 231–249.

Foss, N. J., Knudsen, C., & Montgomery, C. A. (1995). An exploration of common ground: Integrating evolutionary and strategic theories of the firm. In: C. A. Montgomery (Hrsg.), *Resource-based and evolutionary theories of the firm: Towards a synthesis* (pp. 1–19). New York, NY: Springer.

Gibbert, M., Ruigrok, W., & Wicki, B. (2008). Research notes and commentaries: What passes as a rigorous case study?. *Strategic Management Journal*, *29*(13), 1465–1474.

Grant, R. M. (1999). The resource-based theory of competitive advantage: Implications for strategy formulation. In M. H. Zack (Hrsg.), *Knowledge and strategy* (pp. 3–24). Woburn: Butterworth-Heinemann.

Grant, R. M. (1996). Toward a knowledge-based theory of the firm. *Strategic Management Journal*, *17*(S2), 109–122.

Gupta, V., & Dias Jordão, R. V. (2021). Beyond the resource-based view: Strategic planning of networks by the small and medium-sized enterprises. *ASBM Journal of Management*, *14*(1/2), 47–75.

Habbershon, T., & Williams, M. (1999). A resource based framework for assessing the strategic advantage of family firms. *Family Business Review*, *12*(1), 1–25.

Hadjielias, E., Hughes, M., & Scholes, L. (2022). External crises and family social capital reconfiguration: Insights from the European debt crisis and the Covid-19 pandemic. *Family Business Review*, *35*(3), 275–305.

Jovanovic, B., & MacDonald, G. M. (1994). The life cycle of a competitive industry. *Journal of Political Economy*, *102*(2), 322–347.

Kellermanns, F., Walter, J., Crook, R. T., Kemmerer, B., & Narayanan, V. (2016). The resource-based view in entrepreneurship: A content-analytical comparison of researchers' and entrepreneurs' views. *Journal of Small Business Management*, *54*(1), 26–48.

Kraaijenbrink, J., Spender, J.-C., & Groen, A. J. (2010) The resource-based view: A review and assessment of its critiques. *Journal of Management*, *36*(1), 349–372.

Lado, A. A., Boyd, N. G., Wright, P., & Kroll, M. (2006). Paradox and theorizing within the resource-based view. *Academy of Management Review*, *31*(1), 115–131.

Lenox, M. J., Rockart, S. F., & Lewin, A. Y. (2011). Interdependency, competition, and industry dynamics. In: G. D. Markman & P. H. Phan (Hrsg.), *The competitive dynamics of entrepreneurial entry* (pp. 54–88). Glos, UK: Edward Elgar.

Leppäaho, T., & Ritala, P. (2022). Surviving the coronavirus pandemic and beyond: Unlocking family firms' innovation potential across crises. *Journal of Family Business Strategy*, *13*(1), 100440.

Lin, Y., & Wu, L.-Y. (2014). Exploring the role of dynamic capabilities in firm performance under the resource-based view framework. *Journal of Business Research*, *67*(3), 407–413.

Lockett, A., Thompson, S., & Morgenstern, U. (2009). The development of the resource-based view of the firm: A critical appraisal. *International Journal of Management Reviews*, *11*(1), 9–28.

Lumpkin, G. T., McKelvie, A., Gras, D. M., & Nason, R. S. (2010). Is strategy different for very small and new firms? *Journal of Small Business Strategy*, *21*(2), 1–26.

Manfield, R. C., & Newey, L. R. (2018). Resilience as an entrepreneurial capability: Integrating insights from a cross-disciplinary comparison. *International Journal of Entrepreneurial Behavior & Research 24*(7), 1155–1180.

Mathews, J. A. (2002). A resource-based view of Schumpeterian economic dynamics. *Journal of Evolutionary Economics*, *12*(1), 29–54.

Newbert, S. L. (2008). Value, rareness, competitive advantage, and performance: A conceptual-level empirical investigation of the resource-based view of the firm. *Strategic Management Journal*, *29*(7), 745–768

Pfeffer, J., & Salancik, G. R. (1978). *The external control of organizations. A Resource dependence perspective*. New York, NY: Harper & Row.

Peteraf, M. A. (1996). Resource-based theory. In: M. Goold & K. S. Luchs (Hrsg.), *Managing the multibusiness company: Stategic issues for diversified groups* (pp. 68–92). New York, NY: Routledge.

Porter, M. E. (1991). Toward a dynamic theory of strategy. *Strategic Management Journal*, *12*(Special Issue: Fundamental Research Issues in Strategy Economics), 95–117.

Prencipe, A., Bar-Yosef, S., & Dekker, H. (2014). Accounting research in family firms: Theoretical and empirical challenges. *European Accounting Review*, *23*(3), 361–385.

Priem, R. L., & Butler, J. E. (2001). Is the resource-based „view" a useful perspective for strategic management research? *The Academy of Management Review*, *26*(1), 22–40.

Rasche, A. (2008). *The paradoxical foundation of strategic management*. Heidelberg: Physica-Verlag.

Ridder, H.-G. (2017). The theory contribution of case study research designs. *Business Research*, *10*(2), 281–305.

Rule, P., & John, V.M. (2015). A necessary dialogue: Theory in case study research. *International Journal of Qualitative Methods*, doi.org/10.1177/16094069156115.

Sandvig, C. J., & Coakley, L. (1998). Best practices in small firm diversification. *Business Horizons*, *41*(3), 33–41.

Santoro, G., Messeni-Petruzzelli, A., & Del Giudice, M. (2021). Searching for resilience: The impact of employee-level and entrepreneur-level resilience on firm performance in small family firms. *Small Business Economics*, *57*(1), 455–471.

Scapens, R. W. (2004). Doing case study research. In: C. Humphrey & B. Lee B. (Eds.), *The real life guide to accounting research: A behind-the-scenes view of using qualitative research methods* (pp. 257–280). Amsterdam: Elsevier.

Schwaiger, K., Zehrer, A., & Braun, B. (2021). Organizational resilience in hospitality family businesses during the COVID-19 pandemic: A qualitative approach. *Tourism Review*, *77*(1), 163–176.

Shepherd, D. A., & Williams, T. A. (2023). Different response paths to organizational resilience. *Small Business Economics*, *61*(1), 23–58.

Starman, A. B. (2013). The case study as a type of qualitative research. *Journal of Contemporary Educational Studies*, *64*(1), 28–43.

Teece, D. J. (2007). Explicating dynamic capabilities: The nature and microfoundations of (sustainable) enterprise performance. *Strategic Management Journal*, *28*(13), 1319–1350.

Tripathy, M. R. (2009). Case methodology in teaching & research: A critical review. *Indian Journal of Industrial Relations*, *44*(1), 660–671.

VanWnysberghe, R., & Khan, S. (2007). Redifining case study. *International Journal of Qualitative Methods*, *6*(2), 80–94.

Zahra, S. A. (2021). The resource-based view, resourcefulness, and resource management in startup firms: A proposed research agenda. *Journal of Management*, *47*(7), 1841–1860.

Zainal, M. (2022). Innovation orientation and performance of Kuwaiti family businesses: Evidence form the COVID-19 pandemic. *Journal of Family Business Management*, *12*(2), 251-265.

Maria Bartekova

The Impact of AI-Induced Downsizing on Family Businesses

Abstract: The advent of artificial intelligence (AI) has significantly influenced business operations, leading to shifts in employment patterns, particularly in family businesses. This chapter offers a detailed analysis of AI-induced downsizing within family firms, known for their unique management styles and deep-rooted values. Unlike non-family businesses, family firms prioritize long-term sustainability and maintain stronger employee relationships, affecting their downsizing decisions. Downsizing, defined as job reduction to enhance efficiency, presents ethical dilemmas, especially in family firms where kinship ties and shared values play a crucial role. Research shows that family businesses are less likely to downsize compared to non-family firms due to their commitment to preserving socio-emotional wealth and maintaining employee trust and loyalty. However, AI integration poses dual challenges and opportunities: it can enhance operational efficiency and competitiveness but also risks job displacement. This chapter emphasizes the importance of strategic intent in adopting AI to balance technological advancements with employee welfare. It suggests future research should focus on frameworks to help family businesses navigate AI-induced transformations while upholding their values and ensuring long-term sustainability.

Keywords: AI, Downsizing, Family Businesses, Resilience

1 Introduction

Downsizing is a common organizational practice employed by businesses to reduce costs, enhance efficiency, or adapt to market demands (Cascio, 1993; Cameron, 1994). However, in family businesses, downsizing decisions are often influenced by more complex factors than in non-family firms. Family businesses prioritize socio-emotional wealth (SEW), which includes preserving family control, emotional attachment, and legacy. This focus on SEW often leads to a heightened concern for long-term orientation (Chrisman et al., 2010) and reputation (Berrone et al., 2010), influencing their unique approach to downsizing.

Studies suggest that family ownership and management play pivotal roles in shaping downsizing practices. Family firms are more likely to avoid or delay layoffs

Acknowledgement: This research paper is a partial result of the multiyear research projects VEGA 1/0465/23 “Generic, convergence and model-based approaches of environmental production and logistics in business development on Slovakia”.

https://doi.org/10.1515/9783110790344-011

to protect their employees, who are often considered part of the extended "family" (Block, 2010). This contrasts with non-family firms, where economic factors and shareholder interests often dominate downsizing decisions (Zellweger et al., 2012). Furthermore, external factors such as globalization, technological advancements, and competitive pressures have also been shown to influence downsizing behaviours, albeit differently for family and non-family firms (Carney, 2005).

Family-owned businesses are generally less likely to engage in downsizing compared to non-family firms. Research shows that family firms' long-term orientation and commitment to preserving socio-emotional wealth make them reluctant to lay off employees, even during financial downturns. Stavrou et al. (2006) found that family businesses are more likely to avoid downsizing, irrespective of financial performance considerations, due to their relationship with employees based on normative commitments rather than financial objectives.

In contrast, non-family firms are driven by performance metrics and are more likely to resort to downsizing during periods of financial distress. Family firms, however, view downsizing as a last resort, often prioritizing employee retention to maintain their social capital and family legacy. Block (2008) supports this argument, showing that family ownership decreases the likelihood of deep job cuts, while family management does not significantly influence downsizing decisions. The concept of socio-emotional wealth (SEW) is central to understanding downsizing in family businesses. SEW refers to the non-financial aspects of the firm that family members value, such as family control, reputation, and employee relationships. Research by Amato et al. (2021) demonstrates that family firms prioritize preserving SEW, which often leads them to avoid layoffs during times of crisis.

Family firms' focus on SEW results in unique downsizing patterns, particularly during economic downturns. During the global financial crisis, for example, family businesses in Spain were found to have a lower propensity to downsize than non-family firms, due to their concern for employee welfare and community relations (Amato et al., 2021). This behavior is rooted in the family firms' long-term orientation and desire to protect their reputation and relationships with employees.

While family businesses are generally resistant to downsizing, external factors such as globalization and sales internationalization can influence their downsizing decisions. Cirillo et al. (2020) found that family firms with higher levels of export intensity are more likely to downsize, suggesting that global market pressures can force family-owned businesses to reconsider their employee retention strategies. The internationalization of sales often requires businesses to adopt more flexible and efficient structures, which may necessitate workforce reductions. However, even in these cases, family businesses tend to downsize less aggressively than non-family firms. This cautious approach to downsizing is influenced by the desire to maintain socio-emotional wealth and protect family legacy.

Family businesses' resistance to downsizing is particularly evident during times of crisis. Research by Amato et al. (2021) highlights that family firms are less likely to downsize during economic downturns, especially if they are territorially embedded in their local communities. This territorial embeddedness strengthens the firm's ties to its employees and community, making downsizing a less attractive option. Similarly, Sanchez-Bueno et al. (2020) found that family firms engaged in R&D activities are less likely to downsize than non-family firms. This suggests that family businesses with innovative strategies may be better equipped to weather economic crises without resorting to layoffs.

Family firms are often motivated by a desire to maintain their reputation for social responsibility, which can influence their downsizing decisions. Block (2010) argues that family owners are more concerned about their social standing and community relationships than non-family firms, leading them to avoid deep job cuts, even when financially justified. This emphasis on social responsibility is particularly evident in family firms' downsizing practices during economic crises. Family businesses often prioritize employee welfare and community relations over short-term financial gains, leading them to adopt more socially responsible downsizing strategies.

While family firms are generally reluctant to downsize, some research suggests that strategic downsizing can be beneficial in certain circumstances. Farrell & Mavondo (2005) found that downsizing strategies that involve organizational redesign, rather than simply reducing workforce size, can have a positive impact on business performance. This suggests that family firms can benefit from downsizing if it is part of a broader strategic reorganization. However, family businesses are often more cautious in their approach to downsizing, preferring to implement gradual changes rather than large-scale workforce reductions. This strategic approach to downsizing allows family firms to maintain their reputation and employee relationships while still improving efficiency and performance.

The study aims to investigate the impact of artificial intelligence (AI)-induced downsizing on family businesses, focusing on the interplay between family firm characteristics, territorial embeddedness, and AI adoption. It contributes to the literature by providing a nuanced understanding of how family firms balance technological innovation with socio-emotional wealth (SEW) preservation and employee welfare. We have formulated the following research question: "How does AI adoption influence downsizing decisions in family businesses, and what role does territorial embeddedness play in moderating this relationship?"

The paper continues with a detailed explanation of the data and methodology, describing the longitudinal panel dataset, sampling strategy, and econometric models used to analyse the impact of AI adoption on downsizing decisions in family and non-family businesses. The next section presents the results, offering descriptive statistics and regression analyses that reveal how family firm status, territorial embeddedness, and AI integration influence downsizing behaviours. Following this, the discussion interprets these findings within the context of socio-emotional wealth, spatial loyalty, and technological adaptation, highlighting the unique resilience and socially responsible practices of family firms.

2 Literature Review and Hypothesis Development

2.1 Literature Review

Downsizing, or downsizing, is a common strategy for organizations to reduce costs, increase efficiency, and adapt to changing market conditions (Cascio, 1993; Cameron, 1994). While in traditional firms, downsizing is often driven by economic factors and shareholder pressure, family businesses also consider non-financial aspects such as the protection of social-emotional wealth (SEW), long-term goals, and the firm's reputation when deciding on this strategy (Gomez-Mejia et al., 2007). These factors lead to different downsizing practices in family and non-family firms.

2.1.1 Socio-emotional Wealth (SEW)

SEW is a key concept in the literature on family firms and refers to the non-financial values that family owners attribute to the firm, such as family control, reputation, and relationships with employees (Berrone et al., 2010). Research shows that maintaining SEWs can motivate family businesses to postpone or reduce the extent of layoffs, even though this may mean lower financial returns in the short run (Chrisman et al., 2012). Stavrou et al. (2006) find that family businesses are less prone to downsizing, especially during economic crises, as their relationships with employees are based more on normative commitments than on purely financial goals.

2.1.2 Territorial Embeddedness

Territorial embeddedness refers to the extent to which a firm is connected to its local environment through economic, social and cultural ties (Dekker & Hasso, 2016). Research suggests that family businesses with deep ties to local communities are less likely to be laid off, as these ties strengthen their accountability to employees and the local economy (Bjuggren & Sund, 2012; Amato et al., 2021). Cirillo et al. (2020) find that international expansion and the pressures of globalization may weaken this effect as they require more flexible structures and efficiencies, but this still does not lead to as aggressive layoffs in family firms as in non-family firms.

2.1.3 AI and Its Impact on Downsizing

The implementation of artificial intelligence (AI) brings both challenges and opportunities for businesses. On the one hand, AI can increase efficiency and reduce costs, but on the other hand, it leads to job automation and the risk of layoffs (Farrell &

Mavondo, 2005). However, family businesses are able to balance technological transformation with employee protection, especially if they have strong ties to their local communities (Berrone et al., 2010). Research shows that family businesses integrated into local communities are less susceptible to mass layoffs when implementing AI, as they are aware of the impacts on employees and the local economy (Sanchez-Bueno et al., 2020).

2.2 Hypothesis Development

The development of the study's hypotheses is grounded in theoretical and empirical research on family businesses, socio-emotional wealth (SEW), and territorial embeddedness. Family firms are distinct from non-family firms due to their emphasis on SEW, which prioritizes non-financial goals such as family control, reputation, and employee well-being (Gomez-Mejia et al., 2007; Berrone et al., 2010). This emphasis often translates into unique decision-making processes, including a reluctance to downsize even under financial pressures. Research has shown that family firms are more resistant to workforce reductions compared to non-family firms due to their commitment to preserving social and emotional ties with employees and local communities (Stavrou et al., 2006; Amato et al., 2021).

Territorial embeddedness adds another layer of complexity to downsizing decisions in family firms. Embedded firms are those deeply rooted in their local communities through long-standing relationships, local market dependencies, and a shared sense of identity with the region (Dekker & Hasso, 2016). Such ties often create spatial loyalty, wherein family firms prioritize community well-being and employee retention over short-term financial gains. This territorial embeddedness is theorized to reduce the propensity to downsize, as family firms recognize the adverse impact layoffs can have on their local stakeholders and reputation (Bjuggren & Sund, 2012; Cirillo et al., 2020).

Hypothesis 1 is based on this understanding, proposing that territorially embedded family firms exhibit a lower downsizing propensity than non-embedded firms. The underlying rationale is that family firms are more likely to align their business strategies with community values and social responsibility due to their deep local connections and SEW priorities. Evidence from previous studies suggests that local embeddedness strengthens the alignment of family firm goals with community expectations, making downsizing a less viable option (Amato et al., 2021; Sanchez-Bueno et al., 2020).

Hypothesis 2 builds on the interaction between AI adoption and territorial embeddedness, positing that the moderating effect of territorial embeddedness on the relationship between AI adoption and downsizing is stronger in family firms. AI adoption poses dual challenges for family firms: while it can improve operational efficiency, it also risks disrupting traditional employment structures (Farrell & Mavondo, 2005). Territorial embeddedness, however, is expected to mitigate these pressures by reinforcing family firms' commitment to employee welfare and local stability. Studies suggest that family firms embedded in local networks exhibit greater resilience to external pressures, such as technological disruption, due to their strong socio-economic ties and spatial loyalty (Berrone et al., 2010; Dekker & Hasso, 2016). Therefore, the interaction between family firm status, territorial embeddedness, and AI adoption is expected to produce distinct downsizing behaviors, supporting Hypothesis 2.

We stated the following hypotheses:

- Hypothesis 1: Territorially embedded family firms exhibit a lower downsizing propensity than non- embedded firms.
- Hypothesis 2: The moderating effect of territorial embeddedness on the relationships between AI adoption and downsizing is higher in family firms.

3 Research Design

This study adopts a quantitative research design, utilizing longitudinal panel data to examine the relationship between AI adoption and downsizing in family and non-family businesses. The longitudinal approach allows for capturing changes in downsizing decisions over time, particularly during the phase of AI integration. By observing firms over multiple time periods, this design reduces the risk of omitted variable bias, offering a more robust examination of how AI influences employment practices in family businesses.

3.1 Data Sources

The dataset used in this study was collected from multiple sources to ensure comprehensive coverage of firms across industries and regions. The primary data comes from a panel survey of firms conducted between the years 2013 and 2023. The dataset includes firms across various sectors, but with a focus on industries most susceptible to AI-driven transformation, such as manufacturing, services, and retail. The panel data set covers the following areas:

- **Firm characteristics**: Ownership structure, family involvement, managerial decisions, firm size, industry sector, location, etc.
- **Employment metrics**: Total employment, layoffs, workforce reductions.
- **Technology adoption**: AI adoption rates, AI expenditure.
- **Financial performance**: Profitability, revenue, debt ratios, cost structures.

Publicly available financial databases, such as Finstat, were also used to supplement firm-level financial information. The sample selection was based on several criteria to ensure the representativeness and relevance of the data. Firms were included if they had:

- **Family Business Identification**: Firms where family members occupy significant ownership or managerial roles. Following prior literature, family firms are defined as those where at least two family members hold managerial positions or a family holds more than 25% of equity (Greenwood et al., 2010).
- **AI Adoption**: Firms with verifiable AI adoption and integration into their business processes. AI adoption was measured based on self-reported data from firm surveys and corroborated by industry sources that track AI usage in businesses.
- **Location Information**: Firms had to be located within regions where territorial embeddedness could be clearly measured, allowing for a distinction between locally anchored and non-local firms.
- **Temporal Availability**: Only firms with data spanning at least five years during the 2013–2023 period were included to ensure longitudinal consistency.

The final dataset consisted of 347 firms, with a nearly equal split between family and non-family businesses.

3.2 Variables and Models

To analyse the relationship between family firm status, AI adoption, and downsizing, the study employs a panel data model, with a logistic regression approach to account for the binary nature of the dependent variable (downsizing). This model enables the estimation of the probability of downsizing, considering various independent and control variables. The logistic regression model is particularly well-suited for this analysis because it accommodates binary outcomes and accounts for non-linear relationships between predictors and the dependent variable (Hosmer et al., 2013; Wooldridge, 2010). Panel data techniques provide additional robustness by mitigating omitted variable bias and capturing firm-level variations over time (Baltagi, 2005). To enhance clarity, the variables used in the analysis are summarized in Table 1.

3.2.1 Dependent Variable: Downsizing

The primary outcome of interest is the firm's downsizing decision, captured as a binary variable. Downsizing is defined as a reduction in the workforce by 5% or more compared to the previous year. This threshold was selected based on prior literature that uses similar cut-offs to distinguish significant workforce reductions from minor fluctuations (Block, 2010; Stavrou et al., 2006).

The variable *Downsizing* is coded as:

- **1**: If the firm's workforce decreased by 5% or more in the given year.
- **0**: If the firm's workforce remained stable or increased.

To ensure robustness, alternate thresholds for downsizing (such as 3% and 10%) were tested in sensitivity analyses, with results being consistent across different thresholds.

3.2.2 Independent and Control Variables

Table 1 provides a detailed overview of the variables used in the analysis, including their codes, names, descriptions, computation methods, and sources, ensuring clarity and transparency in the study's methodological framework.

Table 1: Independent and Control Variables.

CODE	NAME	DESCRIPTION/COMPUTATION	SOURCE
FB	Family Business	Dichotomous variable: coded as (1) if family members are involved in ownership and management roles; (0) otherwise.	Basco (2013); Sanchez-Bueno et al. (2020)
AI	AI Adoption	Composite index measuring AI integration: includes AI expenditure as a percentage of total revenue.	Self-reported data; Industry reports
TE	Territorial Embeddedness	Dichotomous variable: coded as (1) if the firm's primary market is local; (0) if it operates at national or international levels.	Dekker and Hasso (2016)
AGE	Firm Age	Number of years since the firm was founded.	Firm records
PROF	Profitability	Gross operating margin, indicating financial performance.	Financial database Finstat
DEBT	Debt Ratio	Ratio of total debt to total assets, controlling for financial stress.	Financial database Finstat
LCR	Labor Cost Ratio	Ratio of labor costs to sales, reflecting workforce-related expenses.	Financial database Finstat
RDI	R&D Intensity	Research and development expenditure as a percentage of total sales, measuring innovation levels.	Financial database Finstat
EXP	Export Intensity	Foreign sales as a proportion of total sales, indicating international market exposure.	Firm records

Source: *authors*

3.2.3 Econometric Model

The relationship between family firm status, AI adoption, and downsizing is tested using a panel data model. Given the binary nature of the dependent variable (downsizing), a logistic regression model (logit) is applied to estimate the probability of downsizing. Logistic regression is particularly suitable in this context because it models the likelihood of a binary outcome (e.g., downsizing occurring or not) as a function of predictor variables, such as family firm status and AI adoption. This approach is well-documented in the literature for its robustness in analysing categorical dependent variables and its ability to handle non-linear relationships between predictors and outcomes (Hosmer et al., 2013; Wooldridge, 2010).

The use of panel data further enhances the analysis by allowing for the examination of within-firm variations over time while controlling for unobserved heterogeneity across firms. Panel data models also mitigate issues of omitted variable bias and provide more reliable estimates by leveraging both cross-sectional and time-series data (Baltagi, 2005). Logistic regression combined with panel data techniques thus provides a comprehensive framework for understanding how family firm characteristics and AI adoption interact to influence downsizing decisions. The panel structure of the data allows for the inclusion of firm-specific fixed effects, which control for time-invariant characteristics of each firm.

The base specification of the model is:

$$\begin{aligned} P(\text{Downsizing}_{\text{it}} = 1) = \alpha + \beta 1(\text{FamilyFirm}_{\text{it}}) + \beta 2(\text{AIAdoption}_{\text{it}}) \\ + \beta 3(\text{TerritorialEmbeddedness}_{\text{it}}) + \gamma X_{it} + \epsilon_{it} \end{aligned} \tag{1}$$

Where:
- $Downsizing_{it}$ is the downsizing decision for firm i in year t.
- $FamilyFirm_{it}$ is the family business status.
- $AIAdoption_{it}$ captures the firm's AI integration.
- $TerritorialEmbeddedness_{it}$ reflects the firm's local anchorage.
- X_{it} is a vector of control variables (firm size, profitability, etc.).
- ϵ_{it} is the error term.

3.2.4 Model Specification and Estimation

The logit model provides estimates of the odds ratios for each independent variable. The inclusion of interaction terms helps to evaluate whether the effect of AI adoption on downsizing differs between family and non-family businesses and how territorial embeddedness influences this relationship (Wooldridge, 2010; Greene, 2012).

Panel data techniques, including fixed and random effects models, are used to account for unobserved heterogeneity across firms. The Hausman test is performed to determine whether the fixed effects or random effects model is more appropriate for the analysis (Hausman, 1978; Wooldridge, 2010).

4 Results

4.1 Descriptive Statistics Results

Table 2 provides descriptive statistics for the key regression variables. Approximately 24 % of firms in the sample engaged in downsizing, while family-owned businesses represent nearly half of the total. Only 8% of the firms report relying primarily on local markets for their sales, classifying them as territorially embedded. On average, the firms have been operating for 15 years, with labour costs making up nearly 28% of their total expenses. Additionally, over 65% of the firms are situated in rural areas.

Table 2: Descriptive statistics – for whole sample.

Variable	N	Mean	St. dev	Min	p25	Median	p75	Max
Downsizing	347	0.242	0.469	0	0	0	1	1
Family firm	170	0.489	0.499	0	0	0	1	1
Non-family firm	177	0.565	0.435	0	0	0	1	1
Territorial embeddedness	347	0.080	0.237	0	0	0	0	1
R&D intensity	347	0.773	2.554	0	0	0	0.397	95.789
AI adaption	347	0.317	0.465	0	0	0	1	1
Export intensity	347	22.032	28.406	0	0	7	39	100
Age	347	15.135	11.238	0	15	17	25	31
Profitability	347	7.297	12.549	−50.5	2.4	7.3	13.3	39.2
Labour cost ratio	347	27.742	16.898	3.901	15.784	23.965	35.859	92.894
Competitors	347	2.027	1.255	1	1	1	3	4
Rural	347	0.650	0.485	0	0	1	1	1

4.2 Regression Analysis Results

We present the findings of our analysis in Table 3. In **Model 1**, we include the family firm variable alongside control variables. The family firm coefficient is negative and highly statistically significant at the 0.1% level, indicating that, all other factors being equal, family firms are more resistant to downsizing compared to non-family firms. Specifically, family firms are 4.5 % less likely to downsize than non-family firms. Looking at the control variables, R&D intensity is negatively associated with downsizing. Similarly, greater profitability is linked to a lower likelihood of downsizing. Firm size does not show a significant effect on downsizing. The labour cost ratio shows that firms with higher relative personnel costs are more prone to downsizing. Additionally, the coefficients for the temporary and part-time worker ratios indicate that firms with more non-permanent contracts have more flexibility when making layoff decisions.

In **Model 2**, we add two more explanatory variables. The coefficient for territorial embeddedness is positive but not statistically significant, indicating no clear evidence that the level of a firm's local ties affects the likelihood of downsizing. As a result, Hypothesis 1 is not supported. However, the AI adoption variable is strongly positive and statistically significant at the 0.1% level, showing that the probability of downsizing in the family businesses using AI was more than 10% higher compared to the family businesses without using AI.

In **Model 3**, we test Hypothesis 2 by comparing family and non-family firms with similar levels of territorial embeddedness. The marginal effect of the interaction between non-family firms and territorial embeddedness, compared to family firms as the reference group, is positive and statistically significant at the 1% level. This suggests that territorial embeddedness affects family and non-family firms differently, with territorially embedded family firms being much less likely to downsize. Specifically, territorially embedded family firms have an 8.8% lower likelihood of downsizing compared to non-family firms with similar local ties. This supports Hypothesis 2. On the other hand, there is no significant difference in downsizing between family firms based on their level of territorial embeddedness, as the interaction term for family firms and non-territorial embeddedness, while positive, is not statistically significant.

Table 3: Family Firms, Territorial Embeddedness, AI Adoption, and Downsizing.

Variable	Model (1)	Model (2)	Model (3)
AI adaptation	−0.047*** (0.008)	−0.041*** (0.008)	−0.041*** (0.008)
R&D intensity	−0.536*** (0.157)	−0.565*** (0.161)	−0.571*** (0.161)
Export intensity	−0.000 (0.000)	−0.000 (0.000)	−0.000 (0.000)
Age	−0.000 (0.000)	−0.000 (0.000)	−0.000 (0.000)
Profitability	−0.002*** (0.000)	−0.002*** (0.000)	−0.002*** (0.000)
Labour cost ratio	0.002*** (0.000)	0.002*** (0.000)	0.002*** (0.000)
Competitors	−0.000 (0.003)	−0.000 (0.003)	−0.000 (0.003)
Rural	−0.009 (0.008)	−0.008 (0.008)	−0.009 (0.008)
Family firm	−0.032*** (0.008)	−0.034*** (0.008)	
Territorial embeddedness (H_1)	0.003 (0.017)	0.003 (0.017)	
Non-family firm * Non-territorial embeddedness * AI adoption			0.054* (0.021)

Table 3 (continued)

Variable	Model (1)	Model (2)	Model (3)
Non-family firm * Territorial embeddedness* AI adoption			0.084** (0.028)
Family firm * Non-territorial embeddedness* AI adoption			0.023 (0.021)
Family firm * Territorial embeddedness* AI adoption (H_2)			0.042** (0.024)

The table presents linear probability model estimates based on a panel dataset over the period 2013–2023. Robust clustered standard errors are reported in parentheses. Level of significance +$p < 0.10$, *$p < 0.05$, **$p < 0.01$, ***$p < 0.001$

The results in Table 3 reveal that family-owned businesses are generally more resistant to downsizing, especially when they are embedded in their local communities. While AI adoption increases the probability of downsizing, the effect is more pronounced in non-family firms. Family firms with strong local ties demonstrate a unique resilience, leveraging their territorial embeddedness to maintain employment levels, even when incorporating technological advancements like AI.

This suggests that the socioemotional wealth and community ties of family businesses can counterbalance external pressures to downsize, particularly in times of technological change.

5 Summary

The study aims to examine the impact of AI-induced downsizing on family businesses, emphasizing the moderating role of territorial embeddedness. It investigates how family firms balance the integration of advanced technologies with their commitment to socio-emotional wealth (SEW), long-term sustainability, and employee welfare. The goal is to understand the unique downsizing behaviours of family firms compared to non-family firms and the influence of local community ties on these decisions.

The study addresses the research question: How does AI adoption influence downsizing decisions in family businesses, and what role does territorial embeddedness play in moderating this relationship? The results reveal that AI adoption increases the likelihood of downsizing across both family and non-family firms. However, family firms exhibit a stronger resistance to downsizing, driven by their prioritization of SEW, which includes employee relationships, family control, and reputation. Territorial embeddedness further strengthens this resistance in family firms, as those with deep local ties demonstrate a markedly lower propensity to downsize, even when adopting AI technologies.

The hypotheses were tested and evaluated as follows: Hypothesis 1, which proposed that territorially embedded family firms exhibit a lower downsizing propensity than non-embedded firms, was partially supported. While family firms generally show resilience to downsizing, the direct effect of territorial embeddedness was not statistically significant for all firms. However, its interaction with family firm status revealed that territorially embedded family firms are significantly less likely to downsize than their non-family counterparts. Hypothesis 2, which suggested that the moderating effect of territorial embeddedness on the relationship between AI adoption and downsizing is higher in family firms, was fully supported. The analysis confirmed that territorial embeddedness acts as a critical buffer in family firms, mitigating the downsizing pressures associated with AI adoption more effectively than in non-family firms.

Analysing the effects of territorial embeddedness and AI adoption separately provides only a limited view of how these contextual factors influence downsizing decisions. When we consider both territorial embeddedness and AI adoption simultaneously, it becomes clear that family firms embedded in local communities are particularly attentive to employee well-being during technical changes. Socially close relationships with the local community, driven by shared norms and strong emotional ties, lead family firms to prioritize their employees, recognizing that mass layoffs could negatively impact both their workforce and the local economy. The difference in downsizing likelihood between territorially embedded family firms and non-family firms was nearly 12%. This enhanced sense of spatial loyalty during technical changes contrasts with the lower effects when territorial embeddedness (8.8% and 3%, respectively). Overall, our study reaffirms the unique role of territorially embedded family firms in mitigating the adverse effects of technical changes on employment.

These findings offer practical implications for family businesses navigating the challenges of AI integration. Family firms should prioritize strengthening their territorial embeddedness by deepening their connections with local communities through initiatives such as sourcing from local suppliers, supporting community projects, and fostering regional partnerships. These efforts can build goodwill and reduce pressures to downsize, especially during periods of technological change. Additionally, family firms should adopt a strategic approach to AI implementation, involving employees, family members, and other stakeholders in the decision-making process to ensure transparency and trust. Gradual adoption of AI, accompanied by robust workforce training programs, can help preserve jobs while enhancing employee skills for new, AI-driven roles.

Family businesses must also find a balance between their socio-emotional wealth priorities and innovation goals. By leveraging AI to improve operational efficiency, they can reinvest the resulting savings into employee welfare and community engagement, thus aligning technological progress with their long-term values. Monitoring the effects of AI adoption on both operational performance and socio-emotional wealth is crucial for continuous improvement and alignment with family business goals.

In conclusion, family firms are uniquely positioned to navigate the complexities of AI-induced downsizing due to their commitment to socio-emotional wealth and territorial embeddedness. By adopting strategies that prioritize employee welfare and local community ties, they can remain competitive while upholding their social responsibilities and family legacies. These findings highlight the importance of integrating family business values into strategic decision-making, especially in the context of rapid technological advancement.

6 Limitations and Potential Implications for Future Research

While this study provides valuable insights into AI-induced downsizing in family businesses, it is not without limitations. First, the sample size, consisting of 347 firms, though adequate for initial analysis, may limit the generalizability of the findings, particularly given the focus on a single country, Slovakia. This geographical limitation restricts the applicability of the results to broader contexts with varying institutional, cultural, and economic conditions. Future research should expand the sample to include firms from diverse regions and industries to enhance external validity.

Second, the reliance on self-reported data for AI adoption and family business identification introduces potential biases, such as over- or under-reporting due to subjective interpretations or social desirability. Although we employed complementary sources like financial databases to mitigate this, further studies should incorporate third-party verification or objective measures, such as technological audits or external certifications, to strengthen data validity.

Additionally, the longitudinal nature of the dataset, spanning 2013 to 2023, captures trends over time but may not fully account for rapid shifts in technological adoption or economic conditions, such as those driven by global crises. Future research could employ shorter, more frequent intervals of data collection to observe immediate impacts and emerging patterns.

Finally, while the study focuses on family and non-family firms, it does not delve deeply into intra-family firm heterogeneity. Differences in generational involvement, governance structures, or levels of professionalization may significantly influence downsizing behaviours and merit further exploration. Addressing these limitations would not only refine the theoretical models but also provide practical insights to help family businesses navigate technological transformations more effectively.

Future studies could employ alternative ways of measuring territorial embeddedness to see if family firms' downsizing tendencies change with different operational definitions of local ties. Potential measures might include the geographic distance from the firm's headquarters (Berrone et al., 2010; D'Aurizio & Romano, 2013), proximity to key stakeholders (Amato et al., 2021a), length of time the firm has been based in a location (Baù et al., 2019), and the percentage of inputs or information sourced locally (Kalantaridis & Bika, 2006). A more promising approach could be to develop a comprehensive or "holistic" measure of territorial embeddedness that captures multiple dimensions of a firm's connection to its local environment, providing a fuller understanding of how local ties shape decision-making and outcomes.

References

Amato, S., Patuelli, A., Basco, R., & Lattanzi, N. (2021). Family firms amidst the global financial crisis: A territorial embeddedness perspective on downsizing. *Journal of Business Ethics*, *183*(1), 213–236. https://doi.org/10.1007/s10551-021-04930-0

Baltagi, B. H. (2005). *Econometric Analysis of Panel Data* (3rd ed.). Wiley.

Basco, R. (2013). The family's effect on family firm performance: A model testing the demographic and essence approaches. *Journal of Family Business Strategy*, *4*(1), 42–66. https://doi.org/10.1016/j.jfbs.2012.12.003

Baù, M., Pittino, D., & Mazzola, P. (2019). Family firms and the impact of longevity: Empirical evidence from Italy. *Small Business Economics*, *52*(2), 459–474. https://doi.org/10.1007/s11187-018-0059-x

Berrone, P., Cruz, C., & Gomez-Mejia, L. R. (2010). Socioemotional wealth in family firms: Theoretical dimensions, assessment approaches, and agenda for future research. *Family Business Review*, *23*(3), 258–279. https://doi.org/10.1177/0894486510375069

Bjuggren, P. O., & Sund, L. G. (2012). A transition cost rationale for transition of the firm within the family. *Small Business Economics*, *29*(1), 1–19. https://doi.org/10.1023/A:1015193003504

Block, J. (2008). Family management, family ownership, and downsizing: Evidence from S&P 500 firms. *Family Business Review*, *23*(2), 109–130. https://doi.org/10.1177/089448651002300202

Block, J. (2010). Family management, family ownership, and downsizing: Evidence from S&P 500 firms. *Family Business Review*, *23*(2), 109–130. https://doi.org/10.1177/089448651002300202

Cameron, K. S. (1994). Strategies for successful organizational downsizing. *Human Resource Management*, 33(2), 189–211.

Carney, M. (2005). Corporate governance and competitive advantage in family-controlled firms. *Entrepreneurship Theory and Practice*, 29(3), 249–265.

Cascio, W. F. (1993). Downsizing: What do we know? What have we learned? *Academy of Management Perspectives*, 7(1), 95–104.

Chrisman, J. J., Chua, J. H., & Litz, R. A. (2010). A unified systems perspective of family firm performance: An extension and integration. *Journal of Business Venturing*, *18*(4), 467–472. https://doi.org/10.1016/S0883-9026(02)00054-2

Chua, J. H., Chrisman, J. J., & Sharma, P. (2009). Defining the family business by behavior. *Entrepreneurship Theory and Practice*, *23*(4), 19–39. https://doi.org/10.1177/104225879902300402

Cirillo, A., Muñoz-Bullón, F., Sanchez-Bueno, M. J., & Sciascia, S. (2020). Employee downsizing and sales internationalization strategy in family firms. *Journal of Family Business Strategy*. https://doi.org/10.1016/j.jfbs.2020.100354

D'Aurizio, L., & Romano, L. (2013). Family firms and financial crisis: Evidence from Italy. *Journal of Family Business Strategy*, *4*(1), 14–25. https://doi.org/10.1016/j.jfbs.2013.01.002

Dekker, J., & Hasso, T. (2016). Environmental performance focus in private family firms: The role of social embeddedness. *Journal of Business Ethics*, *136*(2), 293–309. https://doi.org/10.1007/s10551-014-2516-9

Farrell, M., & Mavondo, F. (2005). The effect of downsizing-redesign strategies on business performance: Evidence from Australia. *Asia Pacific Journal of Human Resources*, *43*(1), 98–116. https://doi.org/10.1177/1038411105050309

Greene, W. H. (2012). *Econometric Analysis* (7th ed.). Pearson.

Greenwood, R., Díaz, A. M., Li, S. X., & Lorente, J. C. (2010). The multiplicity of institutional logics and the heterogeneity of organizational responses. *Organization Science*, *21*(2), 521–539. https://doi.org/10.1287/orsc.1090.0453

Hausman, J. A. (1978). Specification tests in econometrics. *Econometrica*, 46(6), 1251–1271. https://doi.org/10.2307/1913827

Hosmer, D. W., Lemeshow, S., & Sturdivant, R. X. (2013). *Applied Logistic Regression* (3rd ed.). Wiley.

Kalantaridis, C., & Bika, Z. (2006). Local embeddedness and rural entrepreneurship: Case-study evidence from Cumbria, England. *Environment and Planning A*, *38*(8), 1561–1579. https://doi.org/10.1068/a37427

Miller, D., & Le Breton-Miller, I. (2006). Family governance and firm performance: Agency, stewardship, and capabilities. *Family Business Review*, *19*(1), 73–87. https://doi.org/10.1111/j.1741-6248.2006.00063.x

Sanchez-Bueno, M. J., Muñoz-Bullón, F., & Galán, J. (2020). Socially responsible downsizing: Comparing family and non-family firms. *POL: Other Strategy & Social Policies (Topic)*. https://doi.org/10.1111/beer.12244

Stavrou, E., Kassinis, G. I., & Filotheou, A. (2006). Downsizing and stakeholder orientation among the Fortune 500: Does family ownership matter? *Journal of Business Ethics*, *72*(2), 149–162. https://doi.org/10.1007/s10551-006-9162-x

Wooldridge, J. M. (2010). *Econometric Analysis of Cross Section and Panel Data* (2nd ed.). MIT Press.

Zellweger, T., Nason, R. S., & Nordqvist, M. (2012). From longevity of firms to transgenerational entrepreneurship of families: Introducing family entrepreneurial orientation. *Family Business Review*, 25(2), 136–155.

List of Contributors

Dr. **Maria Bartekova** attained her doctoral degree in Management from Comenius University in Bratislava in 2018. Presently, she spearheads the OpenmusE research project under the Horizon Europe grant at the University of Economics in Bratislava, representing Slovakia in an international consortium. Her research focuses on the creative industries. Since 2023, she serves as a member of the Academic Senate at the Faculty of Business Management. Additionally, she has chaired sessions at various conferences including the ESD Conference in Rome, Italy; the 41st IBIMA Business Conference in Granada, Spain; the Global Business Conferences in Dubrovnik, Croatia (2022) and Zagreb, Croatia (2023); and the 3rd Global Conference on Entrepreneurship and Economy in an Era of Uncertainty in Pattaya, Thailand (2023).

Dr. **Bernhard Baumgartner** holds a PhD in Social and Business Administration from Karl-Franzens University Graz, a master's degree in Civil Engineering from Technical University Graz, and an MBA from IMD in Lausanne. He completed the ISMP Program at Harvard Business School and is a Fellow of the Family Firm Institute, where he has also spoken at international conferences. Dr. Baumgartner has lectured at the University of Graz, Harvard Business School, and the Management Center Innsbruck (MCI), where he co-founded the Center for Family Businesses and taught for over 12 years. He is the author of *Family Business and its Future* and co-author of *Entrepreneurship and Tourism*. With extensive international experience across Asia, South America, India, the Philippines, and the USA – including Silicon Valley – he has served on global company boards and specializes in restructuring and succession planning for family businesses.

Dr. **Sascha Frohwerk** is senior lecturer and program director for IT-Management at Salzburg University of Applied Science. His research interests are in spatial data science and small and medium size companies. He is also associated at KCE Competence Centre for Entrepreneurship & Small and Medium-sized Business.

Petter Gottschalk is Professor in the Department of Leadership and Organizational Behaviour at BI Norwegian Business School. He received his education at Technische Universität, Dartmouth, MIT, and Henley. Dr. Gottschalk has published extensively on knowledge management, police intelligence, corporate investigation, theory of convenience, white-collar and corporate crime. He has held the position of chief executive officer (CEO) at several companies.

Sophia Hornung, B.Sc., is a business and psychology student at the University of Innsbruck. She holds degrees in both International Business Management and Psychology, enabling her to integrate research from both fields. In addition to her academic pursuits, she has extensive experience as an HR associate and specializes in leading employee workshops focused on behavioral change.

Dr. **Juha Kansikas** is a Senior Lecturer and Founding Director of the international B.Sc. program at JSBE. He co-led a research project on executive education and business elite formation (2020–2024), funded by the Academy of Finland, and conducted research for the Finnish Education Council in 2021 on the development of entrepreneurship education. He holds postdoctoral qualifications in both business and education sciences. Dr. Kansikas has been a visiting researcher at Copenhagen Business School and the Telfer School of Management (University of Ottawa) and an invited speaker at the University of Lausanne. His research has been published in leading journals such as *Technological Forecasting and Social Change*, *Business History*, and the *Journal of Entrepreneurship*. In 2024, he received the Outstanding Reviewer Award from the Emerald Literati Awards.

https://doi.org/10.1515/9783110790344-012

Dr. **Markus Kathan** holds a doctorate in business administration. He has held several management positions in the private sector and has been a Senior Lecturer at the Department Business & Tourism, Salzburg University of Applied Sciences, Puch/Salzburg, Austria since 2017. He is engaged in teaching, interdisciplinary projects, practical collaborations, and research. His research activities focus on strategic management, management accounting, and digitalization.

Carsten Kruppe is Professor of General Business Administration, in particular Finance, at the FOM University of Applied Sciences in Berlin and works as a freelance consultant for medium-sized companies. His professional and research activities focus on issues from the spectrum of corporate finance, such as strategic planning and company valuations, as well as the implementation of sustainability aspects.

Prof. (FH) Dr. **Michael Kuttner** is a Professor of Accounting & Financial Management at the Department Business & Tourism, Salzburg University of Applied Sciences, Puch/Salzburg, Austria. His teaching activities include management accounting, risk management, cost accounting, capital budgeting, corporate finance, and supervising theses at different universities in Austria and abroad. His research focuses on management accounting, risk management, resilience, digitalization, and sustainability, considering various contingency factors (e.g., ownership structure and company size). In addition, he works as a reviewer for several scientific journals and conferences, as an author, editor, and speaker, and as a military expert (business and finance) for the Austrian Federal Ministry of Defense.

Aino Leino, B.Sc., holds a degree in International Management from the University of Augsburg. She brings extensive expertise as a Quality Manager in the Swiss insurance industry, specializing in the implementation of high operational standards. In addition to her work in quality management, she has significant experience in digital marketing and business development, having managed her own SME in the health and wellness space and contributed to the growth of other SMEs across various industries.

Sophia Maier, BA, studied Business Management at the Salzburg University of Applied Sciences, Puch/Salzburg, Austria, and works in a family business in the wood industry. Her responsibilities in the family business focus on finance, including overseeing accounting and payroll management. Additionally, she is also in charge of marketing and human resource management.

Julia Riepl, MSc, is a research associate and PhD candidate at the Institute of Finance, Department of Corporate Finance, at Johannes Kepler University Linz, Austria. Additionally, she serves as an external lecturer at the Department Business & Tourism, Salzburg University of Applied Sciences, Puch/Salzburg, Austria. Her current research interests encompass risk governance and risk management, ESG, family businesses, and corporate finance.

Prof. (FH) Dr. **Stefan Märk** is program director and professor at the University of Applied Science. His research topics are in SME (small and medium-sized enterprises) studies, with a specific focus on entrepreneurship, opportunity identification, and the transformation of families within family businesses. Along with Mr. Mario Situm, he has authored the book *Family Entrepreneurs and Their Stakeholders* (Springer Verlag). Additionally, he is involved with several journals. For more than 20 years, he has been teaching various business-related subjects at numerous universities. Strategically, he can be described as a versatile expert, with a strong affinity for family businesses and their often-intricate characteristics, which result from the interplay between family and business.

Martin Pfaffinger, MA is a postgraduate of MCI The Entrepreneurial School ®. He holds a bachelor's degree in European Economy and Corporate Management at FH Vienna as well as a master's degree in Entrepreneurship and Tourism at MCI, and a master's degree in business at LUISS Guido Carli University.

As an entrepreneur, he has a vast amount of experience in the field of hospitality and international management and is currently taking over a family business himself. His passion lies in understanding the complexities of family business management.

Dr. **Jaana Seikkula-Leino** serves as Professor of Pedagogy at Mid Sweden University and as Associate Professor of Entrepreneurship Education at the University of Turku, Finland. Her expertise spans entrepreneurship, change management, education reform, pedagogy, teacher education, and digital education. With over 150 publications, also in high-impact Scopus journals, her interdisciplinary career has encompassed roles in education, technology, and business. She's also lent her expertise to governments, the EU, the UN, the OECD, and Cedefop. Prof. Jaana Seikkula-Leino also has substantial experience in the private sector.

Prof. (FH) Dr. Dr. **Mario Situm** is a program director and professor at the University of Applied Sciences Kufstein, Austria. His expertise spans financial services, real estate, and banking, alongside his work as an independent consultant for SMEs and family businesses. He is a partner at DANISTER GmbH in Munich and DANISTER Development GmbH in Linz. His academic background includes advanced degrees in Business Administration, Finance, and Economics from universities in Austria, Germany, and Switzerland. His research focuses on controlling, family businesses, finance, crisis and insolvency forecasting, risk management, and corporate branding. He is also active as an author, reviewer, and editorial board member in international journals.

Ante Vuletić is Associate Professor at the Faculty of Economics, University of Zagreb. His expertise includes business continuity, resilience, and artificial intelligence in security. He has extensive academic experience, having taught courses such as Organization, Management, Strategic Management and Business Continuity. His research also covers the integration of artificial intelligence into security frameworks. Prof. Vuletić has held various academic positions at the University of Zagreb, progressing from research assistant to associate professor. His teaching portfolio includes management, business continuity, and artificial intelligence and security. He is also active as a researcher, author, and contributor to international journals.

Holger Wassermann is Professor of General Business Administration, in particular Accounting and Controlling, at the FOM University of Applied Sciences Berlin and Academic Director of the KCE Competence Centre for Entrepreneurship & SMEs. With his company Wassermann/Nachfolge, he provides various solutions in the field of business succession for SMEs and large corporations.

Prof. **Anita Zehrer** is Head of the MCI R&D Unit Management & Society and the Family Business Center at MCI. Her research interests are diverse and include entrepreneurship and leadership and family business management. She holds a doctorate degree from the University of Innsbruck and has been a professor at the Catholic University of Eichstätt-Ingolstadt since 2015. She has broad competence in interdisciplinary research and teaching in tourism and business. She has conducted several projects with national and international partners in research and industry in the field of family business management.

List of Figures

https://doi.org/10.1515/9783110790344-013

List of Tables

https://doi.org/10.1515/9783110790344-014

Index

https://doi.org/10.1515/9783110790344-015